Native American Writing in the Southeast

Native American Writing in the Southeast

An Anthology, 1875–1935

Edited, with an introduction by
Daniel F. Littlefield, Jr.
and *James W. Parins*

UNIVERSITY PRESS OF MISSISSIPPI
JACKSON

Copyright © 1995 by the University Press of Mississippi
All rights reserved
Manufactured in the United States of America

98 97 96 95 4 3 2 1

The paper in this book meets the guidelines for permanence and durability of the
Committee on Production Guidelines for Book Longevity of the Council on
Library Resources.

Library of Congress Cataloging-in-Publication Data

Native American writing in the Southeast : an anthology,
   1875–1935 / Daniel F. Littlefield, Jr., and James W. Parins.
      p. cm.
   Includes bibliographical references.
   ISBN 0-87805-827-3 (alk. paper)—ISBN 0-87805-828-1 (pbk. :
alk. paper)
      1. Indians of North America—Southern States—Literary
collections. 2. American literature—Indian authors. 3. Indians of
North America—Cultural assimilation—Southern States. 4. American
literature—19th century. 5. American literature—20th century.
I. Littlefield, Daniel F. II. Parins, James W.
PS508.I5N375 1995
810.8'0897075—dc20   95-18038
                                                           CIP

British Library Cataloging-in-Publication data available

Contents

Preface

Creation of an anthology is a difficult task. Invariably, original plans are more inclusive and larger in scope than the finished product will allow. Giving in to constraints on space, compilers compromise, seek the best options, and work for balance as we have done, aiming at a fair representation of the literature. Our objective is to offer such a representation of the literature written in English by Indians of the American Southeast during the period 1875 to 1935.

We chose this period for two reasons. First was its historical integrity, beginning with the close of the treaty-making period and ending with the advent of the Indians' New Deal. During this period, the Indian wars ended, the "frontier" closed, and the United States adopted a major policy of liquidating tribal domain and assimilating Indians into American society. For Indians of the American Southeast, it was the most devastating and destructive policy since removal. Official assault on tribal domain and native identity proved fruitful ground for native writers, and the literary response was dynamic. Hence the focus of this anthology.

We began with a list of writers who were popular or were recognized as outstanding by their contemporaries and who would have been likely candidates for inclusion in even general anthologies of native writers: DeWitt Clinton Duncan, John M. Oskison, Will Rogers, Rollie Lynn Riggs. Our selection resources for these writers as well as the remaining authors and works before 1925 were our *Biobibliography of Native American Writers, 1772–1924* (Scarecrow Press, 1981), its supplement (1985), and their update maintained by the American Native Press Archives at the University of Arkansas at Little Rock. For works after 1924, we relied on in-house bibliographies of native writers maintained by the Archives.

The difficulty in selecting writers derived from our desire to create an anthology that was representative of the vast body of native literature generated during the period. We read hundreds of pieces. Though we had hoped to include works from writers of most tribes of the region, we found in the end that, because of the social, political, and economic realities of the era, some tribes carried on little literary activity and others none that is presently known. Thus the collection we offer here contains works by Cherokees (from both the Cherokee Nation and the Eastern Band), Choctaws, Chickasaws, Muscogees (Creeks), and Yuchis.

In making our selections, we considered a number of criteria. First was genre. Our goal was to present selections in as many literary forms as possible to reflect the range of literary production, from the conventionally aesthetic pieces to letters to editors. The second criterion was literary self-consciousness, particularly author concern for audience and author intent. We sought works written for publication, preferably those which demonstrate that the authors considered themselves writers who had ideas that they wished to put forward for a purpose. We sought pieces in which writers consciously shaped arguments, created scenes, or manipulated elements of style with the intent to persuade, arouse emotion, or trigger an aesthetic response. The third criterion was length. In an effort to include as many works as possible within our page constraints, we selected short pieces, and because we chose not to include any excerpts, works such as novels, multi-act plays, and book-length biographies produced by some of these writers are not represented. Though a number of the writers included here wrote extensively, we can include only a sampling of their work. Finally, we sought works that were largely self-explanatory regarding such matters as tribal history, had broad readership appeal, and needed little annotation. However, where esoteric information might appear to be especially troublesome, we have provided notes.

Believing that the writers should be allowed to speak for themselves, we have done only light editing. Occasionally we have edited out brief, irrelevant passages, whose omissions are indicated by ellipses. We have silently corrected misspellings and typographical errors, except where they are used deliberately as stylistic devices, and have supplied some identifications in brackets where such insertions are necessary. After each reading, we have indicated the date of publication on the right; if the date of composition is known to be different, we have indicated that date on the left. A source list giving specific publication information appears at the end of the volume. Finally, we have supplied a historical introduction to the volume and author headnotes, which provide brief biographical sketches of the writers and orient the reader to their works. The arrangement of the texts roughly reflects the time in which the writers were active or, if their careers were long, in which they flourished.

Daniel F. Littlefield, Jr.
James W. Parins

Introduction

The Trans-Mississippi and International Exposition, held at Omaha, Nebraska, from June through October, 1898, was a spectacular affair with its Grecian and Romanesque architecture, courtyards, and lagoons plied by gondolas and a large motorized boat shaped like a swan. There were halls of industry and agriculture, displays of the latest technology and agricultural methods, a huge midway, jinrickshas to carry the tourists about, and thousands of incandescent bulbs that illumined the whole affair by electricity. This backdrop was the setting for a so-called Indian Congress. One misguided exposition goer believed that the gathering was what the name implied and, upon arrival, asked what addresses were going to be made and what papers were going to be read in the congress that day.[1] She did not know that the Indians were there as an exhibit like so much garden produce or poultry and so many head of livestock, electric generators, or cream separators.

This was the first such exhibit at an exposition, and it symbolized the prevailing public opinion and governmental policy regarding American Indians. It began as an ethnologic project by Edward Rosenwater, owner of the *Omaha Bee* and one of the managers of the exposition. In theory, tribal representatives were to go to the exposition site, erect traditional abodes, wear traditional dress, go about everyday traditional chores, and engage in traditional arts and crafts work. The purpose of the exhibit was not to show the Indians as they were in 1898 but, as nearly as possible, what life was like in the aboriginal state.[2] The exhibit was based on the assumption that the Indian was vanishing from the face of the earth.

1. Horace M. Bebok, "The First Continental Congress of North American Indians," *Midland Monthly Magazine* 11 (February 1899): 107.
2. For background on the congress and analysis of its failures, see James Mooney, "The Indian Congress at Omaha," *American Anthropologist* n. s. 1 (January 1899): 126–49.

Though the congress was a dismal failure, its significance was clear. One writer who attended the exposition reminded his readers that within the memory of people then living nearly every foot of land in the Trans-Mississippi West had been ruled by Indian tribes. "The Omaha Exposition," he wrote, "signalizes the triumph of the Anglo-Saxon pioneers, first, over the aborigines, and, second, over the forces of nature."[3]

Much had happened in Indian affairs in the thirty years just past that might have led to this writer's statement, which so well epitomized American thinking about the American Indians. First, the treaty-making policy, which had begun with the nation's founding, was no longer pursued. The last treaty had been concluded in 1868, and in 1871 Congress decided that the government would no longer make treaties with the Indians. It no longer considered Indian tribes "domestic dependent nations" as it had done for the previous forty years. Congress could now deal with the Indians unilaterally, even imperiously, if it chose. Second, the Indian wars had come to an end. In the decades of the 1870s and 1880s, the U.S. Army had brought tribe after tribe under its control so that by the decade of the 1890s, except briefly during the height of the Ghost Dance movement, whites in Indian country had had only minor bouts with war fever. Third, the Department of the Interior, especially the Office of Indian Affairs, had embarked on what its bureaucrats called a "civilization" policy for the American Indians. If Indian tribes or nations were not considered autonomous social or political entities, then they must be absorbed into the American nation. Thus the "civilization" policy's aim was assimilation of the American Indians into American society by requiring them to conform to American values and life ways. To achieve this goal, the Office of Indian Affairs had taken two distinct paths, education and allotment of tribal land to individual Indians, both well under way by the time of the Omaha Exposition.

Education was the first of these policies undertaken. Assimilationists placed their hopes in the off-reservation boarding schools. This effort began in 1878 with the joint education of Indians and blacks at Hampton Institute. The first all-Indian school was established at Carlisle Barracks, Pennsylvania, the next year, to be followed by Forest Grove, Haskell Institute, Chilocco, and others. In theory, these schools would remove the children from the tribal environment for a number of years in order to

    3. Albert Shaw, "The Trans-Mississippians and Their Fair at Omaha," *Century Magazine* 56 (September 1898): 847.

break the ties of language and culture, which would be replaced by English education and skills that would make them employable in an off-reservation, preferably urban, setting.

The second thrust of the "civilization" policy, land reform, was justified by the argument that private ownership of property was a requirement for one to be an American. This policy was given a "reform" label because it had the backing of a number of Eastern humanitarian reform groups, who believed that the reservation system was destructive and that the Indians were doomed if they did not assimilate. Assimilation was impossible as long as tribal members held their land in common; the common title must be put aside and the lands divided into plots to which tribal members were given individual titles. With the backing of the reform groups, Congress shaped legislation that became the General Allotment Act of 1887, one of the most destructive pieces of Indian legislation ever passed. Reformist backing allowed legislators, politicans, and bureaucrats to take a high moral tone in justifying their actions, but as the policy was applied, it became apparent that the real impetus behind the legislation was economic. It pandered to the interests of corporate America, particularly the railroad industry, and of land hungry American farmers and ranchers. Instead of instilling the pride of individual land ownership in the American Indians, it divested them of millions of acres during the next forty years through fraud, legal and illegal sales, and guardianship systems.

The theory behind the "civilization" policy and the reality of its operation were two different things. By the time of the Omaha Exposition, Americans thought the country was well on its way to solving the "Indian problem." It was popularly believed that those Indians who refused to wade into the mainstream had either vanished or were in the process of doing so and that those who survived the process were destined to become part of the mix in America's melting pot. Many Indians themselves believed these results were inevitable, and in the next few decades would advocate the abolition of the Office of Indian Affairs, but the majority, by far, tenaciously persisted in maintaining that they were, after all, Indians. Thus during the first three decades of the twentieth century, policy makers realized that the "civilization" policy had failed. The Indians neither assimilated nor disappeared. The allotment policy had resulted in severe attrition of the Indians' land base. In general, the people were poverty ridden, disease was rampant, and education was in decline.

By the early 1920s another reform movement was under way, this time to counter the disastrous effects of the earlier reform policy. Organized reform efforts began in 1923 with the founding of the American Indian Defense Association to assist the Pueblos in protecting their land titles then under attack. This group was headed by John Collier, who became a major figure in reform efforts in the 1920s and later served as Commissioner of Indian Affairs in the Roosevelt Administration. Efforts by Collier's group and others led to legislation granting citizenship to all Indians in 1924, establishment of the Meriam Commission in 1926, and the publication of the commission's report in 1928, which gave a realistic assessment of the sad conditions prevailing in Indian communities and laid the groundwork for reform in the administration of Indian affairs. Many of the report's recommendations were transformed into law in the Indian Reorganization Act of 1934, which among other things, provided for the cessation of allotment, reorganization of tribal entities under constitutions, economic development, improved education, and cultural revitalization. Indian opinion was divided regarding these developments. While most Indians believed that reform was necessary and would prove beneficial to Indian communities, many who had embraced the concept of assimilation believed that it was regressive and relegated the Indians to second-class citizenship, and some believed that the Indians' New Deal was communist inspired.

How the broad lines of assimilationist federal policy of the reform era between the end of the treaty period and the New Deal affected Indian tribes varied greatly according to their particular history and their status in relation to the federal government when the era began. Good examples are the tribal peoples who had occupied the Southeastern United States. They fell roughly into three groups.[4] First were the tribes who had been removed from or forced out of their traditional homelands into the Indian Territory and elsewhere west of the Mississippi during the early decades of the nineteenth century. These included the Cherokees, Choctaws, Chickasaws, Creeks, Seminoles, Quapaws, and Caddoes and represented by far the largest population of identified tribal members. Second were tribal remnants who had somehow escaped being removed with the masses of their tribes and remained in the vicinity of their traditional

4. These convenient groupings are derived from Walter L. Williams, ed., *Southeastern Indians Since the Removal Era* (Athens: University of Georgia Press, 1979), which is the best single comprehensive source on the history and conditions among the Southeastern Indians during the period covered in this volume and which is the source for the commentary here about the Indians who remain in the Deep South.

lands. Included among these were the Cherokees in North Carolina, the Seminoles in Florida, the Creeks in Alabama, and the Choctaws in Mississippi. Third were groups who had not been subject to removal and had maintained an identity as Indians, at least in their local communities, such as the Catawbas, Lumbees, Houmas, and Tunicas.

The peoples who made up these three groups varied greatly in racial makeup, cultural practices, social structures, and political history—in fact, in most ways one might choose to consider peoples who identify themselves as Indians, including the ways in which federal Indian policy affected them. Among those who remained in the Deep South were some recognized as tribal entities by the federal government and others who were not. Some of the latter were recognized by the states, but others were not. Some had a tribal land base while others had none. All, however, were placed in the anomalous position of maintaining themselves as a third racial group in a society that usually thought in terms of two, white and black, and most groups constantly struggled to prevent being classified with blacks. As a result, all lived under marginal economies.

In contrast were the large tribes who had been removed from the Deep South in the early decades of the century. They recovered from the disastrous physical, cultural, and economic effects of removal, only to have their nations devastated by the Civil War. At the end of the treaty period, they were on the verge of rebuilding their nations once more. However, their struggle during the ensuing years was not one of economics or identity, like that of their kinspeople and others in the South, but of maintaining tribal sovereignty, based on existing treaties and the patents they held to their lands. They were exempted from the provisions of the General Allotment Act of 1887, but in 1893, Congress created the Dawes Commission, whose task was to negotiate with the tribes to set aside their treaties, allot their lands in severalty, and prepare for eventual statehood for the Indian Territory. The tribes effectively resisted negotiation until an exasperated Congress gave in to the demands of American corporations and farmers who were clamoring for the opening of Indian Territory and passed the Curtis Act, which provided for the allotment of lands without the Indians' consent if necessary. The Curtis Act became law in June 1898, the month the Omaha Exposition opened, underscoring no doubt the belief that Anglo-Saxon pioneers had triumphed over the aborigine. They had, in fact, triumphed in the struggle over land as the large Indian republics of the Indian Territory were on the verge of dissolution.

It might appear that the Indians of the American Southeast were better prepared than most to make the social, economic, cultural, and political transitions sought by the government's assimilationist policy during the reform era. They had been among some of the peoples who first experienced European incursion into America, had undergone centuries of acculturation, and had traveled far down the road of assimilating to European American culture. The large tribes who had been removed to the Indian Territory had so advanced in that direction that the Americans began to refer to them commonly in the Reconstruction period as the Five Civilized Tribes. Still, after losing the battle to preserve their tribal autonomy, they insisted on preserving their Indian identity, and large numbers of them lost their land and became just as poverty ridden as Indians elsewere in America.

One important way in which the tribal peoples of the Southeast responded to their long history of cultural discontinuity and struggle to survive was a written literature. The period from 1875 to 1935 was marked by tremendous literary energy and extensive production of a rich literature, which blossomed in the late nineteenth century and bore fruit in the twentieth. Literary expression conformed to various genres: nonfiction in the form of essays, letters, addresses, historical narratives, and biography; fiction in the form of short stories, novels, and dialect humor; poetry; and drama. Though the expression took the forms that were familiar to readers elsewhere in America, the themes were usually—not always—distinctly Indian. Dominant among them were the ideas that the Indians were here first, that their treatment by the larger society was unjust, that they had contributed significantly to the making of modern America, and that they remained—and intended to remain—a part of the American scene.

The large tribes that had experienced removal—with the singular exception of the Seminoles—dominated the literary scene for significant reasons: a high level of literacy, locally controlled educational systems, and a flourishing publishing industry. Sequoyah's invention of the syllabary for the Cherokee language resulted in a high literacy rate among the Cherokee people in the third decade of the nineteenth century. Extensive translation of English texts into Cherokee occurred during the decade before removal, and the first native newspaper, the *Cherokee Phoenix*, was published in both English and Cherokee from 1828 to 1834. Development of the Pickering alphabet resulted in a written language for the Muscogees (Creeks), Seminoles, Choctaws, and Chickasaws. After removal, translation and printing of texts in these languages continued, and newspapers were established among the Cherokees, Choctaws, and Chickasaws. English education had got under way early in the century with the establishment of mission schools, which continued after removal, but the Cherokees, Choctaws, and Chickasaws established systems of public education and continued, as they had done before removal, to send some of their students to the United States for further education. After the disruption caused by the Civil War, these tribes reestablished their educational institutions, and the Muscogees and Seminoles created educational systems of their own. Thus during the last three decades of the nineteenth century, there was a rising literacy rate among all of the tribes. After Oklahoma's statehood in 1907, education continued as Indians were integrated into the public school systems. Literacy was also bolstered during the territorial period by a thriving publishing industry. By the end of the century, most towns in the Indian Territory (there were no towns in the Seminole Nation) had newspapers, and the larger towns had more than one, including a small number of dailies. These publications provided the major outlet for literary expression, which continued in state and national publications after 1907.

Despite the social and cultural discontinuity forced removal and the Civil War brought to the tribes, their members engaged in a surprisingly high level of literary activity. This activity took a number of forms: for example, translations of the Bible and religious and inspirational tracts by Cherokees Elias Boudinot, David Brown, and George Lowrey; letters by statesmen John Ross (Cherokee) and George W. Harkins (Chickasaw); published addresses by Boudinot, Peter P. Pitchlynn (Choctaw), and E. C. Boudinot (Cherokee); fiery polemical pieces by E. C. Boudinot and John Rollin Ridge (Cherokee); and journals by diarists such as Pitchlynn. Certain themes dominated the works of this period: tribal sovereignty, definition of the tribes as domestic dependent nations, native identity, and removal and its consequences. The most productive writers were Cherokees, who during the two decades before the Civil War produced works in more sophisticated aesthetic forms than others, such as lyrical poetry by John Rollin Ridge, William P. Boudinot, and Joshua Ross and fiction and literary criticism by Ridge.

Such literary activity received some publicity outside the Southeast. Tribal peoples in other regions of America took note, particularly the Six Nations in New York, who were experiencing their own literary genesis in this era. Young Seneca intellectuals such as Maris Bryant Pierce used the Cherokees as their literary model in their fight against removal, and

Ely Parker greatly admired the young Cherokees and Choctaws he met for their diplomatic and literary skills. The vigorous literary activity among the Southeastern Indians before the Civil War established a literary tradition that resumed in the post-war years, when writers would find new themes in the pressures placed upon them by the encroachments of American society, which was rapidly becoming industrialized, urbanized, and technologically advanced.

The struggle of these peoples against the dissolution of their tribal governments dominated the themes in their literature before 1900 and, in large measure, determined its form. By far, the preferred forms during this period were essays, addresses, and letters. Essayists such as Coleman Cole (Choctaw), Richard Fields (Cherokee), T. J. Bond (Choctaw), George Washington Grayson (Muscogee), and Walter Adair Duncan (Cherokee) delineated such issues as the social and religious values, the educational goals, political aspirations, and legal rights of their people. Orators such as George W. Harkins (Chickasaw), William Penn Adair (Cherokee), and William McCombs (Muscogee) spoke eloquently on such topics as the encroachment upon their nations' sovereignty by congressional attempts to establish a territorial government over them, allotment of tribal lands, and the extension of federal court jurisdiction over their territory. They found their audiences in their national councils, at barbecues and political rallies, and even in the chambers of Congress. Added to these voices were those of a myriad of letter writers, who addressed every major concern facing their nations. Two series of letters—the Too-qua-stee letters of DeWitt Clinton Duncan (Cherokee) and the Fus Fixico letters of Alexander Posey (Muscogee)—became well known for their criticism of federal policy and its application to their nations. Among the political writers were some of the most fiercely patriotic. A number of them were born before removal and had twice witnessed the destruction of their nations, once in removal and again in the Civil War. As the federal government pursued its allotment policy, they became embittered and, finally, resigned at what they perceived to be the third and final assault upon their nations. After the tribal titles were dissolved, the popularity of essays, addresses, and letters as literary forms declined.

Historical narratives and biography were important forms throughout the reform era. Early in the period, Coleman Cole and Israel Folsom recorded the traditional history of the Choctaws, Henry Reece (Cherokee) wrote his White Horse series to inform young Cherokees about their society before removal, and DeWitt Clinton Duncan sought to expose the injustice and violence of Cherokee removal. Near the turn of the century, Charles Gibson (Muscogee) recorded the traditional and recent history of the Muscogee people as did James Roane Gregory (Yuchi), who also wrote about the intertribal warfare between the Muscogees and Pawnees after removal. In the twentieth century, Mabel Washbourne Anderson (Cherokee), Muriel H. Wright (Choctaw), and Rachel Caroline Eaton (Cherokee) wrote extensively about the history of their tribes. All of these writers drew heavily on the oral histories of their people to produce their written records. Knowing that their nations were passing through a dramatic time in their history, they realized the importance of writing tribal history long before it became fashionable among non-native historians to do so. The same was true of biography. Writers in the nineteenth century had cast figures such as Sequoyah and Pushmataha as national heroes, but it was not until the twentieth century that writers such as Mabel Washbourne Anderson and Rachel Caroline Eaton attempted full-length biographies of important tribal leaders of the nineteenth century, in this case, Stand Watie and John Ross, respectively. And John Oskison (Cherokee) wrote a biography of Sam Houston, who had close connections to the Cherokees.

Humor, like historical writing, was produced from the 1870s to the New Deal. Early in the period, Cherokee and Choctaw writers created personae who wrote dialect letters to editors, modeled after the work of popular American dialect humorists. By the turn of the century, dozens of Indian dialect writers had been published in territorial newspapers. The form reached its peak in the Fus Fixico letters of Alexander Posey, published between 1902 and 1908. Posey's satiric attacks on politicians, federal policy, graft, and bureaucrats of the allotment era attracted national attention. Dialect humorists who followed him included Royal Roger Eubanks (Cherokee), Elias M. Landrum (Cherokee), and Jesse McDermott (Muscogee). All of these writers took the personae of fullblood Indians who spoke English as a second language, the humor quite frequently turning on the Indian's supposed misunderstanding of realities that were well understood by the readers. The popularity of this type of humor waned by World War I, after which emerged the greatest humorist America has known in the twentieth century, Will Rogers (Cherokee). Rogers delighted his audience through not only his writing but his stage performances, radio shows, and movies.

Fiction writing did not become a popular genre among the writers of these tribes until the 1890s. Writers of short stories in that decade included Will T. Canup (Eastern Band Cherokee), Carrie LeFlore (Choctaw), DeWitt Clinton Duncan, and John Oskison. Of these, only Oskison continued to write stories in the twentieth century; other writers in the early years of the century included Mabel Washbourne Anderson, Ora Eddleman Reed (Cherokee), and Royal Roger Eubanks. These writers modeled their fiction after that of the local color writers of America and wrote about the Indian Territory in the fashion that writers in other geographical regions wrote about their locales. Of these writers, only Oskison achieved a national reputation. A less popular form of fiction was the novel. Only two writers worked in this genre: Sophia Alice Callahan (Muscogee), who wrote in the 1890s, and Oskison, who wrote in the 1920s and 1930s. Both novelists made extensive use of Indian Territory characters and settings in their fiction.

Poetry written by Southeastern Indians, though produced throughout the reform era, did not come into its own until the twentieth century. That written in the late nineteenth century by writers such as Israel Folsom, David J. Brown (Cherokee), and John Lynch Adair (Cherokee) was derivative and sentimental, modeled after the romantic poetry of earlier decades. The most prolific poet of the period was Alexander Posey, who produced more than 250 poems, but among them only a handful are innovative. Though poetry remained a popular form for Indian writers in the twentieth century, only one achieved national stature, Rollie Lynn Riggs (Cherokee). Strongly influenced by the American poet Vachel Lindsay, Riggs was closely aligned with the Imagist poets who were associated with *Poetry* magazine at Chicago after 1912. Poets before Riggs favored the landscapes, people, and customs of their native nations as subjects for their poetry, while Riggs turned his attention to contemporary America.

Drama was the last literary genre to be taken up by Southeastern Indian writers. During the 1920s and 1930s Riggs became one of America's best known writers of folk plays, making much use of Indian Territory and early Oklahoma settings and characters in both his one-act and multi-act plays. During this same time, Finis Fox (Chickasaw) became well known as a writer of screen plays for the movie industry.

The native voices reflected in the wide-ranging literature of the reform era are as varied as the genres in which they found expression. There was consensus that destruction of the native nations was unjust and that cultural bias and racism abounded, but writers differed concerning what actions their people should take in the face of changes being wrought by reform Indian policy. Once tribal autonomy was destroyed, they disagreed about how they should conduct themselves as American citizens in the modern, technological society of the twentieth century, the approach of which the Omaha Exposition of 1898 had hailed. Some writers nostalgically recollected the Indian national status, romanticized its history and people, and bemoaned the loss of tribal culture. Others seemed willing to put that era of their history behind them and move on, some gladly and some simply resigned.

Whatever the personal stands taken by the writers of the reform era, their works stand as testimonials to endurance. The American writer who wrote that the Omaha Exposition of 1898 signalled the triumph of the Anglo-Saxon pioneer over the Indians may have spoken accurately regarding the contest for the possession of land. But the native voices speaking through the literature of the era demonstrate that there was no corresponding triumph over spirit and intellect and identity.

Of course, literary production by Southeastern Indians did not end with the reform era. Some who began writing then—Riggs and Wright, for example—remained productive well beyond World War II. Alexander Posey served as a model for later dialect humorists such as Thomas E. Moore (Muscogee), Acee Blue Eagle (Muscogee/Pawnee), and Daniel Madrano (Caddo). The reader who reads closely in the literature of later periods, especially of recent decades, will hear echoes of other voices from the reform era, which, in that crucial period in American Indian history, gave definition to themes that remain significant for Indian peoples today. Native writers whose ancestral homelands were in the American Southeast have contributed significantly to the dramatic outpouring that has characterized Native American literature during the last three decades. Among them, to name only a few, are Linda Hogan (Chickasaw), poet, novelist, and short story writer; Robert J. Conley (United Keetoowah Band Cherokee), novelist and short story writer; and poets Louis Oliver (Muscogee), Joy Harjo (Cherokee/Muscogee), and Jim Barnes (Choctaw). Like native writers of earlier times, they draw on their tribal heritage, history, and culture and frequently grapple with issues of culture, identity, and sovereignty that are their legacy from the reform era.

In marked contrast to earlier writers, however, contemporary writers have generally not produced nonfiction prose, which dominated the literature of the reform era. Instead, they have followed the examples of Adair, Posey, Oskison, Riggs, and others and have been concerned with aesthetics. In doing so, they have helped earn a place for Native American literature in the American literary canon. Thus the native voices from the reform era represent a significant stage in native literary history of the American Southeast. As such, they provide a vital link between earlier, tribal times and the contemporary realities of Indian America and its literature.

Native American Writing in the Southeast

Israel Folsom

CHOCTAW

(1802–1870)

The Reverend Israel Folsom was born in the Choctaw Nation in Mississippi, the son of Nathaniel Folsom, a white trader, and his Choctaw wife. In the wake of the Treaty of Dancing Rabbit Creek (1830), Folsom assisted in moving the Choctaws to lands in the Indian Territory west of Arkansas, settling near old Fort Washita in the western Choctaw Nation. As his poem reprinted here indicates, he recognized not only the injustice of Indian removal but also the social and cultural discontinuity it created for his people. However, he was thoroughly Christian and was a member of the first generation of native preachers among the Choctaws. Still, like other native writers of his generation, such as William Apess (Pequot), he recognized that the Christian promise of equality of God's grace through Christ was not matched by a similar promise of equality in earthly affairs, and admitted the distinction between what Frederick Douglass called the Christianity of Christ and the dollar-driven Christianity of white America. Despite his conversion Folsom found nothing mutually exclusive in being Choctaw and being Christian. However, like many of his generation, he believed traditional Choctaw culture was passing away and wished to preserve the traditional history though it had acquired, by the second half of the nineteenth century, what appeared to be Christian elements. The selections reprinted here recount the Choctaw migration from the west to Nanih Waiya, the sacred mound that is central to Choctaw traditional history and is located in present-day Winston County, Mississippi. Here, as elsewhere in his writing, Folsom found parallels—perhaps because he looked for them — between the traditional history of the tribe of Chahta and some episodes in the biblical history of the tribes of Israel.

Lo! The Poor Indian's Hope

Land where brightest waters flow,
Land where loveliest forest grow,
Where warriors drew the bow,
    Native land farewell.

He who made yon stream and tree,
Made the White, the Red man free,
Gave the Indians' home to be
    'Mid the forest wilds.

Have the waters ceased to flow?
Have the forest ceased to grow?
Why do our brothers bid us go
    From our native home?

Here in infancy we played,
Here our happy wigwam made,
Here our fathers' graves are laid,—
    Must we leave them all?

Whiteman, tell us, God on high,—
So pure and bright in yonder sky,—
Will not then His searching eye
    See the Indians' wrong?

1875

Choctaw Traditions: Introductory Remarks

The history of the aborigines of America has been one of the most prominent and interesting subjects of inquiry and research of the present age. The manners, habits, customs and peculiarities of the different Indian tribes, have, for many years, formed a theme of deep interest and praiseworthy investigation to the philanthrophic and scientific world. While their traditions are worthy of being preserved, on account of their simi larity to some of the wondrous and attractive events recorded in the Old Testament, various and unsatisfactory are the conjectures set forth regarding their parent root or origin. Some, with a good show of plausibility, have attempted to prove that they are of Jewish extraction and constitute a remnant of the lost ten tribes of Israel; others as earnestly agree, that they are but a branch or offshoot from the Tartar, or Sclavonic or Tyrus race;[1] while on the other hand, a class of speculative historians make bold to assert that they are not of Asiatic lineage, and do not, therefore, owe in common with mankind their descent from Adam. This latter view is supported by the Indians themselves, but gives no strength or additional force to the argument. Whatever value, or otherwise may be attached to one, or all of these theories, which to a large extent they only are, one thing is clear and beyond contradiction, that the white people in general, have, comparatively speaking, but a very imperfect knowledge of the Indian race.

During the earlier period of the history of America, and shortly after its discovery, the monarchs of Europe, fired with the lust of conquest and spoil, attempted, but in vain, to subjugate the Indians and rivet the shackles of slavery upon them. They, however, carried this purpose so far into execution, as cruelly to tear them away from their peaceful homes and endeared families, and transported them, by thousands, into various parts of the world. Those unjust proceedings, instead of quenching the indomitable love of liberty, which so strongly and brightly burned in their breasts, served only to arouse the full power of resistance against the oppressors, which ultimately had the effect of freeing them from such bondage.

> They may bury the steel in the Indian's breast;
> They may lay him low with his sires to rest,
> His scattered race from their heritage push,
> But his dauntless spirit they cannot crush.

From that period up to the present time the Indians have been and are still receiving everything but justice. In fact, ever since the Christian world gained a foot-hold upon the American continent and erected the cross on its shores, they have had no rest, but have been defrauded, trodden down, oppressed, scattered and weakened. Their condition has been one of constant suffering and injustice. Avarice, the civilized man's

---

1. That is, the Tatars of central and western Siberia, the Slavs of eastern Europe, and the Tyrians of ancient Tyre.

demon, has worked heavily upon them, the result of which is, that only a sad and melancholy history can be written in regard to their past and present conditions. Yet a people possessed of such rare and remarkable traits, should not be permitted to pass away without some notice and record of their history. As comprising an important chapter of this great subject, I will now proceed to give a brief narrative of the Choctaw tribe of red people—their traditions, government, religious belief, customs and manners anterior to the introduction of the gospel among them. To guard against any misconception, however, I deem it proper to state that their traditions and history are so much commingled it is difficult to separate them without destroying, in a great measure, the interest of the subject, and I have therefore, to some extent, interwoven them.

1875

Choctaw Traditions: Name and Migration from the West

The name Choctaw or Chahta, is derived from a prophet warrior who flourished at a time too remote for fixing any date, as it is only handed down by tradition from one generation to another. Headed by him, tradition informs us, the people in one grand division migrated to the east from a country far toward the setting sun, following the Cherokees and Muskokees, who had moved on four years previous, in search of a suitable spot for a permanent location. He is said to have been possessed of all the characteristics essential to the carrying out of such an enterprise to a successful termination. His benevolence and many other virtues are still cherished and held in sacred remembrance by his people. The country from whence they migrated, or the causes which induced them to seek another place of habitation is wrapt in mysterious oblivion, as their tradition begins abruptly with the epoch of migration. In moving from place to place, Chahta is said to have carried a high staff or pole which, on encamping was immediately placed in front of his wigwam, where it remained from day to day, and from night to night until they broke up encampment. His wigwam is represented to have been placed in the van of all the tribe. When the pole inclined forward—a power which it was believed to possess—the people prepared to march. This is somewhat analagous to the cloud by day and pillar of fire by night, by which the Lord, through his beloved servant, guided the children of Israel from Egypt.[1]

After many years of wanderings, during which they, in common with those who have ever engaged in similar enterprises, suffered many trials and privations, they at length arrived at a certain place, where the staff stood still and instead of bending forward, inclined backward, which was regarded as a sign they were at their journey's end. To this place where the staff stood still, Chahta gave the name of Nunih-Waiya. The exact period of the termination of their wanderings is unknown. So soon as they got in some degree settled, Chahta called the warriors together for the purpose of organizing a code of laws for their government. At this place of rest, Nunih-Waiya, they built strong fortifications in order to protect themselves from any foe who might conceive hostile intentions against them. Whether or not they were ever assailed is unknown. The remains of the fortress, however, is still to be seen in Mississippi. A long time did not elapse before their newly acquired territory was found to be too limited to hold their rapidly increasing numbers, and they were in consequence compelled to spread themselves over the adjacent country, and form settlements in villages. It is a well authenticated fact, that from this out-pouring or scattering, sprung the Indians called Shukchumas, Yazoes and Natches.[2]

1875

1. See Exodus, Chapters 13 and 14.
2. The Chakchiuma allied with the French in the early eighteenth century against the Natchez, Yazoo, and other tribes. The Natchez, whose settlements were destroyed by the French, scattered and were absorbed by other groups, principally the Cherokees and Muscogee (Creeks). Remnants of the Yazoos probably merged with the Choctaws or Chickasaws.

David J. Brown

CHEROKEE

(1856?–1879)

More is known about the death than the life of David J. Brown, who had apparently written only a handful of poems before he was shot down in the streets of Muskogee, Creek Nation, in early 1879. He was the son of John L. and Ann Schrimscher Brown of Fort Gibson, Cherokee Nation, and at the time of his death was considered one of the promising young men of the nation. Brown graduated in 1878 from the Cherokee Male Seminary near Tahlequah, his nation's capital, where, as a student, he had written most of his poems. Though his poems deal with Cherokee subjects, they reflect the instruction in Classical literature that he received at the seminary. In the poem reprinted here, Brown praises Sequoyah, inventor of the Cherokee syllabary, which revolutionized Cherokee society after 1821 by enabling great numbers of the Cherokee population to become literate. Like Cadmus of Thebes, who in Greek mythology invented the alphabet, Sequoyah is associated with Kee-too-whah, the legendary ancient tribal town, with which Brown symbolized the Cherokee Nation. By comparing Sequoyah to Cadmus and to Moses, the lawgiver, Brown became the first of many Cherokee poets to romanticize and praise this Cherokee national hero.

Sequoyah

Thou Cadmus of thy race!
Thou giant of thy age!

In every heart a place,
In history a living page;
The juggernaut chariot time,
May crush as she doth give;
But a noble name like thine,
Shall ever with Kee-too-whah live.

Orion-like thou dost stand,
In any age and clime,
With intellect as grand,
As ever shown by time,
'Twas thy hand lit the spark
That heavenward flashed its ray
Revealing the shining mark
The straight and narrow way.

Ignorance and superstitious awe
From high pedestals toppled o'er
When as the ancient giver of law,
Smiting, thou mad'st the waters pour;
Stand thou didst on Pisgah's[1] height,
And gazed into the future deep.
But day was ne'er unclasped from night
E'er thy spirit silently fell asleep.

1878   1879

---

1. Nebo, a mountain in Jordan near the Dead Sea.

James Harris Guy

Chickasaw

(?–1885)

If the inhabitants of the Chickasaw and Choctaw nations had presumed to label James Harris Guy, they might have called him the "singing lawman" or the "Chickasaw balladeer." Though Chickasaw, Guy was reared at Boggy Depot, Choctaw Nation, one of the nine children of William R. and Jane McGee Guy, whose descendants figured prominently in Indian Territory and, later, Oklahoma history. Guy served as both a deputy U.S. marshal and as a member of the Indian police force in the Chickasaw Nation and was killed in a shoot-out with outlaws in early 1885. Guy was knowledgeable about the recent history of the Chickasaws and was deeply concerned about the rapidity with which United States citizens were overrunning the Indian Territory. He expressed his concerns in letters to publications like the reform magazine *The Council Fire* but more frequently in poetry in which he attacked American incursion upon Indian rights and romanticized the recent past, recalling nostalgically pre-Civil War settlements in the Choctaw and Chickasaw Nations such as Boggy Depot and Fort Arbuckle. At the time of his death, Guy had made an agreement with H. F. O'Beirne, editor of the *Atoka Independent*, to publish a volume of legends and poems. However, none of the legends and only a handful of poems are known to have survived.

The White Man Wants the Indians' Home

The White man wants the Indians' home,
He envies them their land;

And with his sweetest words he comes
To get it, if he can.

And if we will not give our lands,
And plainly tell him so,
He then goes back, calls up his clans,
And says, "let's make them go."

The question in the Indians' mind
Is, where are we to go?
No other country can we find;
'Tis filled up with our foe.

We do not want one foot of land
The white man calls his own;
We ask of nothing at his hands,
Save to be let alone.

1878

Lament of Tishomingo[1]

From the door of my cabin I sit and gaze,
With sad and tearful face,
As Memory brings forth those other days,
And the fearful fall of my race.

For you must know I come from a band
of honest and fearless men,
And when we in friendship gave our hand,
You need not have feared us then.

But they say we are changed entirely now,
From what we were in the days of Penn,[2]
And the question arises why and how
Are we changed from what we were then.

---

1. Tishomingo was an important chief of the Chickasaws during the removal era.
2. William Penn (1644–1718), the Quaker founder of Pennsylvania, who purchased land from the Indians to found his colony.

As long as the whiteman kept his word,
    As *men* should always do
The vows of friendship were often heard,
    For we were honest and true.

But there has dawned a day of deepest woe
    Upon us and the white man's sight;
For the white man's honor has fallen so low
    That evil has conquered the right.

1879

Fort Arbuckle

The day has been long and dreary;
I halt with the setting sun
To gaze on the open world,
And the work that the years have done;
And a vision rises before me,
Of the past as it hath been,
And all that the rolling hills have heard,
And the bright-eyed stars have seen.

Full many a thrilling story
Could the echoing rocks repeat,
And methinks I hear in the forest
The tramp of hurrying feet.
The yells of the great Commanche[3]
Ring once more in my ear,
And files of the ghostly warriors
Appear and disappear.

I see the dusky phantoms
Rise from their graves to-day,

3. In the wake of removal, the Comanches raided the Chickasaws, whom they considered intruders into their territory. In 1851, the War Department built Fort Arbuckle in the central part of the Chickasaw district. After the Army abandoned the post in 1870, it was occupied and claimed by Thomas Grant, Guy's friend, who ran a store in the old sutler's building.

With the war paint still upon them
As they started for the fray;
They scorned the white man's promise
And refused to be his slaves,
But their ranks were few and feeble,
And the sun sets on their graves.

Once more from the hill above me
The painted warriors ride,
And fall upon Fort Arbuckle
Like rocks from the mountain side;
But now the bow and the quiver
Give place to the plodding plow,
A bible, a hut, a handful of corn
And a Christian's broken vow.

Oh, mystical Fort Arbuckle,
The sun is falling aslant,
And a friend stands out in his doorway;
God speed thee, Thomas Grant;
For thou hast ever a seat at thy board,
And in thy heart a place,
For him who would sing the wide world o'er
The songs of a ruined race.

1891

John Lynch Adair

CHEROKEE

(1828–1896)

John Lynch Adair, Sr., was born in the Cherokee Nation in
Georgia, the son of Thomas Benjamin Adair, a white man, and
Rachel Lynch Adair, a Cherokee, but was orphaned early and
reared by relatives. After removal of the Cherokees to the West
in 1838–39, he was sent to Moravian mission school, then put
under the tutelage of the Reverend Cephas Washburn at Benton-
ville, Arkansas, before attending Ozark Institute near Fayette-
ville. There, he found language a favorite study, doing well in
Latin but less well in Greek. Finding no family support for additional education, Adair went to the gold fields of California in
1849, returning to the Cherokee Nation in 1853, when he married and settled down to farm. He fought for the Confederacy
during the Civil War, after which he moved to Tahlequah, the
Cherokee capital, and in the following years served as national
auditor, clerk of the Cherokee senate, and executive councilor
under Chief Lewis Downing, and filled as well a number of other
significant posts, including three times his nation's delegate to
Washington, D. C. He was also editor of a number of newspapers: *Cherokee Advocate* (1873–75) and the *Tahlequah Courier*
(1893) at Tahlequah and the weekly *Indian Chieftain* (1885–89),
the *Daily Indian Chieftain* (1891), and *World* (1891) at Vinita.
Though Adair supposedly wrote a number of poems, the two
reprinted here are the only lines that are known to have survived.
Adair's poetry follows the lyrical tradition of the British and
American Romantic poets of the early nineteenth century. In that
respect, his work is more akin to that of his fellow Cherokee
John Rollin Ridge (1827–67) than to the topical poetry com-

monly written by other poets who resided in the Indian Territory
in the late nineteenth century.

Hec Dies

To him whose hopes are far away,
　To where life's sunset scene discloses
　First of spring flowers and roses,
　Of summer next, and winter snows
　Further on, knows or thinks he knows
That far this scene beyond is day.

That to behold it, as we may,
　It's but little more than a dream,
　And of events, this turbid stream—
　Beginning, ah where? and ending,
　Ah where? and forever wending—
Is not a real scene to-day.

That we'll fall to sleep, as we say,
　And, weary, would have it night
　While the sun is yet warm and bright;
　Will wake from sleep to find
　That all we say and left behind
Was nothing but a dream that day.

Wonder how long we slept that way.
　Think we've been dreaming—nothing more—
　And to those who had woke before
　From sleep, will wish to tell our dreams,
　Of the unaccountable scenes,
We beheld as we slept that day.

That our loved we'll find, as we pray,
　Who had grown weary and had slept,
　And in their dreams had laughed and wept
　O'er scenes that were so real
　That nothing could be ideal
Of what they saw and felt that day.

Believe we were dreaming, some way,
　　When we thought it was more than sleep—
　　It was so cold and calm and deep—
　　In which they lay, and sorrow's tears
　　We'll think were strange, as were the fears,
That made sad our dreaming that day.

　That the gleams from the faraway
　　We sometimes have of better things—
　　Like strange birds upon helpless wings,
　　Blown from some isle in tropic climes—
　　Are memories of other times,
As we'll find when we wake that day.

1877?   1892

Joy Returneth with the Morning

A great storm had blown out the stars,
　　And the winds, rushing from their caves,
　　Lashed the sea into mountain waves;
And the ship, under bending spars,
In utter darkness plowed the deep.
　　Unto Him whom the winds obeyed
　　On Galilee, I humbly prayed
That in his keeping I might sleep.

In a haven, calm and bright
　　With tropic sunshine, where the scent
　　Of orange blooms made redolent
The breeze that was so soft and light
That scarcely there a wavelet broke
　　Upon the bosom of the bay,
　　When next morn' our good ship lay—
To glad consciousness I 'woke.

So may it be, good Lord of all,
　　When into darkness sinks my sun,
　　And my stars go out, one by one,

To such calm slumber may I fall.
And that which only faith had been,
    Awake to find a truth to be,
    Where no white sails go out to sea,
But are forever coming in.

1889   1892

William Trenton Canup

EASTERN BAND CHEROKEE

(1866–1902)

A native of Cherokee County, North Carolina, William Trenton
Canup was the son of F. M. Canup, a Frenchman, and Eliza
Payne Canup, a member of the Eastern Band of Cherokees. The
young Canup went to college in Texas and then worked for the
Dallas Herald. Then, like many North Carolina Cherokees in
the late nineteenth century, he migrated to the Western Cherokee
Nation, where he was known primarily as a journalist. He settled first at Vinita and then in 1887 became local editor of the
Telephone at Tahlequah and later bought the paper, then sold it
and served as its business manager (1889). He edited the *Tahlequah Bazoo* (1888) with Frank J. Boudinot and founded the
Indian Sentinel (1890) at Webbers Falls but sold it shortly thereafter and worked for the Fort Smith, Arkansas, *Elevator* (1891).
He also wrote for the *Capital City Daily News* (1891) at Tahlequah and served as a special correspondent for newspapers in
Dallas, Fort Worth, Cincinnati, New York, Atlanta, St. Louis,
and Kansas City. Though Canup was primarily a journalist, he
was also a cartoonist and occasionally wrote fiction, like the
story reprinted here, based loosely on the lives of people he met
in the Cherokee Nation. One of his best known, this story is set
at Fort Gibson, Cherokee Nation, which had been the site of a
military post established to assist in the removal of the Indians
to the West.

Alluwee Brown, and the Tragic End of Unlearned "Jim"

It was an evening during the melancholy days of October a number of years ago that the writer of this little sketch had occasion to spend a day and night at the old military post of Ft. Gibson in the Cherokee Nation—a place that has been the scene of more real romance and the home of more great men than any hamlet on the frontier—and the environment of its picturesque location is only exceeded by the rich beauty of its halfbreed Cherokee girls. Here it was that the illustrious Sam Houston just subsequent to his departure from Tennessee lived, loved and wedded a pretty Indian maiden—a fact that the biographers of the great Texas statesman for some reason have failed to record. In this village Gen. Zack Taylor resided for a number of years, and the house that the late Jefferson Davis once called his home is still standing—now a weatherbeaten and somewhat dilapidated reminder of the ex-Confederate chieftain.

Outside the barracks is the pretty little town nestling on the east bank of the beautiful Grand river, whose crystal waters flow peacefully by and mingle with the muddy Arkansas a mile below.

Here the writer found himself on the occasion referred to with an evening before him and nothing to do but to pass it off as best he could. The sun was low in the west and was shedding its streams of mellow light over the land and bathing the house-tops and a quartette of wooded hills in its hues of gold. The cow-boys came up on their Indian ponies and dashed away again with the reckless air peculiar to that class of westerners. A few Indians and half-breeds in sombreros, cotton-shirts, and leather breeches came lazily up and moodily departed in the twi-light—to the stranger, perplexing enigmas of the gloaming; to one acquainted with them, the lingering remnant of a once great people.

On that memorable evening—memorable for its remarkable quiet—Simon Brown was standing with the writer on the veranda of his dwelling overlooking the beautiful little town. We had been talking about his pretty half-breed daughter—his wife being a Cherokee, although with but little resemblance of an Indian, and one who spoke only the English language. The girl, with a pan of salt, was sprinkling it upon some big flat stones that were in the meadow just in front of the house and the sober cows were coming up to lick it.

"Yes, we allus give 'em salt when it looks like rain—an' when they smell the damp in the air they cum up regular to git it. Them stones is rubbed smooth as glass where they've licked 'em fer the last twenty years."

"The girl always sprinkles the salt for them," I interposed.

"Yes, 'cepts when she's at school; then Jim 'tends to it."

Jim was the farm hand, and was now sitting out in the lot on a stump whittling a piece of soft pine with hook-pointed jack-knife, seemingly in a profound study.

"I don't know what I'm goin' to do wi' Jim," continued the old man after a brief pause. "He use to be one o' the smartest han's in all this country, but he's gitting awful nocount—drinkin' an' fighting."

"Drinking! isn't it against your laws to sell liquor in the Indian country?"

"O, yes, but Jim gets it somehow."

After a little further talk, the old man strolled down to the barn to turn out the horses for the night and the writer joined Jim in the lot.

"Jim?"

"Yes."

"You were not raised in this section, were you? You have seen considerable of the world I imagine?"

"Yes, 'bout as much of it as most fellers of 30."

"How long have you been here?"

"Where; wi' the old man?"

"Yes."

" 'Bout fifteen years."

"Jim," said I, "we've only known each a little while, and perhaps it isn't any of my business, but are you not getting tired of your life here? The old man says you are not—well—not as steady as you were at first. What is the trouble? Now to-morrow I am going away—perhaps will never see you again—and it kinder occurred to me that you would like to talk about yourself. I believe everybody feels that way sometimes."

Jim whittled a long time—so long that I feared that he was going to rebuke me with his silence—and then—

"Them meadow larks—hear 'em?—they make me bluer'n death—them an' that girl there by the cows."

The plaintive whistle of the meadow larks was to be heard on all sides, and the figure of the pretty Indian maiden, duskily outlined against the evening sky, suggested the etching of the Angelus.[1] No wonder poor Jim felt blue.

"When I fust come 'ere I was 17 years old. My home was in Texas, but I'd been rambling around everywhere. I'd been all over the United States. Alluwee there, was only six, a little half-breed Injun gal, but purty to kill. I taught her letters to her, and taught her to spell, an' then to read a little, and when she was nine she could read the newspapers."

Jim looked up at this for some appreciation of his work. His lips were shut and his nostrils dilated in a swelling pride at the recollection, and then as memory carried him on from that to something that struck him deeper, the lines of the face came down and the shadow of the evening crept into the manly blue eyes.

"Then her father thought the child know'd enough, but I know'd she didn't; I know'd she or'ter be sent to school. The Nation was just startin' a sem'nary at Tahlequah, an' I got the old man to let me take 'er there. I'd rather not tell this—but the way I got him to do it was by paying her expenses myself, tho' I wouldn't let the girl know it. I'd never had any sister or mother to take kere of, and I thought I would do what I could for this little gal. It's 20 miles to Tahlequah, an' I would take her over there in the wagon, an' go after 'er Christmas times and vacations. When the school term was long once or twice I went back to the States to rustle up a little extra money, but I would allus come back in time to go after her. I wish I could tell you how she grow'd, an' how she got purtier every day; how her face got brighter than the faces 'round her, as she le'rned and le'rned. She used to ask me questions 'bout the States, and everything, an' 'bout towns. That was when she'd come home, an' sometimes at school she'd write me letters with questions in 'em, an' I'd sit up all night answerin' 'em. Sir, do you know I got to longin' for them letters, an' a-waitin' for 'em? Yes sir—"

Jim was thinking again. Once he got down from where he was sitting and kicked mechanically at the small stones that lay on the ground. Then he picked up one and, boy-like, sailed it off into the field. But he couldn't shake off the weariness of his mood.

"I don't know how it happened," he finally continued, "but when she was about 15 she quit asking me questions and commenced tellin' me things 'bout histery, an' stories. I 'member one 'bout a man Max'ell killin' a feller an' hiding him in a trunk, an' was hung for it. Did ye ever hear

1. *The Angelus*, an 1859 painting by Jean François Millet, now in the Louvre.

o' that? Yes? well I s'posed ye had, but there was lots of things like that she'd tell me; and then—an' then—"

"What, Jim?"

"Then—I was tryin' to think how to tell it—but anyhow, when I'd try to tell her anything, instead of lookin' interested an' her brown eyes getting bigger like they use to do, I'd catch her laughin' at me—quiet-like—just as if she know'd all about it, an' was 'mused at my poor way of tellin' it."

Jim paused again, and gazed vaguely at the little stars that had begun to twinkle in the evening sky. His case was no longer an enigma to me. He was in love—desperately in love with the pretty Cherokee maiden. But by his kindness to her he had ruined his chances of ever winning the fair girl. Through his instrumentalities she had been educated and elevated far above him. Tho' once a simple little girl who looked up to him as a superior, she was now accomplished, educated and his superior in society. As I left Jim in the lot that memorable evening I could but sympathize with him and regret that he had not had the same peculiar advantages of an education that the pretty girl that he had learned to love had had. But such is fate.

Three years passed, when one evening at about the same time of year, when the sere and yellow leaves were beginning to fall from their branches and drift in the October winds, and the prairies were brown and dry, my business called me again to the Territory and to Fort Gibson. Simon Brown and his pretty daughter, now in the bloom of womanhood, were still there, but my friend Jim, whom I had often thought of, was not with the family. I made inquiries of him of one of the villagers before I left and learned his sad fate. Driven to desperation by his uncontrollable love for pretty Alluwee Brown, Jim turned out bad—as I had expected. He finally joined a band of burglars who were then operating in the Territory. One dark night Jim and two of his associates planned the robbery of the house that he had for so many years made his home. As Jim was acquainted with the place so well he was selected by the other two to enter and conceal himself in the house that had been marked for robbery. Just after dark the three men might have been seen talking in a subdued tone in front of the house. After his companions left him, Jim muttered: "Yes, I belong to the fraternity now; I am here to rob this house that was so long my home. I hav' the mask, an' the pistol in my pocket. Yes, I'm a full-fledged burglar—but how different it might o' been. I wonder what Alluwee would say if she could see me—if she knew—"

The fallen man stopped himself with an oath—seemed, with a motion of his hand, to cast away the thoughts that were upon him—and in a moment more was making his way noiselessly through the window into the house. He made no sound as he moved and, guided by a dark lantern, was looking for a place of concealment. It soon presented itself—in a long wardrobe he hid himself.

He heard, after a while, a woman's voice which he at once recognized as that of Mrs. Brown. She was talking to her daughter, whose musical voice was heard a moment later answering her.

"I am so frightened to be left alone as we are," said the voice. "Your father was called away so unexpectedly this evening. The very thought, dear, of being alone almost makes me ill."

"I am never nervous, mother," said Alluwee as she crossed the room and stood so near Jim that he could almost hear her breathe.

"I am as good as a man about the house," Alluwee continued, "I've hunted imaginary burglars until I believe them not half so bad as most women think."

"Don't speak of them!" said the mother, with a shudder; "this house would be more of a temptation to them to-night than it has ever been before since we lived here. Simon left $8,000 with me this evening, Alluwee. He hadn't time to take it down to the store and deposit it. They said that Mr. Harris was dying, and it's 20 miles to Tahlequah. He hasn't arrived there yet."

As the matron made this confession, Jim, concealed so very near her, listened with his very heart in his ears. But it was not to the statement so well calculated to rejoice a burglar's heart. No, not that. He heard only the soft voices of the mother and of pretty Alluwee as she tried to calm the mother's fears. After all, what was Alluwee to him? True, he had been her protector and benefactor and had learned to love her with a mad love, but her haughty pride had driven him to desperation. Jim placed his face to the keyhold in the wardrobe door, and he could see the beautiful face and graceful figure, and then he thought how unworthy he was, even before he was a robber, of so fair a woman.

"I wish Jim was at the house to-night," said Alluwee after a pause.

"We could feel more secure, after all my bravery. When he becomes tired of rambling I hope he will come straight back to us; for mother, do you know that since he left I have realized that he was the best fellow that ever lived—and I—I would love much to see him."

The man who had stolen into the house to rob it—the man of whom they spoke—could bear no more. His heart was softened as it had not been for months and years. It was as if an angel was talking in his presence.

Then Jim remembered why he was hidden in that closet—and kneeling he kissed the door that was between him and the dear girl who had saved him from a desperate deed. He crept out, found his way to the window through which he entered, and departed as he had come, vowing to lead an honest life, and sometime—perhaps when he was dying—to see his dear Alluwee again. At least always the memory of that face and the words she spoke would keep his heart tender and life pure, lonely as might be his lot.

With these thoughts in his mind he stood beside the house and remembered with a pang who would arrive soon and what their errand would be, and that, while he scorned to betray them, he must stand between them and their purpose, and save the house from burglary, and perhaps the lives of the two women. He felt in his bosom for his pistol. He knew well enough the unforgiving ferocity of those with whom he had to deal, and he uttered a little prayer for aid—the first he had breathed for many a day—as he heard soft footsteps approaching.

"He is opening his eyes," said a soft voice.

Jim heard it, and wondered what had happened, and who it was that spoke. Then came the remembrance of a quarrel, a conflict and the report of a pistol. He knew all now. His fellow burglars had shot him and left him for dead.

"Mother, I think he is opening his eyes," and then they did open and Jim saw two women bending over him with a light.

"Jim, do you know us?" said Alluwee, as she peered sadly down into the wounded man's face.

"Yes, I know you both," answered Jim faintly.

"We found you wounded—dead we thought—here at our gate," said the mother. "It was Alluwee who knew you first. We don't know how it happened, but you can tell us when you get better."

Jim knew that it did not matter whether he told them how he came to be at their house that night or not. He knew that in a little while he would neither see their faces nor hear their voices. He was dying.

He turned his dimmed eyes to those of Alluwee and said in disjointed gasps:

"If I was going to live I would not ask it, but you used to kiss me long ago, Alluwee. Will you kiss me now—just once more?"

The girl with tears trickling down her cheeks knelt by Jim, and he took her in his arms.

"God is merciful," he said, "more merciful than love; perhaps we shall meet again, dear Alluwee."

Those were the last words that Jim ever spoke.

1891

William Eubanks

CHEROKEE

(1841–1921)

William Eubanks (or Unenudi), the son of a white adopted father
and Cherokee mother, was one of the outstanding Cherokee intellectuals of the late nineteenth century. As a young man he
joined the Confederate army in the American Civil War under
the celebrated Cherokee general, Stand Watie, and reached the
rank of captain. After the war Eubanks taught school, but distinguished himself as a translator for the Cherokee Nation from
1870 until the nation was dissolved in 1906. For many of those
years he translated for the *Cherokee Advocate*, the official newspaper of the Cherokee Nation. He also translated the constitution and laws of the nation in 1893 and later in that decade
served as translator for the commission appointed by the Cherokee Nation to confer with the Dawes Commission. A self-taught
linguist, in 1891 Eubanks invented a shorthand for the Sequoyan
syllabary. He was also an essayist, whose subjects included his
amateur studies of astronomy, unusual theories on the origins of
the Indians, and his researches into ancient languages, religions,
and philosophies. In 1893 he toured the South, lecturing on
those subjects. Eubanks also wrote political commentary under
the pen name Cornsilk. The context of the two Cornsilk pieces
reprinted here was the establishment of the Dawes Commission
by Congress in 1893. The commission's purpose was to prepare
the way for breaking up the Five Civilized Tribes and prepare
their members for statehood and U. S. citizenship. To do this,
the commissioners proposed to negotiate agreements by which
the tribes agreed to dissolve the common tribal land titles and to
allot individual parcels of land to tribal members. The sarcasm

and bitterness in Eubanks' works reflect the view most Cherokees held of the Dawes Commission's purpose and of the changes in Cherokee life ways that purpose portended.

For Lands in Severalty, and Statehood

This is an age of freedom, in which a man can express his opinion on anything without fear. And taking advantage of this privilege, I wish to say, as far as I am concerned, I am in favor of lands in severalty and statehood. I am a progressive man and wish to keep up with the age of progress. I want a state so that we could have everything that people have in the States of the United States, such as whiskey, saloons, gambling halls, poor houses and other kinds of houses, such as we find all over Christian America. These, in my opinion, would be a great blessing to the Cherokee people. Another great privilege we could have if we were a state, and that would be the right to kill our old mothers and grandmothers for sixteen dollars and forty cents.

If we were citizens of a state we could be frauds, thieves, robbers, cutthroats and sneaks and if we felt any ways modest after learning all these things we could join the church, same as they do in the states.

More than this I am an educated man, or in other words I am an enlightened man and don't believe in a God, don't believe in any spirit, don't believe in the law of retribution, or the theosophical karma, I don't believe in justice. I believe in nothing but gold and silver and land. I believe in that Brother-in-red kind of religion that can ask the U. S. Government in the name of Christ to crush the Indian out of existence so that we can get his land.

I want courts of injustice established all over this country every two miles. Let us in these courts construe the treaties. If any part is in favor of the U. S., let's get on the house tops and talk loudly about the treaties being the *"Supreme Law of the land,"* but if it favors the Indian let's see if it won't bear another construction.

1894

Measure for Measure

"That which you measure out to other men shall be measured to you again."

The above words were favorite expressions of the ancient Essenian initiates,[1] when imparting to their pupils the accumulated wisdom and experience of the past ages. One of the masters using these words was said to have spoken as one having authority. "That which ye mete out to other men shall be measured to you again," is one of the grandest truths that ever was uttered by man, and is strikingly illustrated in the treatment of the Indians of America by the so-called Christian government of the United States.

Sacred treaties have been made with these Indians and before the ink, with which the agreement is written, is dry, schemers have been allowed to intrude upon the Indians' country against treaty agreements. They are used as battering rams to tear down the nationalities of the Indians and get up disputes that the government may find a pretext to show its animal power. We are harassed by an innumerable long haired, dirty, greasy and black skinned white men who have come into this country claiming to be Indians, but the government seems to look upon this as a very fine scheme and winks approvingly, being too ignorant to fully appreciate the grand truth, that which she is measuring to us Indians shall be measured to her again.

The measurer is in fact, already within her borders with the measuring rod in his hand. The United States with ignorant liberality has thrown wide open the doors and entrance ways to her country and admitted that class hostile to her welfare and prosperity, with not an iota of gratitude, but of the same element of our intruder and some citizens, continually squalling out for a change of government.

Think of the nihilist, the anarchist, the striker, the uprising of that foreign pauper against the capitalist of your country—think of our petitions, prayers, and the oft repeated request to you to honor your sacred obligations to us, and then ponder on the true meaning of the above caption to our warning: "That which ye measure out to others shall be measured to you again."

1. See Matthew 7:1, Mark 4:24, and Mark 6:38. The Essenes were an ascetic brotherhood of Jews in Palestine from the second century B. C. to the second century A. D.

Yes, pour out the vials of indignation on the head of the despised Indian. Violate your sacred obligations which bear your signature. Trample the patent to his lands in the dust. Exterminate him from the face of the earth—but remember that according to the just laws of a just God—"That which you measure out to others shall be measured to you again."

1894

DeWitt Clinton Duncan
[Too-qua-stee]

CHEROKEE

(1829–1909)

DeWitt Clinton Duncan was born at Dahlonega in the eastern Cherokee Nation in Georgia, the son of John and Elizabeth Abercrombie Duncan, who removed to the West with the tribe in 1839. Young Duncan attended mission and Cherokee nation schools before going to Dartmouth College, from which he graduated in 1861. Because of the Civil War, Duncan did not return to the Indian Territory but taught school in northern states before finally settling in 1866 at Charles City, Iowa, where he practiced law, held petty political offices, and taught school. For more than a decade after 1880, Duncan divided his time between the Cherokee Nation and Iowa, but served the Cherokees in various capacities: as attorney for the nation; teacher of English, Latin, and Greek at the Cherokee Male Seminary; and translator of the Cherokee laws. Throughout this period and beyond, he attempted to write a linguistic analysis of the Cherokee language. In the early 1880s he also began to write for Cherokee newspapers, particularly the *Indian Chieftain* at Vinita, where he took up permanent residence in the 1890s, and the *Cherokee Advocate* at Tahlequah. Though he became known locally as a poet and fiction writer, Duncan was best known for dozens of letters that appeared under the pen name Too-qua-stee. While the range of subjects in the Too-qua-stee letters is great, the predominant subject is the United States attack upon the sovereignty of the Cherokee Nation. Though himself a product of assimilation, Duncan complained of that process. Yet, ironically, because of it, he believed the Cherokees were better equipped to understand the whites and to resist encroachment upon their national sovereignty. It allowed them to escape altogether the degradation of the reservation system to which other tribes were subjected in the last half of the century. They escaped, as well, the resulting poverty and disease that so decimated the ranks of native populations. Yet the price of the Cherokees' escape was the dissolution of their nation and citizenship in the United States, as provided for by the Curtis Act of 1898. Though Duncan saw these ironies, he raised his voice to the last in opposition to the destruction of his nation and, after the fact, lamented its passing and attempted to prick America's conscience about its unfair dealings with the Cherokees. The letters reprinted below reflect his fierce Cherokee nationalism as well as the emotional appeals and the clear, rational arguments he made in behalf of the Cherokees. The poems reflect the sadness and bitterness engendered by his nation's demise and his pride in his people's achievements.

A Momentous Occasion

There occurred recently in the senate chamber at Tahlequah an incident which, from a moral point of view, equaled, and perhaps surpassed in grandeur and pathos, anything that ever happened in all the history of human affairs, the tragic day of the crucifixion alone excepted; and yet like that awful scene of Calvary, it passed off as but a commonplace phenomenon and, at the time, left no abiding impression upon the public mind.

The Dawes commission were there; they had come to confer with the Cherokees in reference to the allotment of their lands, the dissolution of their tribal government, and their becoming citizens of the United States.

For nearly a week the commission had been exceedingly beset by a swarm of importunate petitions praying for various personal advantages to be secured to them by means of special stipulations to be embodied in the treaty which, as supposed, was soon to be concluded. These were mostly white men who had come into the country under the franchises of marriage, and were insisting on their right to share with the Indians in the distribution of their lands, together with a like number of mixed-bloods who were equally obtrusive in demanding that suitable provisions should be made in the treaty for the protection of certain speculations which they had ventured in town lots.

The fullbloods were plentiful about the council ground; but they neither sought, nor seemed even to desire, any contact with the commissioners. They had no sordid favors to ask, no axes to grind; but, in the meantime, they kept themselves quite aloof and solemnly counseled with one another, in reference to the momentous propositions which had been submitted by the government.

At length, all economic questions pushed aside for a moment, the commissioners expressed a desire to see, and hear from the real people of the country. Accordingly, in response to a special invitation, a courteous reply was returned to the effect that they would be pleased to appear by representation before the commission the next day at their morning session.

On the morrow, at the appointed hour, as many as three portly men of decidedly aboriginal appearance came filing into the chamber and took their seats in the auditorium. The commissioners, also three in number, had already entered and resumed their positions of state. The house had been early crowded with a mixed concourse of people, all on the tiptoe of curious expectation; for the occasion had been looked upon by all as one likely to be attended with something of dramatic interest. The words of the government in regard to pushing forward the negotiations had been preemptory, while at the same time it was well understood that the ultimate terms conceded by the commission were only such as could never possibly prove acceptable to the inflexible patriotism of the full-blood mind. Indeed every circumstance seemed to point forward very clearly to a season of intense feeling and earnest words; and as the full-bloods had always enjoyed the reputation of wielding a controlling influence in shaping political results, everybody was anxious to be present in order to hear and learn the position they would take in reference to the great question before the convention.

The moral aspect of the meeting thus constituted was remarkable; it was virtually the coming together of two of the principal races of mankind to discuss no less a subject than the surviving chances for further national existence. The white men had literally summoned the red men before them to show cause, if any they had, why their name, as a people, should not be expunged from its ancient place upon the annals of time; why their national history, coming down through a countless series of centuries and redolent with so many cherished traditions, should not be brought, once for all, abruptly to a close.

All were seated and a few moments of suspense ensued, affording a solemn interval for the study of character and melancholy reflection upon the terrible vicissitudes that are wont, in the course of time to betide the nations of earth.

Conspicuous on the one hand sat the commissioners on the part of the United States, the accredited representatives of the all-conquering white men; and facing them, equally prominent in the midst of the expectant multitude, sat the dark-skinned, stalwart personators of the once independent, but now subjugated, proprietors of the western world. Each side was characterized by a peculiar and very interesting dignity of its own; that of the former was indeed reverend, yet it was of that tame and unpoetic kind which usually shows itself in connection with a consciousness of acknowledged superiority over environment; it was the dignity of the lion as he sits in a state of quietude by the side of the prey which he has crushed. That of the latter, on the other hand, was all of dignity in the truest sense—dignity adorned with every conceivable element of grandeur; that heroic kind which, when defeated hopelessly at all points in the open field, retires into the citadel of its own great being and there, with unyielding fortitude, welcomes and at the same time defies the peltings of "outrageous fortune."

Each side, too, had a biography which, when touched by the wand of reminiscence, yielded abundance of rich material for enhancing the general interest of the occasion. The two had been brethren once, a few millenniums ago, upon the lovely plain of Shinar; but, becoming alienated from each other by so foolish a matter as a diversity of language, they quarreled at the foot of old Babel, and parted company, the one toward the east, the other to to west.[1] Each having made a semi-circumference of the entire globe, they met again on the opposite hemisphere, but only to renew the absurd wrangle. In the meantime, one had multiplied in numbers amazingly, and had become what is called civilized; that is to say, they had acquired a knack for invention, had mastered the arts of comfort and gratification, and had learned how to use the destructive elements of material nature for the purposes of aggression and defense.

1. See Genesis, chapter 11. A Christian, Duncan accepted the general theory of human descent from Adam. The theory that the natives of America descended from a lost tribe of Israel was popular in the nineteenth century. For reference to other theories of racial and cultural descent of aboriginal peoples in America, see Israel Folsom.

But their social system had become miserably corrupted by the substitution of conventionalisms for natural principles. They deemed, for instance, the rule of the majority to be *right* without regard to the sanctions of the moral law. "The greatest good to the greatest number," they held, was the legitimate and only end of all human government; and under the influence of this political heresy, plighted faith ceased with them to be a binding guaranty any further than it happened to be endorsed by majorities sufficient to avenge its infraction. Solemn treaties were held to be *repealable.*

Between two families of people who had been so long and so widely estranged from each other, and between whom there had sprung up such incompatible notions of honor and moral obligation, anything like harmonious intercourse and good neighborhood could not, of course, be expected. Accordingly unwarranted aggression on part of the white men early provoked a conflict of races; and a ceaseless repetition of the same offense, under various sophistical pleas of jurisdiction, kept the flame of war alive for more than three hundred years, and down to the present day. The red men were beaten in the field. Finding arms and valor insufficient as a means of defense against the attacks of their overbearing brethren from the east, they determined, (and it was the best thing that they could do,) to test the effect of moral forces; they endeavored to bind the evil hands of the white men with the ligatures of treaty stipulation; and, in order to give the restraint thus imposed all the needed force for the purposes of future safety, they adopted the practice of granting to them large scopes of their valuable territory in consideration of the pledges received. But it was all to no purpose; for no sooner had the land thus ceded been fully occupied, (and often times even before,) than renewed intrusion had given rise to new hostilities, necessitating a new treaty of peace, an additional cession of lands, and the further retirement of the red men beyond the confines of present aggression. The futility of any effort to purchase peace and immunity of the white men in this way, soon became obvious, and the red men were fain to abandon the scheme. But it was too late; the plan had worked well, to the notion of the former, and it at once became, with them, a very favorite mode of procedure. Hence as additional territory became desirable from time to time, old guarantees were claimed to be incompatible with the demands of civilization, and armed forces were sent into the country of the red men of sufficient power to extort from them an *amicable* agreement called a treaty;

and the work was done; the red men retired as usual and the white men sat down upon their estate.

But not to digress further; the Dawes commission had by means of official declarations, given the Cherokee people to understand that the reforms proposed would be consumated either with or without, their consent; and that they should not deceive themselves by trusting to their treaties as matters of sufficient moment to stay the hand of the government; for it was the intention of congress to override all these guarantees by means of arbitrary legislation.

The speaking began; and the three orations occupied the whole of the forenoon. The language used was the unadorned, laconic Indian. It is not within the power of English translation to do full justice to these three speeches; yet thought after thought was regularly snatched up as it came glowing from the furnace of inimitable eloquence, and shaped somewhat to the comprehension of the commissioners by means of skillful interpretation. Each oration had its own leading idea; that of the first was, the effect of the reforms proposed, (if adopted,) upon the well-being of the fullblood people. "What," he exclaimed in a torrent of language, thought, feeling and argument equal to anything ever seen in Grecian or Roman classics, "What will become of that class of people whom I today have the honor to represent? We know the white men; they are a proud and overbearing race. We fullbloods can never live with them. Their laws are too many; they are written in big books, and in a language, too, which we cannot understand. We shall never know when we are violating their laws until we are arrested and dragged away to trial. Your judges, too, will be white men; they will not be able to talk to us. When on trial, we shall be at the mercy of the white men; when convicted, we shall not know the nature of our offense; and when punished, we shall not know whether we have been punished according to the law or against. We can never live with the white men. If it be indeed the intention of the government to annul our treaties and turn the white men in upon us, it would be much the same as if the great father at Washington should take us up and plunge us all headlong into hell; death would be preferable."

The prevailing idea of the second oration was the sanctity of treaty obligation. He said:

"You ask us to make a new treaty; but we can not see the need of any new negotiations. You tell us that our old treaties are not good; but there was a time when you did not think so. When did they lose their force? Who is it that has spoiled them? It is not we. We have violated no treaty;

we have broken no law. What is the matter with our great father at Washington? What is the cause of his offense, that he should annul our treaties and destroy our nation? Treaties never die except by the consent of the parties. The United States makes treaties with England, and they live forever. The great father at Washington never thinks of spoiling them. Why should he consider the treaties which he has made with us any less sacred than those he has made with the men on the other side of the big water? It is unjust to spoil our treaties. We are a small people, much smaller than we used to be. I know we shall have to yield to the wishes of the government. The great father has many big guns; their protection was promised to us. Yet we know that unless we obey him, they will not be our protectors; they will be turned against us. Yet if resistance were practicable, and it were at all availing, I should willingly pour out my blood in defense of the rights of my people."

The words of the third speaker were different from those of the other two in tone and elevation of spirit. Said he:

"I am an old man. I have spent the greater part of my lifetime going about trying to do good. My business has been to preach the gospel. It has been my special care to look after the young men of our country and lead them in the right way. I have pointed them to the Savior of the world who died on the cross; and in doing this, I have also been in the habit of recommending to them the ways of the white men as something worthy of their imitation. But I begin to doubt whether I have been doing the right thing. If what I hear from the commissioners be indeed the words of the white people—if they really mean to annul our treaties and break faith with us in that way—then their example will be no more worthy of an Indian's imitation. The good results of my labors among my people will be blasted. I shall not feel like preaching to our young men any more; they will laugh at me and ask me if I would like to have them do like the white men.

"I am not in favor of making a new treaty; our old treaties are all that we need. It is said we have a great deal of crime in our country; there would not have been so much if the United States had complied with her treaties with us. We have laws, and we have courts of justice. When one of our own people commits a crime, we can try him and punish him. But the government allows white people to come into our country contrary to our treaties. They commit crimes, but we are not allowed to handle them. They are allowed to stay here, and it makes our country look like a hiding place for criminals, when we are not at fault. All we want is peace; we only want to be let alone. I am not in favor of treating."

At the close of the speaking, one of the commissioners arose and, for himself and his associates, said in substance:

"We have heard what you have had to say. We have felt the force of your words, and appreciate your feelings. We sympathize with you from the bottom of our hearts. But what you want is beyond our power to grant. Congress had determined to make a change in the political condition of your country, and we can't help it. We can only advise you to be wise, improve the opportunity offered you, and prepare for the inevitable."

The scene, from a moral point of view, was indescribable; it was simply awful. It was a spectacle never to be forgotten. It was the white man's boasted civilization brought down to lick the dust at the feet of the red man's so-called barbarism; an exhibition at which the moon might well blush in blood, and the sun hide his head forever in the caverns of universal night, from motives of intolerable shame.

1897

The Indian's Hard Lot

The Indian now has a hard time of it in Washington. He is looked upon here somewhat as an outlaw—not indeed a criminal, that is not what we mean exactly—but as a man whose rights (if he can be said to have any at all,) have no reliable foundation in law, a man who is politically just what he is, and has what he has, merely as a matter of sufferance; a man whose status in the world is only a question of public policy; a thing which may be this today, and that, or something else, tomorrow, just as the popular choice may chance to require at the hand of arbitrary legislation. His condition, from a legal standpoint, is truly anomalous; it seems especially so in a land like this, where we have a right to claim and expect for him a state of things much better than this—where, for instance, the light of civilization is so bright and pervasive; and all the fine humanities suggested by the divine law are thought to bloom and fruit so grandly.

There is something curious in all this; something truly unique.

There is no class, or race, of men now on the earth who, when they come up to the seat of government on errands of business, have to contend with an array of disadvantages so formidable as those which, on such occasions, usually confront the Indian. If it be a citizen of the United States, his power of the ballot invests him with respectability, and introduces him at once to favorable attention; if a foreigner, the backing which he has from his home government throws around his person the charm of safety and shelters his rights under the aegis of law; if a stranger from the islands of ocean, he is received with demonstrations of cordiality, and, when civilization has done parading him as a proud trophy of its own missionary benevolence, he is dismissed and sent back to his wave washed home loaded with gifts and godspeeds.

But how is it with reference to our own continental Indian, the man without a flag behind him; that familiar football of civilization, whose importuning presence at the capital comes up more in the nature of an indictment than a compliment?

There is, and has been for a long time, something of a controversy between him and his Great Father at Washington; and he happens to be in the predicament of one of those unfortunate sons from whom paternal affection has been withdrawn, and yet of whom are expected nevertheless the usual manifestations of filial devotion. Consequently when he comes to Washington to make known his wants and grievances, the justness of his cause is but a secondary matter, and usually insufficient to secure him a suitable hearing. The first question which he has to answer is, "How much are you disposed to concede?" He must needs bring along with him a basket, or some such thing, stuffed with conciliatory concessions; otherwise he forfeits the pleasure, as well as the advantage, of a cordial reception at the parental mansion.

The government, wisely, or unwisely, early adopted the policy of dealing with the Indians as with men; that is to say, in matters of intercourse, it respected their rights and, in reference to them, generally deferred to their wishes. This practice was certainly fair and honorable; yet, it proved to be the origin of all the most perplexing problems that have been met with in the administration of Indian affairs. During the first years of its existence, the government, in getting along with the Indian tribes, endeavored, in general, to proceed on the theory of amicable agreement; instances of absolute coercion, though not entirely unknown, were rare. Many treaties were made with them very solemn in form, and abounding in guarantees purporting to endure forever. But the arrangements with them attained in this way were not generally in accord with the aggressive spirit of the white population; and however satisfactory they may have seemed to be at first, they soon came to be regarded in every instance, as serious obstructions in the way of legitimate emigration. Popular clamor arose denouncing them as nuisances and demanding their abrogation; and the government never failed to find itself, in due time, confronted with the alternative of either allowing these treaties to be shamefully overriden by the lawless multitude, or to save its honor by securing amicable concessions from the Indians. This practice, from a moral point of view, proved to be correct, in many instances, only in theory; for many of these "amicable" concessions were obtained by the most galling of coercive measures. Indeed, the most of these so called treaties seemed to have been made for the sake rather of guarding the good name of history, than for the benefit of the Indians. Though appearing to be exceeding fair upon the printed page, there were but few of them but what, if tested by the rules of equity in a court of competent jurisdiction, would be annulled on the ground of fraud and duress.

Speaking more particularly in reference to the Cherokees—there was a time in their early history when it was quite an easy matter for them to comply with these periodical demands for concession in a way that was really magnificent—when they were rich and the United States was young and poor. In those early days of thoughtless affluence, ere the malignant beam of fortune had been tipped the other way, they were in the habit of regarding it as but a light thing to bring along now a state, and then a state, and again, and again, a state, and throw them down as love gifts at the feet of the stripling who was soon to fatten upon their liberality, grow mighty and finally arrogate to himself the mastery of his old host and benefactor. In this way, it was, that Virginia, the mother of presidents, was "conceded;" in the same way, too, the Carolinas were "conceded;" and Georgia, the golden, and wild Kentucky, with Alabama, the beautiful land of plenty and rest, were all "conceded." And yet, in return for all these imperial benefactions at the hand of the Cherokees, what have they ever received but a transient smile of ungrateful satisfaction, and a wretched little volume of false promises called treaties?

But the time came at length, in the course of years, when it was deemed by the Cherokees that this extravagant species of liberality had needs to be discontinued. It had been found to be trenching so seriously upon the amplitude of their original domain, that the motives of self-preservation suggested with much emphasis the impracticability of further "concessions;" they could give no more. "Concessions," with them, came to bear the significance of expatriation, impoverishment, starvation, beggary, and despised tramps and strolling from door to door in quest of ill-paid labor and poor bread.

In their new home west of the Mississippi, they had been induced by the flattering promises of the government, to entertain very cheerful hopes of a future eternity of repose; but in this also they were deluded. The old demand for "concession," like a trailing spectre, hung upon their heels, and, at the close of the late war, found out their retreat and set upon them with renewed and quite unexampled ferocity. At the first note of alarm, heralding the breaking out of hostilities, the government hastened to withdraw her troops from the south, leaving her helpless wards, the Cherokees, to shift for themselves in the heart of the Southern Confederacy. At the close of the struggle, Congress professed itself to be seriously offended with them, because they had, in the meantime, failed to keep the Union flag aloft over ground upon which even Mr. Lincoln's armies had deemed it unsafe, at the time, to bivouac for a single night. The result was, they had to "concede" the western half of their country as a penalty for disloyalty. Nor was this the whole of that most unjust and unreasonable punishment. The Cherokees were, at this time, owning a handsome tract of eight hundred thousand acres, lying, like a jewel, snug down in the southeastern corner of the state of Kansas; this was included in the penalty, and had to be "conceded" accordingly. Nor was this the whole of it. It was found that those ancient surveyors who ran the western boundary line of the state of Arkansas and the southern line of Kansas, had made a mistake, fixing the former, in many important places, much too far toward the east, and the latter throughout, some miles too far to the north. Hence it came to pass, apparently as an uncontrived necessity, that, when these two lines were corrected by the modern sticklers for "concession," the Cherokees found that they had again to "concede" many thousand additional acres, to be shared by these two states in proportion to the gravity of the wrong which had been practiced upon them respectively in the old survey. Nor was this all; the penalty was still further enlarged in the following manner.

The Cherokees were required by the government to assent to the construction of as many, at least, as two railroads through their lands, and to "concede" to these corporations, as a mere gratuity, all and whatever of their realty that might be needed for such a purpose. This, however, was but a little matter conpared with the magnitude of the injustice by which this measure was subsequently supplemented. Congress, without the knowledge or consent of the Cherokees, and in violation of the most sacred forms of plighted faith, made a conditional free gift to one of these corporations of about eight hundred thousand acres in the very center of the Cherokee home lands. Now, the government had, for valuable consideration, engaged with the Cherokees to keep them in peaceful possession of this, their home tract for all time to come; but instead of observing this promise, she in this way virtually subsidized one of the most powerful agencies on earth to annoy them without ceasing. Accordingly, for the last thirty years this corporation has been tireless in contriving schemes for the bringing about of that specified condition (the extinguishment of the Cherokee title,) which, according to the terms of the grant, was to perfect its own title and give it possession of these Cherokee lands; while, during the same long period of tedious years, the harassing apprehension, kept ever alive by the threatened consummation of this great wrong, has never allowed these people the enjoyment of a single hour of undisturbed repose.

But all the "concessions" so far made by the Cherokees, however extensive, were not enough. Accordingly, at a late day, the Dawes commission was authorized to pay them a visit with propositions asking them to "concede" some more. They said, "We have not come to discuss with you the question of your rights, we have come simply to tell you what the government wants of you. It desires you to 'concede' the abolition of your tribal existence, to allot your lands, and become citizens of the United States, and the less fault you can find, and the quicker you can come to terms with our commission, the better, far the better, it will be for you, for if you defer, and prove so unfortunate as to fall into the hands of Congress, you will be sure to be made to feel all the rough treatment due to your folly."

These dishonorable, and yet very fearful, words of prophecy are just now seeming to have been only too true. The Cherokees refused to "concede;" hence they are enjoying at Washington just now the reputation of being a bad set of Indians, the most "unconceding" and impractical tribe on the continent. On this account, while the reconciled countenance of the great Father is dispensing the smiles of summer in every other direction, the Cherokees are left out to shiver alone in the dreary winter of disapprobation. Be assured, the chilliest thing that the Indian has to encounter in the world, is the "cold shoulder" of his great Father at Washington; it is the frostiest thing imaginable.

With these words it has been the mind of the writer to close this article, but just now word comes to him that the senate committee of Indian affairs has finished its review of the Curtis bill and that the results of their labor is now before the senate. In some respects they have improved it, in others, they have most unfortunately degraded it. It is hardly credible, yet it is true as the decalogue, they have admitted a section confirming that fraudulent and most infamous Clifton freedman roll.[1] With the unquestionable evidence of its infamy in writing now on file in the office of the Secretary of the Interior, it is hardly thinkable that it can possibly become a law. The section will undoubtedly be stricken out. It is well known in all quarters that should that roll be confirmed by legislation, the mouth of a hideous pit of corruption would be closed forever; a pit which might otherwise continue to send up its stench and stink through the annals of all future history.

Let it be conceded that the Cherokees showed themselves to be bad boys in declining to treat with the Dawes commission; let it also be admitted that the great Father has had some good ground for the exercise of parental displeasure, yet there is, in the nature of things, no vanity of ill humor possible that could justify him in treating his helpless children unjustly.

1898

Passage of Curtis Bill

The second session of the fifty-fifth congress was rapidly approaching its close. Members that felt themselves free from the pressure of any legislative burden, had packed their trunks and were making ready to be off for their respective homes. The "Curtis bill" had been at last hurried through the lower house, and was now pending before the senate. When the bill

1. The treaty of 1866 had required that the Cherokees adopt their former slaves and free blacks. In the Dawes Commission era, it became apparent that these people of African descent would share in the allotment. This roll, compiled by William Clifton, William Thompson, and Robert H. Kern in 1896–97, was challenged by the Cherokees for containing hundreds of names of freedmen with fraudulent claims to Cherokee rights. The Curtis bill to which Duncan refers became law on June 28, 1898, and provided for the breakup of the tribal domain and allotment of lands without the Indians' consent.

was called up for action before that body, the chamber was presenting the appearance of a vast den of deserted magnificence and tremendous memories. The roar of excitement that attended the quarrel with Spain and the declaration of war, had passed away, but its echoes were still there whispering dreadfully in the still ear of the imagination. The sunbeams that came down through the crystal skylight, dropped upon the glistening furniture, and laughed, as it were, in mockery of the inhuman solemnity of the place. The galleries would have been clear, but for the presence of a few Indian delegates, who sat and leaned over the railing, gazing contemplatively down on the sea of vacant seats below them. There was no quorum present—far from it; had the roll been called, scarce a half-dozen members could have been had to answer to their names. The vice-president was in his place, and, lodged backwards in his great easy chair, read from a fresh paper the news of the day. Senator [Richard] Pettigrew of South Dakota, chairman of the senate Indian committee, had charge of the bill, and was apparently the only man in the chamber, except Senator [William B.] Bate and Senator [John T.] Morgan that felt the least concern in reference to the legislative action that was being taken. Neither of these gentlemen professed any friendship for the bill, yet they did not deem it prudent, under the circumstances, to interpose any decided opposition to its passage. Senator Morgan maintained that the bill was, in many of its provisions, an obvious violation of both the Indian treaties and the constitution of the United States. Senator Bate took still higher ground: that while the government might easily enough, and with practical impunity, repudiate its treaty obligations to these helpless Indian people, nevertheless the honor of the country should be a consideration of sufficient moment to check all attempts at arbitrary legislation, and confine all proceedings looking to a reconstruction of tribal institutions of the territory entirely to fair and amicable negotiation. Senator [Matthew] Quay, of Pennsylvania, was in his seat. Outside of his own consciousness, perhaps there was no motive for his presence generally known except a friendly purpose on his part to do the Indians a kindly turn in this supreme hour of their struggle for justice. The Cherokee delegation had previously waited upon him, and, laying the true nature of their cause before him, had elicited from him expressions of sympathy and interest in their behalf which promised very hopefully to be of material service to them upon the floor of the senate when the bill should come up for action; but when the attempt was made to put the section in reference to mineral leases upon its passage, the man from Pennsylvania arose from his seat, and stepped across the aisle to the desk of Senator [Thomas] Platt, of Connecticut. A brief whispered interview ensued, mingled with a few mutually assenting nods of the head; at the close of which, he again returned to his own place and for the remainder of the hour leisurely busied himself in the midst of a pile of folios that lay on the desk before him.

Senator Pettigrew, as we have said had control of the bill, and led in the process of legislation. For two long hours he stood at his place in the senate, moving amendments to the bill. With little outside of the Indian ring, besides the gloomy walls of the old chamber, to witness, or care for what was going on, all these amendments, in rapid succession, and with scarcely the formality of a motion were declared by the president of the senate to be adopted. The formula of his announcement ran like this: "If no objections to the amendment it will be adopted, hear none 'tis adopted." These words were run off with a racing precipitation without the least change in his supine position, or turning the eye or attention from the printed page before his face.

When the bill, through this sham process of legislation had become a law, it was not, in fact an act of congress, but simply the formulated plan of three or four men who had wormed themselves into the Indian committee and got themselves constituted virtually the administrators of the Indian estate.

In the meantime, the Indians sat alone in the empty gallery, wrapped in gloomy silence, and looked down with mingled feelings of helpless contempt upon the false assumptions of fact, the hypocrisies of argument, and the injustice of conclusions, which pushed on to consummation, this most remarkable act in the great drama of civilization; they saw the sweet angel of plighted faith taken and knifed by christian hands, and laid upon the altar of insatiable greed, and offered up as a sacrifice to the god of mammon; barbarism quaked at the spectacle with a sense of insupportable horror, and with just aversion turned its swarthy face from the gleams of Calvary, as only the delusive lights of pride, power, arrogance and oppression.

They saw more than that; their own homes, the uninterrupted possession and enjoyment of which these same senators or their lineal predecessors, had but a short time ago, solemnly guaranteed to them forever, they saw taken and handed around as gratuities to unentitled strangers; they saw themselves taken and imprisoned upon a narrow strip of 80 acres, with their enjoyment of the same limited to the dusty surface, while everything beneath them—the gold and the silver—is "reserved" and handed over into the hands of the rich, the cherished gods of the dollar.

But this is not all those poor wronged Indians saw there that day; but space fails us. The tragedy was played out; the curtain fell. With the fortitude of true philosophy these native sons of the continent rose solemnly from their seats, filed quietly out of that great den of legislation, and down the white marble stairways of the capitol. At the great door of egress the bright setting sun, far away in the west, dashed his beams into their faces, laughed graciously, and said: "Good cheer! good cheer, my children! The day is coming! coming! coming! Egypt, Greece, Rome, and all other nations whose wrecks adorn the shores of time have paid the penalty of such conduct; and the United States cannot expect to escape."

1900

The Dead Nation

Alas! poor luckless nation, thou art dead
 At last! and death ne'er came 'neath brighter bows
Of flattering hope; upon thine ancient head
 Hath late-time treason dealt its treacherous blows.

When out the watery chaos rose the land
 And built this continent thy venturous foe
Were first to tread the new-born world; a hand
 Divine had given it thee thy restful seat.

Here with thy God, without such wars as tore
 The entrails out of cultured Rome and Greece,
Thou didst abide ten thousand years or more,
 Thy wants by Him supplied, in halcyon peace.

But then came Art, in rouge and ribbons dressed,
 The scourge of woe, borne on the winged hours,
And squat upon thine own salubrious west,
 Bred pestilence and rot within they bowers.

Smit by the blast of her contagious breath
  Thy children fell in armies at thy side;
And struggling in the grip of a strange death,
  Exclaimed, "O white man!" closed their eyes, and died.

Came also Might, the adjutant of Art,
  Wrenched off the hinges from the joints of truth,
And tore its system into shreds apart—
  Repealed, in short, the moral code, forsooth.

Then first it was, that on thy peaceful plains
  The roar of onset and the saber's gleam,
Began—but hold! humanity refrains,
  And genius cannot paint a dying scream.

Thus rotting Pestilence, and Art, and Might,
  In moonlight orgies o'er thy children's bones,
To honor civilization, hands unite
  And dance the music of their dying groans.

'Twas civ'lization, (said to be,) at work,
  To proselyte thy sons to ways of grace;
With savage means, the rifle, sword and dirk,
  To slaughter night, that day might have a place.

And so, indeed, they made the day to shine
  Upon thy callow brood, and with the light
Awoke those worms of greed that always twine
  In breasts exposed to suns too strangely bright.

Thy sons, touched by these strange transforming rays,
  Withdrew their love; to "end the strife,"
They said, they aped the white man's heartless ways,
  And tore the breast that nursed them into life.

Dear Cherokee nation, with the right to live,
  Art dead and gone; thy life was meanly priced;
Thy room to civilization hadst to give,
  And so did Socrates and Jesus Christ.

                                        1899

Sequoyah

Great man! Or wondrous, should I say?
　For, like a comet bursting into sight,
Launched unexpected on its arctic way,
　　Through boundless fields of rayless polar night,
　　Eclipsing constellations in its flight—
A flaming orb thou wert, and unforetold,
　Whose distance, altitude, and awful size,
No man, no kalendar however old
　　Could tell; and sweeping through the frigid skies,
　　In its own distance fades from human eyes.

So thou, Sequoyah, from thy Maker's hand,
　Was hurled prodigious through the skies of time,
Untaught, original, and strangely grand.
　　Thy mighty genius rose and shone sublime,
　　The wonder of all eyes, in every clime.

'Twas meet that, when thy day was spent, the ground
　Should fail to give thy sacred ashes room;
No low-built grave for thee shall e'er be found
　　Beneath the sky;[1] 'tis needless to inhume
　　A Sun gone out—the universe its tomb.

1904

1. Sequoyah disappeared in 1843 while on a journey to Mexico to look for Cherokees who had migrated there years earlier. The Cherokee Nation sent a delegation in search of him but found no traces.

Mabel Washbourne Anderson

CHEROKEE

(1863–1949)

Mabel Washbourne Anderson descended from two well-known families in Cherokee history. Her paternal grandfather was Cephus Washburn (the name subsequently changed), the founder of Dwight Mission to the Cherokees, and her maternal grandfather was John Ridge, the well-known leader of the Treaty Party of Cherokees. Anderson attended Cherokee public schools, graduating from the Cherokee Female Seminary in 1883. Upon graduation, she became a teacher at Vinita, where in 1891 she married John C. Anderson. The family moved to Pryor Creek in 1904, living there until 1930 when they moved to Tulsa. Anderson taught in the public schools throughout this period. In the early 1890s she also began to write for local newspapers and to make presentations before local literary societies. She wrote poetry, fiction, and essays, in which she treated such subjects as Cherokee history, folklore, art, and literature. Some of her works were picked up by out-of-territory publications. In the early years of this century, Anderson contributed to Indian Territory and Oklahoma magazines and newspapers and in 1915 published a biography of her grandfather's cousin, the well-known Cherokee general, Stand Watie. The biography, like much of her writing, including the biographical article on Watie reprinted here, reflects the tendency among Cherokee writers of her generation to romanticize Cherokee national heroes. As the first selection below demonstrates, her romanticism is also reflected in her treatment of the folklore related to the Osages, whom the Cherokees displaced when the government forcibly removed them to the West and resettled them on territory claimed by the Osages.

Both articles reflect the ethnocentrism of the Cherokees and their recognition of the effects of acculturation upon them.

An Osage Niobe

Years ago when the Indian Territory was a wild, uncultivated land, the Osages wandered over its plains and hills, claimed it as their own, and no man disputed their right. At that time a portion of Georgia belonged to the Cherokees, and was known as the Cherokee Nation. But the white man had become covetous of the soil, and congress agreed to remove the unhappy Indian from the state. Thus, forced by oppression and necessity, they sought an independent and separate existence in the wilds of the West. Leaving their beloved and familiar haunts behind them they wended their way to that part of the country west of the Mississippi now known as the Cherokee Nation, Indian Territory. About twenty years previous to this final emigration, which occurred in 1837, a portion of the tribe voluntarily emigrated to the Indian Territory. Hoping to find it uninhabited, they were surprised and disappointed to find themselves among the wild and warlike Osages. These wild Indians did not like the intrusion of a superior and more civilized race, and immediately began hostilities.

The Old World at that time was the scene of innumerable civil and political wars. Napoleon had been overthrown, the French monarchy re-established and many of his followers were compelled to seek safety and protection on the shores of the New World. Among these adventurers was a young Frenchman of the name of Claremont, who, having take refuge in flight from his native country, landed in New Orleans, then composed principally of French descendants. Still influenced by the spirit of adventure, he sailed up the Mississippi to the mouth of the Arkansas River, where he landed, and so continuing his explorations, he found himself in that portion of the country now known as the Cherokee Nation, which was then occupied, as has been said, by the Osages. With the ease and versatility characteristic of his nationality, he at once adapted himself to their aboriginal habits and customs, and so won their confidence and admiration by his courage and military bearing that he soon became one of the leaders of the tribe, and finally its chief. By this time the Cherokees were emigrating from the old Nation by scores and hundreds and encroaching with vigor upon the supposed possessions of the Osages. The Cherokees wished to be at peace, and overlooking the first attacks of their would-be enemies, their chiefs and principal warriors visited the Osage villages and proposed a treaty of amity, which was concluded, the tomahawk was buried, the calumet of peace was smoked, and tokens of fidelity were exchanged. The Cherokees, well pleased with the attainment of their object, took up their march to their own homes, but while on their way hither a party who had been sent out to kill game for food to supply them with provisions for the the journey were waylaid and murdered by the Osages, a number of whom had followed them thus far.

After this violation of the treaty the Cherokees took up arms against their treacherous neighbors; their warriors, amounting to some 250, met the Osages numbering some 2000 warriors. On the very first fire scores of the Osages were slain. Very soon after this victory a man by the name of Tak-ah-to-kuh emigrated from the old nation. This man was descended from the ancient priesthood. He had been a chief and a brave warrior. He was immediately regarded as the highest authority by the Cherokees. Having been told the situation, he approved of their open declaration of war. The Cherokees, though greatly outnumbered by the Osages, were uniformly victorious. In the western part of the Cherokee Nation a dreadful and final battle took place in which Claremont, the chief, was slain, with scores of his followers. The remainder took refuge in an inglorious flight. The signs of this battle are yet to be seen in the hecatombs of the fallen braves known as the Claremore mounds. These mounds are a short distance from the thriving town of Claremore, which name is a corruption of "Claremont," the name of the adopted Osage chief, for whom they were both called. On one of those mounds this famous Osage chief was buried with all of his possessions, but his remains were afterward exhumed, and every bone and personal belonging was carried away by the Osages, thereby proving their affection and appreciation of him. These mounds are easily seen from the passing trains, and are landmarks of interest and curiosity, and to this day people in quest of curios, by diligent search, may find buried relics of the Osages. Many of the adjacent farms are Osage graveyards, where human skulls and personal belongings are yet turned up by the plow. Thus disappeared from the land of the Cherokees the last of the Osages, taking up their abode in that portion of the country purchased by them from the United States government.

This battle has furnished the subject of a pretty Indian legend, accounting for the origin of the Salt Springs near the Cherokee Orphan Asylum.[1] In a valley between the hills of Saline district, on the shores of the Grand River, in the center of what appears to be an arid waste, where neither sprig of grass nor green shrub is to be seen, so impregnated is the soil with saline matter, boiling up to the height of several feet are a number of salt springs, which are not only objects of curiosity, but of usefulness as well, for years ago they furnished the entire supply of salt consumed by the Cherokees in that part of the country. To the present day the old iron kettles, portions of the engine and pipes, and other instruments used in the manufacture of salt may be seen, now spoken of as the ancient salt works of the Cherokees. Beneficent nature, who never does anything by halves, has not belied her reputation in this instance. A few yards opposite the boiling salt springs may be seen a number of other springs, at whose fresh and sparkling waters the Osage maidens had often quenched their thirst and bathed their shapely limbs.

Years ago, so the story runs, near the present site of this natural wonder, dwelt an Osage maiden, Palisha, a daughter of one of the chiefs, whose ponies, trinkets and gorgeous blankets were the envy and admiration of every other young squaw of the tribe, and whose hand was sought in marriage by many a stalwart Osage brave; but Palisha, after the manner of all maidens since the days of Eden, had smiles and glances for only one Adam, a brave and youthful warrior in Claremont's army at the battle of the mounds. During this battle runners were sent as newsbearers between the Osage village and the scene of the battle, some twenty-five miles distant. As the news of the battle fluctuated from victory to defeat, the hopes of the young girl rose and fell; she neither ate nor slept during its progress, but kept a constant vigil awaiting the arrival of the messenger, whose coming held such fatal interest for her, for all too soon the tortures of uncertainty were replaced by her melancholy cries to the Great Spirit to sustain her in her grief, for the dreaded news had reached her that the battle was over, and her lover was slain. At the foot of a gigantic oak she threw herself prostrate upon the bosom of mother earth and gave herself wholly to her despair. Like the Grecian Niobe of old,

1. The asylum was located at present-day Salina, Oklahoma. The salt springs, one half mile south of there, are now under the waters of Lake Hudson.

she wept and wept without ceasing till the Great Spirit in pity transformed her into the artesian-like springs, whose salty waters shall forever perpetuate her tears.

1900

General Stand Watie

America has done scant justice on the pages of history to the first citizens of this country, the North American Indian. It is a matter of regret and a loss to posterity that we possess, comparatively so little written matter of the life and traditions of the Five Civilized Tribes, whose achievements made possible the earliest history of Oklahoma. Research students know that the history of the country, embraced within the boundaries of this state, began with its Indian civilization long before the run of 1889, or the later advent of statehood, relating in fact, to the old tribal nations in the different states from which they came to re-establish their governments in the now Indian Territory. From the background and fertile soil of this civilization, blossomed in all its magic growth and progress, the young star, Oklahoma.

General Stand Watie was one of the most influential characters in the early history of Oklahoma. Some of the salient points in his eventful career will, no doubt, be of interest to readers of the Chronicles.[1] He was a North American Indian, one of the noblest sons of the Five Civilized Tribes. His courage and military prowess were known far beyond the limits of his activities, and his loyal service and constructive influence were a potent force in the history of his people.

He was born at the Watie home on the Coo-see-wa-tee stream in the old Cherokee Nation in Georgia, near the present site of the city of Rome, December 12, 1806. His kinsmen were among the prominent leaders of his people, his father David Oowatie, being the younger brother of Major Ridge, a well known chief and orator of the Cherokees. His mother Susannah, a descendant of Charles Reese of North Carolina, was one-half Cherokee and like her husband spoke the Indian language

1. *The Chronicles of Oklahoma*, in which the article appeared, is the publication of the Oklahoma Historical Society.

altogether. She was a member of the Moravian Church, the first to establish missions among the Cherokees. His father, a quiet, retiring man, took no active part in National affairs, either in the old or new country. General Stand Watie was one of eight children, three daughters and five sons, two of whom rose to places of eminence in their tribe.

In those days a Cherokee child was usually given an Indian name with some special meaning and sometimes an English name as well. Often these personal names, or their English interpretation, were taken as surnames which accounts for the difference in the family names of own brothers, as in the case of Watie, Ridge, and Boudinot, though this last was an adopted name as is explained later in this sketch. The name of General Watie is especially significant. At his birth he was called "Taker-tawker," meaning "To stand firm; immovable." Surely an appropriate name for one so steadfast in character and so ready to support his convictions of right at any cost.

Watie spoke only his native tongue until twelve years of age, when his parents sent him to the little Moravian school at Spring Place where he simplified the spelling of Oowatie, dropping the "Oo"; and though his mother had named him "Isaac" also, he retained the English meaning of his Cherokee name, "Stand," and ever afterward wrote his name simply "Stand Watie." The family name from that date was always spelled "Watie," often mis-spelled "Waite."

His brother Elias, and his cousin John Ridge, were sent East to school, but Watie's education was limited to the meager advantages of his own nation. This is proof of the fiber of his intellect and ability, for he attained a distinguished place as soldier, statesman, and leader despite this educational handicap. He was never an orator, even in his native tongue, but wrote with ease, as is characteristic of the Indian.

General Watie was a man of action and few words. No one ever rose to a place of such importance who had less to say. He was not a handsome man as was his brother, Elias, but his features gave evidence of the strength of his character and courage. His friendships were slowly made but loyally retained. His sympathies were easily touched. Little children loved him and the needy were glad to call him friend.

To better understand this remarkable man who was so intimately associated with the Cherokees during the most turbulent period of their history, both in the old nation and the new, it is necessary to touch briefly upon some of the contemporary events which so profoundly affected his life.

At the time of Watie's early manhood, the Cherokees, due to certain factors, had reached a high state of culture and civilization among the North American Indians. Missions were more common among them; many of their young men had been sent away to school, often to Eastern colleges, and returned to lend more progressive ideas. Sequoyah had invented the Cherokee alphabet. At New Echota, Georgia, their national capital, the first newspaper ever printed in both English and an Indian language had been established, with Elias Boudinot, Stand Watie's elder brother, as first editor. This brother earlier known as "Buck Watie," a name originating from his Cherokee name which meant "Male Deer," had been educated by a well known philanthropist, Dr. Elias Boudinot, of Princeton, New Jersey, with the request the boy should take his name. This Buck Watie did and when his education was completed, he returned to his own country, where he was destined to play so influential and tragic a part. His descendants, some of whom still reside in Oklahoma, retained the name of Boudinot.

Watie was thirty-one years old when he emigrated with family and kindred to the new Territory, now Oklahoma. Though he was clerk of the Cherokee National Supreme Court in 1829, he had taken little part in politics. The more active and eventful years of his life followed the emigration.

The story of the exodus of the Cherokee and other Southern Indians is a subject in itself, and too involved to include in any detail here. Two factions or parties arose among the Cherokees over the question of removal, one headed by Major Ridge, John Ridge, and Elias Boudinot known as the Ridge or Treaty party. This party advocated a treaty of removal with the United States Government, not from choice but as an acceptance of the inevitable, the oppression of their people having become unbearable. The other faction known as the Anti-Treaty party, headed by John Ross, then principal chief of the Cherokees, opposed a treaty of removal. This difference and division led to bitterness and tragedy as is ever the case when feuds arise within a nation.

The final result, emigration, was inevitable from the first, and history has proved the wisdom and foresight of those who advocated removal at the price of their personal safety. Unfortunately, the enmity and lust for power occasioned by the controversy, was carried from the old nation into the new by the Ross party, and this finally culminated in the tragic assassination in one night of Major Ridge, John Ridge, and Elias Boudinot, three of the most powerful men in the nation. Stand Watie was slated to die the same night, but was away from home and so escaped.

Responsibilities seem to gravitate to the shoulders that will carry them. Although burdened and saddened by the fearful murder of his uncle, cousin, and beloved brother, Stand Watie now became the acknowledged leader of the Ridge or Treaty party.

This tragic event proved a turning point in the career of Watie, one that thrust him from the home life he loved into a position of activity and prominence in the political affairs of his people. Unshaken by feuds and factions, which constantly threatened his life, from that time on his power, purpose, and courage proved of lasting influence.

The internal difficulties of the Cherokees were finally settled by the Treaty of 1846, and Watie as a leader of his party played a prominent part in bringing about this treaty, which ushered in a brief era of peace and prosperity for the Cherokees. He was speaker of the Council from 1857 to 1859, and a member of the Council from 1846 to 1861.

Stand Watie was married in the new Nation, September 18, 1842 to Sarah Bell. The two families were friends of long standing, and his wife's brothers, Colonel Jim Bell and Jack Bell, were schoolmates of Watie. Of this union there were three sons, Saladin, Solon, and Cumiska, and two daughters, Minnee and Jacqueline. His home life was congenial and very happy, darkened only by the unfortunate political conditions of his time, and the separations and suffering occasioned later by the War of 1861.

In the years that intervened, from the Treaty of 1846 until the outbreak of the war, Watie had some time to devote to his personal interests and fortune. He accumulated some valuable properties, and built a number of substantial homes. During this interval he lived quietly, enjoying the love and esteem of his neighbors and friends.

This era of peace, all too brief, was broken by the shadow of suffering and division into which the war plunged the entire nation. In the conflict that followed Stand Watie naturally assumed the place of leadership, for which he was so well qualified. A Southerner by birth and breeding, he unhesitatingly cast his lot with the Confederacy.

The military career of General Watie comprises the whole of the Confederate History of the Indian Territory. Many people have believed, erroneously, that little war activity took place in the Indian Territory, and that little was in the nature of guerrilla warfare. Nothing could be further from the truth. Long before the Treaty of 1861, made with General [Albert] Pike as Indian Commissioner of the Confederacy, large numbers of the Cherokees and whites had offered their lives to the cause of the Confederacy, and pledged to follow where Watie led.

So at the very outbreak of the war, Stand Watie had organized, and been made Captain of a troop of Cherokees and whites, for the purpose of protecting the Indian Territory, especially the Cherokee Border, from the federal forces stationed at Humboldt, Kansas. Between this point and the Cherokee Nation were the Osage Indians, who were nearly all Unionists, and ancient enemies of the Cherokees. There is no doubt that the wisdom and timely action of Watie and his men saved his people during these early days from even greater hardships than those they later experienced.

In May, 1861, Watie offered his services to General [Benjamin] McCulloch of Texas, who had been given the command over the military district of the Indian Territory. His offer was gladly accepted. He was given a Colonel's commission and authorized to raise an Indian regiment, which was known as "The Cherokee Mounted Rifles." Watie received high commendation from General McCulloch, and was ever in harmony with his superior officers, and acting under regular army orders.

At the beginning of the war, John Ross, as principal chief, had signed the Treaty of Alliance with the Confederacy, but afterwards renewed his policy of friendship with the Federal government, and went to Washington, where he remained until the close of the conflict, the Cherokee Nation being left at this crucial period without an official head.

In 1862 a National Convention of the Cherokees was held, at which time John Ross was deposed from office of principal chief, and Stand Watie elected to succeed him. Federal members of the council, said to have constituted a quorum, refused to recognize this election; but from that time on the Cherokees had two tribal governments, and all official business of the United States Government with the Southern Cherokees at the close of the war, was conducted through Stand Watie as their head.

Space does not permit details of any of the battles fought on Indian Territory soil—some eighteen or twenty in number, in which Stand Watie and his command did such heroic service. Some of these engagements were in important battles that took place on the borders of Arkansas and Missouri, but the larger number occurred in such familiar localities in Oklahoma as Fort Gibson, Webbers Falls, Bird Creek north of Tulsa, Muskogee and nearby points. His men declared that General Watie and his Indian Brigade marched over as many miles, had as many independent conflicts and skirmishes, captured as many trains of wagons, horses and mules as any one brigade west of the Mississippi.

Stand Watie showed such efficiency as a leader and commander, that on May 10, 1864, he received from President [Jefferson] Davis the appointment of Brigadier General in the Confederate Army, and later was brevetted. Except for Alexander McGillivray, who was commissioned as General in the United States Army in 1790, Stand Watie is said to be the only North American who ever attained this rank. He was the only Indian to received this distinction in either the Union or Confederate Army.

After this promotion, the Indian Territory troops were re-organized with General Watie as commander-in-chief, being known as General Watie's Indian Brigade, and included all Confederate Cherokees, as well as Creek and Seminole Troops, the Choctaws and Chickasaws being largely under the command of General Douglas Cooper, though they too were later attached to Watie's command. As many know, General Watie had the honor of making the last surrender of the war, which occurred at Doaksville, in the Choctaw Nation, June 23, 1864, nearly three months after the surrender of General Lee.

When the dark shadow of Reconstruction days enveloped the South, no section was found to have suffered greater devastation than the Cherokee Nation, for that region, though small and remote, had been occupied by both armies. What had been a scene of prosperity and rapid progress in 1861 was now almost a destitute wilderness. The losses of the Union Indians were provided for by the United States Government, but the Southern Cherokees had not only the loss of property, but also of citizenship to reclaim. It was during these days that General Watie proved a savior as well as a leader of his people. Throughout the war he had taken upon himself the task of rescue and relief for helpless Confederate families, and now he took upon himself the gigantic burden of alleviating the distress of reconstruction, extending his personal help and financial aid to all he could.

Internal discord, as well as the hardships resulting from the war again beset the Cherokees. The Northern branch confiscated the property of the Southern Cherokees, and denied them the right of suffrage. General Watie with many other prominent Cherokees was untiring in his efforts to bring about harmony and the restoration of the rights of the Southern branch. The controversy was finally settled by the Treaty of 1866, which procured re-instatement of the Southern Cherokees, but at a costly price to them. Many phases of this treaty were objectionable, but the most unjust clause was that which demanded of the Southern Cherokees an equal division of his lands and inheritances with his former slaves and their posterity, which was not required from any other Southern state.

The war ended, his people reinstated as citizens, General Watie retired from the public life which Fate had thrust upon his home-loving nature. Impaired in health, and broken in fortune, he engaged for a time in the mercantile business in Webbers Falls, Oklahoma, later moving to his farm near Bernice, where he spent his remaining years.

Sadness and suffering did not end with the close of the war for General Watie. His youngest son had died while a refugee in Texas, and in 1868, Saladin, his eldest son, was taken after a brief illness. Solon died just one year later. The loss of these sons, so full of promise, forms the saddest page in the life of this great man. His magnificent constitution had been weakened by the hardships of war, and these sorrows which followed so rapidly seemed to hasten the end which came to his own courageous spirit September 9, 1871, while on a visit to his old home on Honey Creek. He was buried with Masonic honors not far from this home, in the old Ridge cemetery, Delaware County, Oklahoma. His daughters did not long survive him. His wife, who had been such a faithful companion to him, died in 1883.

It has been the privilege and pleasure of the Southern women of Oklahoma, through their Division of the United Daughters of the Confederacy, to pay a long neglected tribute to the memory of Stand Watie by erecting a simple, yet dignified, monument at his grave, and a large and beautiful memorial on the Cherokee Capitol grounds at Tahlequah, where once his power and influence were so potently felt.

A careful search of the official war records reveals nothing but praise and commendation for Watie. Some of the finest tributes paid him as a man and an officer came from the North, as well as from the men who served under him. In return for the justice and consideration he accorded his soldiers, they gave him a devotion that was touching in its loyalty, from the highest in rank down to Dutch Billy, the bugler and John, the Swedish cook.

In this connection I am reminded of the many stories told me by "his boys" as they called themselves, and indeed, most of them were mere boys when they enlisted. Of how after long and wearisome marches, food being scarce, he would refuse some specially prepared dish, because his men could not share it. How often they had awakened at night to find him sitting by the fire, his blanket covering some soldier who needed it.

He never ordered a charge that he did not lead, yet he never received a wound in battle. The full-bloods believed that he possessed a charmed life and no bullet was ever moulded that could kill him. His personal acts of courage furnished full foundation for this belief, and his name stands for the very definition of bravery among his people today.

To students of the subject perhaps no Indian character appeals with such great force as that of Stand Watie. He was indeed a man of powerful personality and magnetism, with a courage and integrity as stalwart and changeless as the granite rocks of his native hills. He was ready as his life shows to make any sacrifice, compatible with honor for the good of his people. He did not thirst for pomp or glory but gave his great heart to duty as he saw it. Simplicity, sincerity and service symbolize his greatness.

1932

John Milton Oskison

CHEROKEE

(1874–1947)

John Milton Oskison was one of the first Native American writers to find wide appeal among American readers. Though he made his living as a journalist, his first love was fiction, and he wrote extensively, drawing upon his early experiences in the Cherokee Nation. Oskison was born at Vinita, the son of John and Rachel Crittenden Oskison. From Willie Halsell College at Vinita, where he was a friend and classmate of Will Rogers, he went to Stanford, graduated in 1898, and entered Harvard graduate school in literature. At Stanford he had begun to write short stories, drawing his settings and characters primarily from the people—Indian and white—and places familiar to him, particularly the ranch lands of Cooweescoowee District, where he grew up. In 1899, his story " 'Only the Master Shall Praise' " won the *Century Magazine* competition for college graduates and was the first of a number of stories and articles to appear in that magazine as well as *Overland, Frank Leslie's Monthly, North American Review, Everybody's,* and *McClure's.* In that story as well as others such as "Tookh Steh's Mistake," "When the Grass Grew Long," and "The Problem of Old Harjo," reprinted here, Oskison capitalized on the widespread appeal of regional writing to American readers. Oskison soon abandoned literature for journalism. Between 1903 and 1912, he edited a newspaper at Ossining, New York, and was an editorial writer and financial editor for *Collier's.* He also was a syndicated writer for other publications. After World War I, Oskison tried his hand at novels, publishing *Wild Harvest* (1925), *Black Jack Davy* (1926), and *Brothers Three* (1935). Oskison also wrote two biographical works: *Texas Titan; the Story of Sam Houston* (1929) and *Te-*

cumseh and his Times (1939). In his novels, Oskison returned to the regional themes and characters that typify his short stories, in which the reader sees a cross-section of the population of Indian Territory of the late nineteenth and early twentieth century: full bloods and mixed bloods, and white outlaws, adventurers, missionaries, and hangers on.

Tookh Steh's Mistake

Tookh Steh was a fullblood and his convictions concerning things were very strong. But Tookh had something of right on his side, when he made the one foolish move of his life, as this story is written to show.

For forty years Tookh Steh had lived in the White Oak hills, a neighborhood not known outside the Indian Territory, or, one might safely say, the Cherokee nation. During this time he had seen many changes come over his country. When he came to these hills with old Wana Steh, his father, he was not old enough to remember anything of his former home down in the Flint Hills, where the "hogbacks" of Arkansas and Indian Territory jostle each other, and throw up boulders into each other's arms. The White Oak hills were neither so high nor so rugged as those down in Illinois district, and it was only a few miles to the prairie in any direction. Tookh grew up half on the prairie and half in the rocky solitude of the timbered hills. The prairie was an inspiration to the boy. From its wide, rolling sweep he imbibed a love of freedom, the love that is not voiced by brazen lunged patriots, but the kind that the coyote pup sucks from its mother's breast, and which prevents you from ever taming the little vagrant. From the hills the boy got that secretiveness which tells you nothing of what a fullblood feels.

Twenty years after the little log cabin was built and hidden away in a ravine far up under the edge of the sandy ridge which separated the waters of Pryor Creek from those of White Oak Creek, Mr. Verte came to live near by. Verte was a white man, and a seeker after solitude. He lived, Indian like, within a mile of old Wana Steh's cabin, and did not come to know his neighbors for more than a year. This insured a lasting friendship between young Tookh Steh and Mr. Verte when they met finally over the grave of the Indian's father. Because an Indian is difficult to know. No other white man came across the hills to settle for many years, and

Verte found his fullblood friends, hunters as well as residents, excellent neighbors. They did not steal his stock, and minded their own business. Verte was a musician, fashioned in the school of Indiana "fiddle parties," or more politely, musicales. He played his violin in the doorway of his cabin when the shadows of the post oaks stretched away into the tangle of underbrush to the east, and Tookh came often to listen. Conversation between them was not extensive, and was carried on in a concessionary mixture of English and Cherokee. If Verte wished to buy a calf from old Acha Dilla, he made Tookh understand in a few words, and the bargain was struck by Verte's friend and interpreter. Verte could be trusted to treat the Indians as men, and they discredited the tales that floated about concerning some whites who had come to the territory and had driven away half of the cattle thrifty old Chief Ross had collected. The railroad came down from the north, in time, and flashed on into Texas, and the intruding whites followed its trail. Stockmen began to realize what a mine of wealth lay in the luxuriant grass growing waist high on the hills and prairies, and soon long trains of cattle were turned loose to get fat and make profits for their owners. The clean-limbed, long-horned Texas steers came up into the hills and nosed about the cabins at times, when some serious-faced Indian boy would come rushing out of the hut waving his arms, and bursting into fits of laughter when the curious beasts stampeded through the brush.

It did not happen that the United States wished to stamp out tribal government in the Cherokee nation until Tookh had lived in his hill home for forty years. The rafters of the cabin were much worm-eaten then, but the old place fitted so well that neither Tookh nor his family, a pleasant faced squaw and a ten year old boy, ever thought of building another. They might have put up a frame house now, for Coxton's saw mill was cutting up the splendid oaks not two miles away. The year the commission came to the territory was a year when the Indian elections were held, and orators from rival parties declaimed loudly and vaguely about the ancient, honorable and inviolable rights of treaty the commission had been sent to abrogate. They left the impression that the United States meant to rob the poor Indian outright. The delegation sent by the senate of the United States was made up of half a dozen sensible, educated and conscientious men. They were acting under instructions from the senate, and tried to do justice in the work. But political ambition is the birthright of a Cherokee, and so those who talked ancient vows hindered the commission's work more than a stranger would imagine.

Tookh Steh showed a lively interest in the negotiations entered into by the nation with the commission, because he desired the best possible results to come of the proceedings. He was not blind to reason, and when Mr. Verte tried to explain that the United States, far from contemplating any robbery, wished to effect an organization along firmer lines and institute a civil and educational reformation, he saw how good might come from a change. The change he had in mind would never disturb the serenity of his life. His small, rail-enclosed corn patch would not be taken away; each citizen would keep the home of his birth. The wild country to the west, where he shot deer and turkeys would surely not be taken up; there were not enough people out of homes to occupy it. Mr. Verte told the trusting fellow that white men were real friends, and wished to do the best they knew by the Cherokees. These men knew that the Indian government was almost efficient, that their schools were ample in number, if poor in teachers; that the Indians were working alone, a splendid solution of the Indian problem. But Verte said that many things could be better, the solution hastened and happiness consummated sooner, with the change. Verte believed what he said. He was not largely experienced in the politics of the world. Tookh believed what Verte said, because he had learned to trust the words of the white man.

When the commission sat in the town nearest to Tookh's home, he rode in one day to hear the proceedings. Mr. Verte told him that a number of fullbloods would meet the commission that day. It was not often that the Indian, Tookh, went to town. His long black hair, dark face and feather-decked hat created no more favorable impression among the snobbish little store clerks, than his dingy, mouse colored pony, blind in one eye for ten years, and his old twine mended saddle did among the bespurred and fully equipped cowboys. But Tookh did not care about such a simple matter as external appearance; he had the welfare of the country on his mind. He felt that he was partly responsible for the action of the nation, whatever it should be, in the issue at hand. No politician had yet explained to him what a difficult matter it is to look after the welfare of one's country, because it was not believed that silent old Tookh Steh had any "pull" with his people. So it came about that he went into the conference of the commission with a mind quite unprejudiced.

The meeting was called, the commissioners announced, to get the sentiment of the fullbloods on the question of the extinguishment of the tribal government, and the substitution of a territorial one, under the laws of the United States. Tookh listened eagerly while the fullblood spokesman set forth the views of his people. The old orator, speaking in his native tongue and very earnestly, said: "We do not want to change. We are satisfied with our own government. You would cut up our land into squares and make us stay on the little chunk we got in the cutting up. You would put down our courts, and drag us into your own docks where we could not understand your strange justice. You made treaties with us. We have kept our part faithfully. You say you will not keep yours. Is the great head of your nation so poor that he must have our lands? Is he such a good father that he must destroy our government, and take us to his own breast, for fear that we can not keep up our institutions? We are not of your race, we do not understand you, and we would rather be left alone. We are not ignorant, we are not savage; and the criminals that you tell us invade our country came from your land. You ought to catch them and hang them, as we do our own law breakers. You tell us that the man with many cattle grazing over our land, and with many miles of wire fences, is the one who is getting the good of our system. We tell you that this man is here because we let him stay. We can drive him out by law, and he will not use up our lands. You tell us we are ignorant. We tell you that we have our schools, our churches, and some of our sons are in the big colleges with your children. They will come back, and will keep up our institutions. They love their country and will make it great. Treat us fairly and we will respect you. Break your treaty and we will despise you."

One of the commissioners spoke next, and told the fullbloods that they had no choice in the matter. They had instructions and those instructions were to make the change. They had already dealt with the tribes in the south, and must deal now with the Cherokees. The United States was sorry that the change would work hardship on the Indians, but sentiment would not control. The Cherokees would no doubt be greatly benefited in the end, and so the change must come. Treaties were good so long as they did not stand in the way of progress, but they could not last forever. It would be better to make the change at once, and get the best terms while there was yet opportunity for securing favorable conditions.

While he was listening to the speech of the commissioner, and with the fullblood's words fresh in his mind, Tookh Steh made a resolve. He would not live in a country where his old freedom would be restricted. They had said that thousands of eager homeseekers were waiting to file into the country to get homes. No more hunting; and even his dear, secluded hills would be peopled, the timber cut down, and his boy would have only the corn patch and the two ponies when the old man was gone. He would go to Mexico. He had heard that there one could find boundless freedom, amid mountains more rugged than any he had ever seen.

"You tell me the white man honest," Tookh said to Mr. Verte a few days later. "You tell me he not want my land. You do not know. He tell me all, we have to give up lands. We no more hunt deer, no shoot turkey. Land all gone. I go to Mexico where Great Father no take my land. I tell you, good-bye." Tookh shook hands with Mr. Verte, and a week later, he left his old log house in the White Oak hills and started south. His poor old horses and tumble-down wagon furnished conveyance. The determined Indian did not know how many long moons he would be compelled to travel before he came to Mexico. He was filled with the idea that he must leave this place where, if he stayed, he would feel like a coyote shut in a box pining to get out.

One day in the middle of winter, a letter came to the officials of the town where Tookh had traded. An old Indian who called himself a seeker after freedom, and who babbled foolishly about Mexico and deer and turkeys, had died in a small Texas town. The old man had said he was dying because he could never reach the land he was going to; his horses were dead. But most of the people believed that he had starved to death, since the wife and boy were almost dead from lack of food. They would not beg, and they would not say they were hungry. The man had died, begging brokenly to be sent back to the White Oak hills. Did any one know of this person? What should be done? The wife and child were in the poor house.

Yes, one knew. He was Tookh Steh's neighbor from the head of Pryor Creek, and he said shortly when he heard of his friend's death: "Big fool, Tookh Steh. Leave his home and go away. Leave his corn not gathered. He starve. Get mad 'cause he take away. Big fool, he!"

Perhaps Tookh was foolish to think that he could change the course of what men call destiny, simply because he had a principle to back him. But then, Tookh was a fullblood, and his convictions concerning things were very strong.

1897

"Only the Master Shall Praise"[1]

On the cattle ranges of the Indian Territory ten years ago he was known as "the Runt," because he was several inches shorter than the average

1. The title is from "When Earth's Last Picture is Painted," by Rudyard Kipling.

puncher. His other title of "Hanner" had been fastened upon him by a ludicrous incident in his youth. "Hanner the Runt" was a half-breed Cherokee cow-boy, who combined with the stoicism of the Indian something of the physical energy and mental weakness of his white father. One of his shoulders was knocked down a quarter of a foot lower than the other, two ribs had been "caved in" on his left side, and a scar high up on his cheek-bone indicated a stormy life. It was a matter of speculation in the cow-camps as to the number of times Hanner had been thrown from horses and discharged by his employers; he would have been called the foot-ball of fate had these cow-boys been modern and college-bred.

No trick that was ever perpetrated upon him, no service that another imposed upon him, no jeer flung straight in his face, could destroy the innocent trust he felt in humanity. Bill Seymour had caused him to break his ribs by falling from a wild pony, and had then thrashed the puncher who laughed at the fall. In this way Hanner had become the slave of Seymour.

The two, Seymour and Hanner, now rode for Colonel Clarke, and were generally together. It was convenient for Seymour to have his "vallet" to do his work, and it was the chief joy of Hanner's uncolored existence to do something for the man who had fought for him. The grotesque little figure never stopped to ask whether his friend were worthy of his devotion. Bill Seymour was a short, athletic fellow, and good to look upon, but he bore in his nature a too large share of the devil to be dependable. Silent, gruff, and capable when sober, he became a laughing, steel-hearted fury when drunk, and he got drunk as often as he could reach liquor. More than Hanner had felt the sting of his quirt as Bill reeled laughing and jesting on the streets, and had feared to show the anger that rose in their hearts. He made enemies when drunk, and gravely apologized to them in his sober days. One man, a traveling cattle-buyer, braver than most, and not knowing his man, had drawn a small pistol and shot the puncher in the body. Bill, who was not hurt at all seriously, laughingly strode up to the shooter, seized the weapon, and pointing at his feet, said:

"Now dance for me, you impident son of a mosquito! Dance till you drop! Tryin' to plug me with a toy like that—a curséd little thirty-two!" He flung the pistol noisily into the street, caught the man by one ear, and slapped his face.

There is one time in the year when the cow-puncher feels that he must get away from his work and indulge in a "good time." He does not know the significance of the Fourth of July except in a hazy way, but he does know that on that day he may have abundant whisky for the buying, even though its sale be prohibited by law. He knows, too, that he will find at the big celebrations in the Territory all his friends and enemies worth meeting and fighting; and this meeting of friends and fighting of enemies give the spice of variety to his life.

As the two companions rode to the largest town in the Territory on the morning of the Fourth, one could see that their outfits were typical of themselves. Bill Seymour rode the best and fastest horse on the ranch; his saddle was new and modern in make, his spurs rare and shanked long— only a leader of cow-boy fashions had dared to wear them; his hat was a Stetson, and hardly discolored by the weather. Hanner might have fitted himself up from the ranch dump-heap. Two old, unmated spurs dangled from a pair of "run-over" boot-heels, the patched corduroy trousers he wore had been traded to him long ago by his champion, and between the bottom of a dirty waistcoat and the top of his trousers there showed a greasy cartridge-belt, with scattering cartridges stuck in it. A "floppy" black hat, which almost concealed his dark, pinched features, completed the queer figure. The pony he rode was called "Pignuts," and was knotty and scrubby and tough enough to deserve the title.

"Bill, ye ain't a-goin' to git drunk to-day, are ye? They say they's goin' to be a lot of extra marshals 'at ain't lettin' any drunk walk the streets to-day. I wish ye would n't drink too much, Bill!" Remembering other celebrations, Hanner wished to get through the day with as little trouble on Bill's account as possible.

"Oh, go to the devil, you old woman! Who said I was goin' to get drunk? Somethin' I never do. Come on; let's ride up," Bill replied shortly; and the two galloped into town through a cloud of dust raised by many incoming wagons.

"Hello, Lem! How 's the Convict? Keepin' healthy now, Smear? What's the show and the price?" Bill greeted the punchers from the ranches in all parts of the country with a familiarity possible only to one who knows and does and dares as much as the best of them.

"Got the dangdest mule fer buckin' down here they's goin' to have rode to-day ye ever seen. Five dollars in it fer the man that rides it. Why don't ye try, Hanner?" The Convict winked at Bill, and insinuatingly confronted the Runt with the question.

"I don't hardly think this here saddle of mine 'u'd stand it," the Runt returned, after glancing at Seymour. "Think I'd better try it, Bill?"

"Get your bloomin' neck broke if you do, but I expect it 'u'd be good for you. Yes, go ahead and ride it, and I'll lend you this saddle."

Bill's words were spoken in jest, but Hanner meditated upon them seriously during the day, and when the vicious mule was led out for its first trial, Seymour noted with some anxiety that his own saddle was buckled upon it. He was careless with drink now, and grinned in anticipation of the sorry figure the Runt would present astride the mule. He made a foolish drunken wager that "Hanner 'll stay with that there mule till its tongue sticks out and it can't hump its back any more."

The bucking mule was the closing scene in the day's spectacle. The high-heeled, stiff-muscled cow-boys had chased a greased pig over a fifty-acre field, and been sadly beaten by the street boys of the town; they had pitched rings at the heads of canes over the handles of cheap penknives, and wasted their efforts trying for a gilded watch pegged down with a large-handled awl; they had ridden in the tourney, flying past rings hung in the air, and picking them off with wooden spears, causing strangers to gaze with open-eyed wonder at their dash and recklessness; they had bucked the scores of games which gamblers had devised to part the fool and his money, and were gathered now to watch a game they could understand and appreciate.

Out of a knot of excited men Hanner went straight to the waiting, restless mule. With a mock air of bravado he struck the excited mule across the flank with his sombrero, after roughly seizing the reins. No one who has not learned by experience how to mount a plunging horse can understand how Hanner lifted himself out of the chaos of rearing mule and struggling attendants into the saddle before he signed to the men to turn the animal loose.

When the mule found itself free to act there was a momentary pause. Then began the short, nasty jumps straight into the air, with the animal's back bowed, its legs stiff, and its head lowered. It was the first powerful effort of the angered beast, made with devilish confidence. Hanner was scarcely shaken by these first straight jumps, but then began the twisting series, which is the second expedient of a bucking animal. A jump high into the air, with a seemingly impossible twist to the side, landed the mule with its head turned almost half round. Before the rider caught his breath another jump and another half-turn were made. These are the motions that make a bronco-buster's life shorter. Hanner was bleeding at the nose in half a minute. The twisting jumps were continued until the strength of the mule was almost exhausted, and as yet only the hat of the puncher had been dislodged. A short pause followed, during which the mule changed its tactics, and Hanner thwacked its sweaty neck with his open hand. The next motion was a sudden rearing by the mule. As it rose on its hind legs the rider yanked fiercely on the reins, and, slipping to the ground on one side, allowed the brute to fall on its back. The saddle-horn buried itself in the earth, and the mule's hoofs beat the air a moment before it scrambled to its feet.

Hanner was cooler than the mule now, and swung himself back into the saddle with the first long leap of the desperate animal. This was the easy part of the trial for the rider, and the spectacular part for the world. The mule ran straight away for the opposite fence of the fair-grounds with long, lunging jumps, rising and pitching forward with the speed of a racing yacht. Hanner brought his craft about before it sailed into the fence, and beat it fore and aft with a flourishing hand. He was wild with triumph now, his hair blowing in the wind. He leaned forward as in a race, urging the thoroughly tired and conquered mule straight for the crowd. A particularly vicious dig with the spurs made the beast plunge into the scattering knot of spectators and rise to a four-barred gate. At the opposite side of the track no fence barred its way, and it ran, frightened and quivering, under the awning of a lemonade-vendor's stand, scattering glasses and confections to the winds, and wrecking the stand. Hanner slowly dismounted, stroked the sweaty flank of the subdued mule, then turning and picking up an unbroken bottle of soda, proposed a toast "to our gentle old family-buggy hoss!"

The punchers cheered Hanner with the heartiness of men who can appreciate the feat.

"Hanner, you're all right. I knowed you could do it." Bill's praise fell sweetly upon the Runt's ears. "Where's that wooley I made the bet with? Hanner, we'll drink; yes, sir, we'll liquor up now and have a good time. I won the bet and you won the five for ridin' the mule. We'll drink, Hanner." Seymour slapped Hanner's shoulder in a cruelly hearty fashion.

"No, Bill; let's not drink any more to-day," Hanner protested, though he had not drunk anything.

"Hanner, I don't understand you; blast me if I do." Bill was argumentative. "Here you are, just rode the buckinest mule in the Territory, and you won't take a drink with your best friend! Now, if anybody else 'u'd refuse to drink with Bill Seymour I think they'd have trouble. But you,

Hanner, I reckon I'll just have to pour it down you." The drunken puncher tried to carry out his plan, but changed his mind at Hanner's appeal.

"Don't, Bill; fer God's sake, Bill, I'm too sick to drink! Let's go home, Bill. I'm shore sick. Won't ye come on home with me?"

"I believe the darn little skunk is sick," muttered Bill to himself. Then aloud: "If you want to go home with me you'll have to come along pretty quick. I'm tired of this show, and, anyway, I've got to get over to the round-up on Big Creek to-morrow. Get your horse and wait for me here; I'm goin' to see Smear before I go home."

Hanner knew that his companion went for another bottle of whisky, but knew also the futility of protesting.

They rode out of the tired, dirty, and heated crowd, where the dance-platforms were beginning to fill up, and where the owner of the two-headed calf, the five-legged mule, and the biggest steer in the world, was beseeching everybody to come and view his collection. Bill rode at a gallop, with his companion spurring at his heels, until they passed quite out of sight of the revelers. Then he turned with an air of real concern to the Runt, and asked:

"You shore 'nough sick, Hanner? That mule shore put up a stiff article."

Hanner was not diplomatic, and spoke out truthfully: "Sick? No, I ain't sick. What 'u'd I want to see ye get drunk an' run in for? They'd 'a' run ye in to-night, Bill, I know. Did ye ever notice the color of the sky this time a day, Bill? Seems to me it ain't so darn purty as some people think." The sun was setting in a dull, coppery sky, the air was sultry, and the dust rose in thick clouds.

For a minute Bill did not reply, but looked at his companion with a half-puzzled expression. Then he broke out:

"Well, you're a nice one, ain't you? Do you know what I'm a mind to do to you for this dirty trick? You think I'm a darn kid to sneak like this to keep from gettin' run in? Oh, you baby! For a cent I'd make you walk all the way home, and lay this quirt over your shoulders every step of the way."

"Oh, no, Bill; ye would n't think o' doin' that. D' ye want to go back? I did n't know ye cared to stay so bad."

"Go back? You think I'm crazy? What 'u'd the punchers say? No, curse you; you've robbed me of my fun. That mule ought to 'a' killed you!"

Hanner had learned long before the value of silence, and rode beside his morose companion with now and then an anxious glance at him. Bill was meditative, and quite forgot the rider at his side. The pale light of a young moon deepened the shadows and illuminated the heavy, sluggish dust-clouds that rose in the wake of the riders. Hungry calves, neglected at the ranches since early morning by the celebrating ranchmen bawled in useless appeal; scurrying, skulking coyotes answered with their threatening cries the challenge of the ranch dogs a mile away, and coming toward them with rhythmic hoof-beat and noisy rattle of hub on axle, the two riders heard a wagon and team.

"Who do ye reckon kin be goin' into town this time of night, Bill?" asked Hanner.

"Hold on here, Hanner; we'll stop." Bill meditated a moment, then went on: "You know what that team is? It's the mail-stage from Coffeyville to Vinita. Darn old rattle-trap; it's a disgrace to the country. Ought to have a railroad through this God-forsaken land. That driver's a fool, and you know what I'm goin' to do? Darn your skin, Hanner, you made me miss the fun at Vinita; now I'm goin' to have some fun of my own. We'll rob the stage! Ever hear about the road-agents, the James boys and the Younger gang? Well, they robbed overland stages and trains for swag; but we won't get anything here, only some fun, and scare the fool driver. Stage-robbers always jump out and grab the horses' heads and poke a gun in the driver's face. We'll tie our horses over there in the gully, and hide in the grass here by the road. You jump out and get the horses, and I'll fix the driver. See? Come on; tie up over here!"

"Ye don't mean that, do ye, Bill? Oh, come on and let's go home." Hanner detected a determined ring in the puncher's voice, and he dared not protest more.

"You don't have to get in on this unless you want to. I can do it myself." Bill considered the plan a good joke, being drunk enough to forget that robbing the mails is a very serious crime in the eyes of the law, and the most serious in the eyes of citizen posses, who sometimes take the law into their hands. He galloped down the rain-washed gully and tied his horse out of sight of travelers on the road. Hanner, expecting an end of the joke, rode with him; but when Bill turned to go back to the road on foot, the little puncher announced his intention of having nothing to do with it.

"Then give me that floppy old hat. I got to wear some kind of a mask. Let me have that old red handkerchief round your neck, too. Now I look like a shore-'nough stage-robber—or like you, and that's worse. Well, ride out of the way if you ain't goin' to help." The amateur highwayman half stumbled, chuckling at the prospect of fun, to a place in the long grass at the roadside.

Hanner rode far down the dry wash, and waited in anxious silence. He heard the scarcely understood command of Bill Seymour to the driver. The rattling of the wagon suddenly ceased. There was a brief moment of absolute silence, and a pistol cracked. Another shot from the same gun rang out. In a short moment an answering shot was heard. Hanner could have sworn that it was the bark of Bill's revolver. An angry shout from Bill was followed by a fusillade of shots. The rattling of harness indicated a struggle with the horses. Then a yell from the driver started the stage-team at a gallop. The firing ceased, and trembling with fright, Hanner heard the noisy wagon pass on toward Vinita.

Thoroughly sobered now, Bill ran to his horse, mounted, and rode to meet his companion. The two galloped on their way for five minutes before Seymour trusted his voice to explain. After breaking into a string of furious oaths, he said:

"What a fool I was! Softy Sam was n't drivin' the blanked wagon at all. When I got holt of the horses they shot at me. I yelled to 'em to stop, that I was only jokin', but the fools kept on pluggin' away at me. I got behind the horses and yelled again. Then I had to shoot. One of 'em fell back off the seat, and then the other one whipped up the horses. I let 'em go quick. That unshot fool plugged at me till he got out of sight. No, I did n't get hurt, but your hat got a hole in it all right."

"Ye did n't kill one of 'em, did ye, Bill? Ye don't think ye did? That would n't do, ye know, at all."

"Kill one? Hit one, all right; maybe killed him. The fool! Oh, that's just my luck. Curse you Hanner, it was your fault, you cur, takin' me away from the fairgrounds with your old-granny tale about bein' sick. Say, what we goin' to do about it now, eh? We got to get out of this, or we'll get strung up, shore—I will, I mean. We'll ride for the Verdigris River timber and hide there. Well, have you got anything better?"

"Bill, could n't we explain, tell the marshals it was a mistake, and—"

"Get strung up to a limb before we got through tellin' that, you darn fool! But it ain't a question of 'we'; I'm the only one in this. You kept out of it, you cowardly skunk, and you're safe. You want to run away now, and keep your skin whole?" Bill grew incoherent, scarcely retaining sense enough to spur on toward his destination.

Meanwhile the stage had reached Vinita, with the wounded man at the point of dying, and the driver too much confused to do anything to help him. Quite by chance, a considerable sum of money had been sent through the mails that day, and the regular driver had been replaced by two well-known deputy sheriffs. After the driver had finished telling of the attack made by a short man wearing a big, floppy black hat, and with a dirty red handkerchief tied over his lower face, a posse was immediately formed to hunt the bandit down. No one could guess who the guilty one might be.

Dick Brewer, the leader of the party, questioned minutely: "Would you know the hat if you saw it?"

"Yes," the driver answered; "Tom Forbes put a hole through it before he got shot. I saw it nearly fall off his head—a great, big, wide-brimmed, floppy thing, with what looked like a piece of rope for a band."

"Somethin' like the hat that Hanner the Runt wore to-day, was n't it, Smear?" the Convict commented. Then he asked: "Where is Bill Seymour and Hanner anyway? You seen 'em last, did n't you, Smear?"

"They started home an hour ago. Bill said he had to get over to the Big Creek round-up to-morrow, an' he got a bottle of my whisky before he went." Smear remembered the unusual incident of Bill's early departure; ordinarily, duty was not allowed to interfere with the puncher's pleasure.

To Smear, who made one of the pursuing party, the words "a big, floppy black hat and a dirty red handkerchief" kept repeating themselves in his mind. At each repetition he recalled with distinctness the appearance of the Runt as he had gone out to ride the wild mule. No other puncher in the country would wear that hat, and none would feel quite respectable with that dirty red rag about his neck at a Fourth of July celebration.

"But, shucks!" Smear muttered to himself, "it can't be him. But he's got nerve, the little devil, ridin' that mule the way he did! He ought to 'a' been with Bill Seymour, though; could n't tear the cuss away from him. Well, we'll see."

Hanner and Bill rode at a steady gallop until, in the middle of the night, they plunged into the Verdigris River timber. No definite plan of action had been formed; they felt only a strong desire to get away out of sight. The horses must rest, and, overcome by fatigue, Bill dropped asleep. The consciousness of a crime done did not disturb him; in his mind it was an accident, the unfortunate result of a joke. Hanner did not sleep. He stared up through the treetops into the starlit sky, and pondered the significance of the deed. The course he had suggested to Bill, that of confessing and explaining the matter, still seemed to be the wisest one to him. "Surely," he thought, "they would understand, for they all know Bill's nature. Did n't everybody know that he must indulge in a joke whenever he could?" A plan began to form in his mind.

"I kin sneak away before Bill wakes up, an' go explain to the marshals. They'll let Bill go, I know they will. I kin do this fer ye, Bill, an' ye'll be glad of it. I don't want to have ye scoutin' round the country; I want ye here, so we kin still ride together. I made ye come away from the fair, an' I got to git ye out of the trouble I got ye into." Hanner scarcely spoke his thoughts. He waited undecided for two or three hours. The dawn was just beginning to filter in to the hiding-place as he stole forth quietly to his horse and rode to find the posse.

More than one gang of outlaws had made the river-bottom their head-quarters and been captured there. The pursuers of the lonely mail-robber inferred that he was one of a number, and that he was very likely to be heard of in the old haunts. So early morning found the posse scouring the country outside the timber, inquiring of ranchmen and the women of the houses for a trace of the man they sought. It would do little good to try to rout him out of the great forest of brush and swamp until some trace of his location had been found.

Dick Brewer and Smear were riding together near the road that plunges through the thickest of the timber when Hanner rode out. They stopped, attracted by his action. The little puncher looked anxiously about until he saw the waiting horsemen, then galloped toward them. Smear felt sick at heart on seeing the floppy hat and the dirty red handkerchief that he wore. Brewer saw them, too, and his hand flew to his revolver. He had not voiced his suspicions before, but now Smear exclaimed with excitement:

"If that there hat's got a hole in it, we've got the man!"

"It's the Runt!" Brewer had not heard the insinuations which were made before the posse started.

The appearance of the bullet-hole in the crown of the old hat sufficed to make Brewer and Smear bring Hanner to a halt before their pointed pistols. At sight of their stern faces and threatening weapons Hanner's power of speech was gone. He tried to say that he wanted to explain, and grew quite incoherent.

"Never mind; explain when you get up before all of us," the leader commanded.

Half an hour of scurrying about by Smear and vigorous blowing of signal-calls brought the party together. Everything was extremely orderly and businesslike. A man who robbed mails and killed drivers had no claim on their consideration; the only question was, to be sure of the man. When they were sure of him, no matter what his former standing, he must be hanged straightway. The effect of a lynching they felt to be good. Dick Brewer called upon the driver of the mail-wagon to step forth and declare truthfully whether or not he recognized the prisoner.

"Yes, sir; I can swear that that hat is the one the robber wore, and allowing for the difference between daylight and moonlight, I'd say that handkerchief was around the robber's face."

"Is he of the same size and build?" asked the leader.

"About the same; but I won't swear to anything but the hat. I know that."

It grew clear to the mind of the confused little puncher that if he told the story which he had planned to tell, Bill Seymour would be caught and hanged within the day. No excuse that he had perfected would stand for an instant against the plain fact that an attempt to rob the mails had been made and a man murdered. He saw, too, just as plainly, that if he did not tell the truth concerning Bill, he, as the owner of the hat, would suffer the penalty. He knew that very soon he would be asked to tell his story, to clear up the evidence against him. There was none of the great excitement present that nerves men to self-sacrifice. The day was young yet, and the air was chilling. The legs of the horses and the boots of the men were dew-splashed and dripping. It was not pleasant to die now, even though life had been hard and mean to him. He felt a shudder of repulsion when he thought of the mode of death.

On the other side he considered what he owed to Bill. Out of a host of cow-boys he had known, Bill was the only one who had ever recognized the fierce desire for comradeship that had consumed him, the only one who had not passed him by in open ridicule.

"Bill fought fer me when I was down," Hanner whispered to himself. "He knowed I was human. An' I brought this on to him. He come away yesterday because he thought I was sick. He'd 'a' got away, maybe, if I had n't left him asleep to explain. If he had to go I would n't have nobody to ride with, an' if I take his place—if I go he'll know an'—" Hanner did not trust himself to go on, but turned to the leader and said:

"I reckon ye got the man all right."

Under the misshapen body and the half-foolish features there was a

stoic in Hanner. To save the life of his friend, the man whom he wor-
shipped and the other punchers respected, was the one great service he
could render. He died there with a blind terror in his heart at the black-
ness of the unknown, and with the thought of Bill Seymour in his mind.
The men who hanged him felt no exultation at having avenged a crime,
but only a nameless pity for the poor fellow.

A day later Bill Seymour, while dodging about in the timber, learned
from a chance-met friend of Hanner's fate. Looking this friend full in the
face, he said:

"The poor little fool, to do a thing like that!"

1900

When the Grass Grew Long

Ten years ago every cow-boy in the northern part of the Indian Territory
knew "Sermon Billy" Wilson, for he was such a slouchy, tireless, moody,
and altogether strange figure that one did not forget his face after once
seeing it. Everybody knew that one of Billy's hips was dislocated, and
that he walked with a difficult sideswing of his right leg, but none knew
or cared how the disfigurement had occurred.

It was when the puncher was seventeen years old that he came to the
Territory, leaving a rather miserable Indiana home and the ridicule of an
Indiana community behind him. His first job, after he reached the coun-
try of wide prairies and wider license, was as a horse-rustler for "Jimmy"
Thompson, whose ranch skirted the edge of the Paw Paw Creek timber.
Jimmy paid ten dollars a month to his puncher, furnished a horse and
saddle, and stood ready to act as schoolmaster to the young rustler.

"Look here, Billy," advised the ranchman one day, "this ranch is a
long ways from any excitement, an' I know how it is with young bucks
like you. Girls an' drink are the general things. I don't like to change
punchers ever' month; an' I'd not care if you went down into the timber
once in a while. There's some half-breed girls, an' full-bloods, too, that
ain't so bad comp'ny as you'd think. Better consider it some."

Billy considered the words of his boss, placing more confidence in them
each time he recalled them. He rode past the cabins of the Cherokees,

stuck on narrow, fertile strips of open land under the shelter of rocky hills, and watched the girls plodding about their outdoor tasks. At first he could not understand how romance might be fostered here. The girls were rather heavy-bodied, with large, regular, and unresponsive faces. They would not talk to him when he called for a gourd of water or asked to be allowed to rest in the shade of a big live-oak. They brought the water and went back to their work, or pointed silently to the tree.

But at "Cherokee Jake's" cabin, one day, he gained the daughter's favor by helping to pen a calf that had wormed its way through the milk-lot bars. When Billy, at the third attempt, swung the noose of his lasso over the calf's head, the Indian girl showed her teeth in a smile, and spoke her thanks:

"Much welcome. Awful nice rope. Bad little *oyah* (sheep)!" And Billy felt that he had made distinct progress.

The little puncher had occasion to ride that way often afterward, and, noting the growing cheerfulness of his rustler, Jimmy Thompson reflected: "If there was any white girls in sight that was n't a darn sight worse than the Indians, I'd rather he'd take up with them; but the way it is, the Cherokees are the best. I reckon he'll marry her some of these days, settle down on his cornpatch, an' raise shoats and two calves ever' year."

It could scarcely be called a courting, this unconscious fluttering of the young puncher about the cabin; for old Jake, Jake's wife, and "Jinnie Jake," as the girl was called, apparently accepted him as only another piece of furniture to be given room, when necessary, in a crowded cabin. But Billy knew they were friendly, and his desire for female companionship was almost satisfied.

Before the great herds of cattle from Texas were turned loose on the prairies, the grass grew incredibly tall and thick every year, and in the late fall great fires raced across the country, leaving it black and bare. Ranchmen who were thus early settled in the country provided fire-guards—strips of grass cut while green, let to dry, and burned—to protect their ranges from destruction. The Indians generally provided the same protection for themselves; but sometimes they would forget, and be forced to build again after the annual conflagration.

A year after Billy had hired himself to Jimmy Thompson, at the end of a remarkably dry and hot summer, the prairie fires began to break out earlier than usual. A black cloud of smoke rolling up from the west side of Paw Paw attracted Jimmy's attention one day. Calling Billy to follow, he rode over to drive his cattle to a place of safety on his own range.

Reaching the open prairie, on the edge of which was Cherokee Jake's cabin, the ranchman took in the situation at once, and instructed Billy: "I can get the steers back all right by myself. You'd better go over to Jake's cabin an' see if they're all safe. If they ain't burnt a fire-guard, get 'em away to my side the creek—an' hurry!" The fire was sweeping across the open furiously.

In this strip of country, west of the creek, and lying east of a range of low, black-jack-covered hills, where few cattle ever grazed, the grass grew to the height of a rider's cinch-buckle. The day was hot, and the air was dry; the long stems of the dried grass were like trains of cotton. From the south the wind carried the flames straight up the valley, forcing the wild prairie-chickens and rabbits to scurry for safety to the timber on each side. Billy spurred his pony in front of the line of fire, beating it to Jake's cabin with a margin of only a few minutes.

As he rode near the cabin he saw Jake, Jake's wife, and the girl standing outside the cabin, apparently unconcerned and delighted with the spectacle. Billy decided that they must have burned a fire-guard about their home since he had been there two days before; but when he came up to the three he saw the mistake. Jake stood near the cabin with an old wet grain-sack in his hand, waiting to beat out the flames when they should come up to him. Jake had never before neglected a fire-guard, and he did not understand the resistlessness of a prairie fire. Jinnie Jake held another wet cloth, ready to help with the fighting, and the mother had carried two pails of water from the spring to keep the sacks wetted. There was an element of humor in the situation that appealed to Billy, and he muttered to himself: "Darnedest funniest bucket outfit I ever seen!" He had seen and applauded the drills of the Plainfield, Indiana, bucket brigade. He turned to Jake, and shouted: "Git out o' here, quick! This way," and he pointed toward the creek. Old Jake only grunted, gripped his sack firmly, and looked toward the roaring line of smoke, which rolled up in thick, black clouds, rose for an instant as the flames leaped out over the tops of the yet unburned grass, then closed down, and pressed forward with new speed. "Git out, git out, quick!" the puncher screamed above the roar.

But now the answer was a half-crazy exultant light in the old Indian's eyes and a vigorous shake of the head.

"Here, you two, git on my horse an' race for the timber!" Billy turned to the two women standing stolidly at one side.

"No," said the girl, shortly; "we stay, put out the fire. You help."

But the old woman weakened. Bits of charred grass-tops, carried up in the billows of flame, fell about them; the crackling of dry stems, snapped by flashes of outreaching fire, could be plainly heard. Billy noticed the woman's willingness, and carried her bodily to his horse. Then he turned to the girl, and tried to place her behind the mother. Jinnie only pushed him away with powerful arms, and stood defiant at her father's side. The mother galloped away safely to the creek when she saw that Jinnie would not come. The young puncher was desperate.

"Don't be such awful fools! Are you crazy?" He shouted the words in Jake's ear, and seized the Indian's arm to drag him away. The fascination of the oncoming wall of destruction was upon the full-blood; he was mad with the impulse to save his home. He grabbed the little puncher as one might grab a furious, irritating terrier and threw him against the corner of the cabin with crushing force. A jutting log left rough and sharp-edged at the corner stopped Billy's fall, smashing his hip and stunning him for a moment. When the girl saw her father fling Billy against the corner of the cabin, and heard the thud of the impact and the groan of pain that escaped him, she ran to the fallen form with a single comprehending cry: "Oh!" In the one exclamation she loosed all of that which we call love and tenderness, which had been so long and so carefully hidden. Billy regained his senses, tried to rise, and fell back limp with pain.

"Git to water—the well—the spring—quick!" he gasped, and the whirling smoke clouds made breathing difficult.

The Indian girl picked him up in her arms and ran to the spring. She shouted over her shoulder for old Jake to follow. As well have shouted to the fluttering frightened bird as it flew into the singeing heat to its late-built nest! Jake put down his head with a fierce shake of his long black hair, and seized the wet rag with both hands and plunged into the consuming flames. The girl saw him disappear as she put Billy on the ground at the edge of the shallow, walled-in well. She dipped some water from the spring with her hands, and dashed it in the face of the young puncher, for she saw the faintness that was coming upon him. The flames leaped up the side of the cabin, and the smoke swallowed it up. Then the fire raced on toward the two at the spring.

"Maybe so, this way!" the girl half sobbed to herself as the heat singed her hair; then she plunged the body of the puncher into the spring. The water was not deep enough to cover the upright man, and she forced him to his knees on the bottom of the pool. She leaned over to see if he was completely covered and conscious, and when she rose, she whispered to herself: "Maybe so, save him, little fellow!" There was no chance for the girl to escape now. She knew that in the narrow spring there was not room for two, and, turning away, she disappeared in the crackling bed of flames. She went into the choking, blinding, cinder-laden smoke to find old Jake.

When Jimmy Thompson rode back with the frightened old Indian woman, he found some twisted bucket-hoops and two charred skeletons. The cabin was blazing furiously, and Jimmy wondered where he would find Billy's bones. While hunting for them, he discovered the little puncher, half drowned, struggling to get out of the spring. Jimmy pulled him free, and allowed him to faint; but before he lost consciousness Billy broke out angrily:

"Fools!" Then questioningly: "What come o' the girl? Think she done somethin' for me, did n't she?"

"Maybe she did," agreed Jimmy, though Billy had fainted and did not hear the answer.

1901

The Problem of Old Harjo

The Spirit of the Lord had descended upon old Harjo. From the new missionary, just out from New York, he had learned that he was a sinner. The fire in the new missionary's eyes and her gracious appeal had convinced old Harjo that this was the time to repent and be saved. He was very much in earnest, and he assured Miss Evans that he wanted to be baptized and received into the church at once. Miss Evans was enthusiastic and went to Mrs. Rowell with the news. It was Mrs. Rowell who had said that it was no use to try to convert the older Indians, and she, after fifteen years of work in Indian Territory missions, should have known. Miss Evans was pardonably proud of her conquest.

"Old Harjo converted!" exclaimed Mrs. Rowell. "Dear Miss Evans, do you know that old Harjo has two wives?" To the older woman it was as if some one had said to her "Madame, the Sultan of Turkey wishes to teach one of your mission Sabbath school classes."

"But," protested the younger woman, "he is really sincere, and—"

"Then ask him," Mrs. Rowell interrupted a bit sternly, "if he will put away one of his wives. Ask him, before he comes into the presence of the Lord, if he is willing to conform to the laws of the country in which he lives, the country that guarantees his idle existence. Miss Evans, your work is not even begun." No one who knew Mrs. Rowell would say that she lacked sincerity and patriotism. Her own cousin was an earnest crusader against Mormonism, and had gathered a goodly share of that wagon load of protests that the Senate had been asked to read when it was considering whether a certain statesman of Utah should be allowed to represent his state at Washington.[1]

In her practical, tactful way, Mrs. Rowell had kept clear of such embarrassments. At first, she had written letters of indignant protest to the Indian Office against the toleration of bigamy amongst the tribes. A wise inspector had been sent to the mission, and this man had pointed out that it was better to ignore certain things, "deplorable, to be sure," than to attempt to make over the habits of the old men. Of course, the young Indians would not be permitted to take more than one wife each.

So Mrs. Rowell had discreetly limited her missionary efforts to the young, and had exercised toward the old and bigamous only that strict charity which even a hopeless sinner might claim.

Miss Evans, it was to be regretted, had only the vaguest notions about "expediency;" so weak on matters of doctrine was she that the news that Harjo was living with two wives didn't startle her. She was young and possessed of but one enthusiasm—that for saving souls.

"I suppose," she ventured, "that Old Harjo *must* put away one wife before he can join the church?"

"There can be no question about it, Miss Evans."

"Then I shall have to ask him to do it." Miss Evans regretted the necessity for forcing this sacrifice, but had no doubt that the Indian would make it in order to accept the gift of salvation which she was commissioned to bear to him.

Harjo lived in a "double" log cabin three miles from the mission. His ten acres of corn had been gathered into its fence-rail crib; four hogs that

---

1. There was an attempt in 1907 to deny Reed Smoot a seat in the U. S. Senate on the basis of a charge of "Mormonism."

were to furnish his winter's bacon had been brought in from the woods and penned conveniently near to the crib; out in a corner of the garden, a fat mound of dirt rose where the crop of turnips and potatoes had been buried against the corrupting frost; and in the hayloft of his log stable were stored many pumpkins, dried corn, onions (suspended in bunches from the rafters) and the varied forage that Mrs. Harjo number one and Mrs. Harjo number two had thriftily provided. Three cows, three young heifers, two colts, and two patient, capable mares bore the Harjo brand, a fantastic "**HH**" that the old man had designed. Materially, Harjo was solvent; and if the Government had ever come to his aid he could not recall the date.

This attempt to rehabilitate old Harjo morally, Miss Evans felt, was not one to be made at the mission; it should be undertaken in the Creek's own home where the evidences of his sin should confront him as she explained.

When Miss Evans rode up to the block in front of Harjo's cabin, the old Indian came out, slowly and with a broadening smile of welcome on his face. A clean gray flannel shirt had taken the place of the white collarless garment, with crackling stiff bosom, that he had worn to the mission meetings. Comfortable, well-patched moccasins had been substituted for creaking boots, and brown corduroys, belted in at the waist, for tight black trousers. His abundant gray hair fell down on his shoulders. In his eyes, clear and large and black, glowed the light of true hospitality. Miss Evans thought of the patriarchs as she saw him lead her horse out to the stable; thus Abraham might have looked and lived.

"Harjo," began Miss Evans before following the old man to the covered passageway between the disconnected cabins, "is it true that you have two wives?" Her tone was neither stern nor accusatory. The Creek had heard that question before, from scandalized missionaries and perplexed registry clerks when he went to Muskogee to enroll himself and his family in one of the many "final" records ordered to be made by the Government preparatory to dividing the Creek lands among the individual citizens.

For answer, Harjo called, first into the cabin that was used as a kitchen and then, in a loud, clear voice, toward the small field, where Miss Evans saw a flock of half-grown turkeys running about in the corn stubble. From the kitchen emerged a tall, thin Indian woman of fifty-five, with a red handkerchief bound severely over her head. She spoke to Miss Evans and sat down in the passageway. Presently, a clear, sweet voice was heard in the field; a stout, handsome woman, about the same age as the other, climbed the rail fence and came up to the house. She, also, greeted Miss Evans briefly. Then she carried a tin basin to the well near by, where she filled it to the brim. Setting it down on the horse block, she rolled back her sleeves, tucked in the collar of her gray blouse, and plunged her face in the water. In a minute she came out of the kitchen freshened and smiling. 'Liza Harjo had been pulling dried bean stalks at one end of the field, and it was dirty work. At last old Harjo turned to Miss Evans and said, "These two my wife—this one 'Liza, this one Jennie."

It was done with simple dignity. Miss Evans bowed and stammered. Three pairs of eyes were turned upon her in patient, courteous inquiry.

It was hard to state the case. The old man was so evidently proud of his women, and so flattered by Miss Evans' interest in them that he would find it hard to understand. Still, it had to be done, and Miss Evans took the plunge.

"Harjo, you want to come into our church?" The old man's face lighted.

"Oh, yes, I would come to Jesus, please, my friend."

"Do you know, Harjo, that the Lord commanded that one man should mate with but one woman? The question was stated again in simpler terms, and the Indian replied, "Me know that now, my friend. Long time ago"—Harjo plainly meant the whole period previous to his conversion—"me did not know. The Lord Jesus did not speak to me in that time and so I was blind. I do what blind man do."

"Harjo, you must have only one wife when you come into our church. Can't you give up one of these women?" Miss Evans glanced at the two, sitting by with smiles of polite interest on their faces, understanding nothing. They had not shared Harjo's enthusiasm either for the white man's God or his language.

"Give up my wife?" A sly smile stole over his face. He leaned closer to Miss Evans. "You tell me, my friend, which one I give up." He glanced from 'Liza to Jennie as if to weigh their attractions, and the two rewarded him with their pleasantest smiles. "You tell me which one," he urged.

"Why, Harjo, how can I tell you!" Miss Evans had little sense of humor; she had taken the old man seriously.

"Then," Harjo sighed, continuing the comedy, for surely the missionary was jesting with him, " 'Liza and Jennie must stay." He talked to the Indian women for a time, and they laughed heartily. 'Liza, pointing to the other, shook her head. At length Harjo explained, "My friend, they cannot say. Jennie, she would run a race to see which one stay, but 'Liza, she say no, she is fat and cannot run."

Miss Evans comprehended at last. She flushed angrily, and protested, "Harjo, you are making a mock of a sacred subject; I cannot allow you to talk like this."

"But did you not speak in fun, my friend?" Harjo queried, sobering. "Surely you have just said what your friend, the white woman at the mission (he meant Mrs. Rowell) would say, and you do not mean what you say."

"Yes, Harjo, I mean it. It is true that Mrs. Rowell raised the point first, but I agree with her. The church cannot be defiled by receiving a bigamist into its membership." Harjo saw that the young woman was serious, distressingly serious. He was silent for a long time, but at last he raised his head and spoke quietly, "It is not good to talk like that if it is not in fun."

He rose and went to the stable. As he led Miss Evans' horse up to the block it was champing a mouthful of corn, the last of a generous portion that Harjo had put before it. The Indian held the bridle and waited for Miss Evans to mount. She was embarrassed, humiliated, angry. It was absurd to be dismissed in this way by—"by an ignorant old bigamist!" Then the humor of it burst upon her, and its human aspect. In her anxiety concerning the spiritual welfare of the sinner Harjo, she had insulted the man Harjo. She began to understand why Mrs. Rowell had said that the old Indians were hopeless.

"Harjo," she begged, coming out of the passageway, "please forgive me. I do not want you to give up one of your wives. Just tell me why you took them."

"I will tell you that, my friend." The old Creek looped the reins over his arm and sat down on the block. "For thirty years Jennie has lived with me as my wife. She is of the Bear people, and she came to me when I was thirty-five and she was twenty-five. She could not come before, for her mother was old, very old, and Jennie, she stay with her and feed her.

"So, when I was thirty years old I took 'Liza for my woman. She is of the Crow people. She help me make this little farm here when there was no farm for many miles around.

"Well, five years 'Liza and me, we live here and work hard. But there was no child. Then the old mother of Jennie she died, and Jennie got no family left in this part of the country. So 'Liza say to me, 'Why don't you take Jennie in here?' I say, 'You don't care?' and she say, 'No, maybe we have children here then.' But we have no children—never have children. We do not like that, but God He would not let it be. So, we have lived here thirty years very happy. Only just now you make me sad."

"Harjo," cried Miss Evans, "forget what I said. Forget that you wanted to join the church." For a young mission worker with a single purpose always before her, Miss Evans was saying a strange thing. Yet she couldn't help saying it; all of her zeal seemed to have been dissipated by a simple statement of the old man.

"I cannot forget to love Jesus, and I want to be saved." Old Harjo spoke with solemn earnestness. The situation was distracting. On one side stood a convert eager for the protection of the church, asking only that he be allowed to fulfill the obligations of humanity and on the other stood the church, represented by Mrs. Rowell, that set an impossible condition on receiving old Harjo to itself. Miss Evans wanted to cry; prayer, she felt, would be entirely inadequate as a means of expression.

"Oh! Harjo," she cried out, "I don't know what to do. I must think it over and talk with Mrs. Rowell again."

But Mrs. Rowell could suggest no way out; Miss Evans' talk with her only gave the older woman another opportunity to preach the folly of wasting time on the old and "unreasonable" Indians. Certainly the church could not listen even to a hint of a compromise in this case. If Harjo wanted to be saved there was one way and only one—unless—

"Is either of the two women old? I mean, so old that she is—an—"

"Not at all," answered Miss Evans. "They're both strong and—yes, happy. I think they will outlive Harjo."

"Can't you appeal to one of the women to go away? I dare say we could provide for her." Miss Evans, incongruously, remembered Jennie's jesting proposal to race for the right to stay with Harjo. What could the mission provide as a substitute for the little home that 'Liza had helped to create there in the edge of the woods? What other home would satisfy Jennie?

"Mrs. Rowell, are you sure that we ought to try to take one of Harjo's women from him? I'm not sure that it would in the least advance morality amongst the tribe, but I'm certain that it would make three gentle people unhappy for the rest of their lives."

"You may be right, Miss Evans." Mrs. Rowell was not seeking to create unhappiness, for enough of it inevitably came to be pictured in the little mission building. "You may be right," she repeated, "but it is a grievous misfortune that old Harjo should wish to unite with the church."

No one was more regular in his attendance at the mission meetings than old Harjo. Sitting well forward, he was always in plain view of Miss Evans at the organ. Before the service began, and after it was over, the old man greeted the young woman. There was never a spoken question, but in the Creek's eyes was always a mute inquiry.

Once Miss Evans ventured to write to her old pastor in New York, and explain her trouble. This was what he wrote in reply: "I am surprised that you are troubled, for I should have expected you to rejoice, as I do, over this new and wonderful evidence of the Lord's reforming power. Though the church cannot receive the old man so long as he is con-fessedly a bigamist and violator of his country's just laws, you should be greatly strengthened in your work through bringing him to desire salva-tion."

"Oh! it's easy to talk when you're free from responsibility!" cried out Miss Evans. "But I woke him up to a desire for this water of salvation that he cannot take. I have seen Harjo's home, and I know how cruel and useless it would be to urge him to give up what he loves—for he does love those two women who have spent half their lives and more with him. What, what can be done!"

Month after month, as old Harjo continued to occupy his seat in the mission meetings, with that mute appeal in his eyes and a persistent light of hope on his face, Miss Evans repeated the question, "What can be done?" If she was sometimes tempted to say to the old man, "Stop worry-ing about your soul; you'll get to heaven as surely as any of us," there was always Mrs. Rowell to remind her that she was not a Mormon mis-sionary. She could not run away from her perplexity. If she should secure a transfer to another station, she felt that Harjo would give up coming to the meetings, and in his despair become a positive influence for evil amongst his people. Mrs. Rowell would not waste her energy on an ob-stinate old man. No, Harjo was her creation, her impossible convert, and throughout the years, until death—the great solvent which is not always a solvent—came to one of them, would continue to haunt her.

And meanwhile, what?

1907

James Roane Gregory

YUCHI

(1842–1912)

James Roane Gregory, a member of Big Spring tribal town, was born near Coweta, Creek Nation, the son of Edward W. and Eliza Roane Gregory. He attended Coweta Mission School, where he developed an appetite for reading, enabling him to continue his education at home. He farmed until the outbreak of the Civil War, during which he enlisted on the Union side. After the war, Gregory resumed farming and made his living for the remainder of his life as a ferry operator and farmer, settling finally near Inola, Creek Nation. He also held political office, being elected to the Creek National Council (1867) and judge of Coweta District (1873 and 1875). He was often appointed to fill unexpired terms of public officials and at the turn of the century served as superintendent of schools for the Creek Nation. In 1903 he was nominated as a candidate for second principal chief. Still, Gregory found time to read and write. He was considered by his contemporaries an authority on the history and lore of the people of the Creek Nation and on their relations with other tribes in not only the Southeast but in the Southwest after removal. His personal experiences also sparked an interest in the Creek Nation's role in the Civil War. Gregory published a number of historical essays and also enjoyed a local reputation as a poet because of the numerous poems on wide ranging topics he contributed to Creek Nation newspapers. The poems reprinted here reflect Gregory's intimate knowledge of ceremonial life, which was still vital in the Creek Nation at the turn of the century, and a turn-of-the-century despair, heightened no doubt by the impending demise of his nation. In the prose selection, Gregory relates the traditional history of the Muscogee (Creek) people and recent history of their conflict with the Pawnees that ensued following removal.

The Green Corn Dance[1]

My children are happy unto this day
   He-yo-we-yoo! my mother! Hi-yo-chee!
The ashes of the fires were cold and gray,
   The paths are long that lead from the blue sea;
The Southern winds breathed and the snow was gone,
   The warm sun counseled with the great dark cloud,
Then He-yo-we-yoo sent down his new corn
   With his lightning fire dancing, singing loud,
      He-yo-we-yoo-hi-yo.

The children of the storms rejoice this day:
   He-yo-we-yoo! my mother! Hi-yo-chee!
The ashes of the fires are blown away,
   The rain came up straight from the deep blue sea.
The Southern winds came blowing the new corn,
   The warm sun counseled with the lightning cloud;
He-yo-we-yoo sends the lightning free born,
   With his lightning fire we dance singing loud.
      He-yo-we-yoo-hi-yo.
My children are happy.

1900

Nineteenth Century Finality

Nineteen hundred and it rains fire and blood,
   Fast filling up hell and the grave;
A million lives trampled in gory mud,
   They kill to kill—killing to save.

---

1. The Green Corn Ceremony, commonly called the "busk" by whites, was an annual celebration held usually in late July or early August. Activities included fasting, taking "medicine," dancing, and playing stick ball. The celebration, which lasted several days, marked the beginning of the new year. Crimes and social offenses were forgiven, names were conferred, family affairs were sorted out, and order and unity among the people were reaffirmed. The ceremony was the most important event in the people's ceremonial cycle.

Great wars fought for paradise by the lost,
   Hark! Widows' cries and orphans' wails!
God of Love! Pierce our hearts with cold death frost!
   Crown Jesus Christ a stone, God Baal!

The love of God for man deified him,
   The Gentiles glorified his name.
The Roman and the Jew crucified him,
   Science covers His love with shame.

1900

Some Early History of the Creek Nation

That portion of the Creek nation lying south and west of the Arkansas River, before the advent of the Creeks, was the common battle ground between the Osages on one side and the allied tribes of the Pawnee Picts, Kiowas, Comanches and Caddoes on the other side. All this country was once Pawnee Pict territory, who are now known as the affiliated tribes of the Wichita agency. In junction with their allies, the Comanches and Kiowas, the Osages were driven from the east by the Chickasaws. The Osages in turn defeated and drove out the Pawnee Picts with great slaughter.

The Pawnee Picts, having formed a strong alliance with the other tribes mentioned, were beginning to cut the Osages short and had them driven from beyond the Arkansas river to the Verdigris swamps and Grand river hills and into the Ozark ranges. The Concharty mountain was the last fortress the Osages were compelled to relinquish to the Pawnee allies south of the Arkansas river.[1] The Cherokee and Osage war followed, being new foes from the east against the Osages.

The first settlers of the Creeks came west and began to build homes, churches and school houses on the lands the Pawnee allies claimed to have recovered as their old ancient homes. Contentions followed. The first Creek killed by these wild allies was named Joe, a member of the

1. Concharty was a tribal town located on the south bank of the Arkansas between present-day Muskogee and Tulsa, Oklahoma. Hitchetee (or Hichitee), mentioned below, was located on the Deep Fork in the central part of the Creek Nation.

Hitchetee town. He was killed within a mile of the present townsite of Muskogee.

This war party was driven west by a war party of Creeks. It was then that Jerry Cates—an inter-married white man—made a remarkable shot at a Pawnee spy disguised as a wolf, who was lying by a point of rocks viewing a passing column of Creek warriors. Jerry's horse began bucking and Jerry fired his rifle from the horn of his saddle, without aim, killing the wolf Pawnee at seventy-six yards distance.

When the Creeks first met these prairie warriors, who circled in open field battalion tactics, covered with snow-white shields, bedecked with war trophies and eagle feathers, they mistrusted the ability of their rifle balls penetrating the shields of these noble wild warriors. On trial, however, they found that these beautiful shields were no defense against a swift half-ounce rifle ball, which gave them great courage.

The Creek frontiersmen pushed forward far west of other civilized outposts. Such men as Can-cha-tee-matha, Au-kan-teen-ne-ya, Cho-la-feksel-ko, Long Tiger and Tiger Bone; also the elder brothers and uncles of ex-Chief Roley McIntosh and others should be recognized as the pioneers and knights who led the present civilization into this country. Creek blood splashed the wild prairie flowers by Pawnee arrows and lance far and near. In sight of Judge N. B. Moore's residence one fell. Just over the succeeding ridge to the west, near the base of the Concharty mountain, Loney Bruner defeated a superior force of the enemy. The rifle being too slow, the Creeks charged the Pawnee Picts, sword in hand, against the lances of the wild men. In battle royal, worthy of the fame of eastern fields, the enemy was driven away. Loney Bruner is the father of Hon. Richard Bruner, now of Coweta.[2] A few miles further on, near Bluford Miller's residence, an entire Creek family was slaughtered. The innocent boys and girls, with the infant child, and both parents, whom the writer well knew long years ago, and still remembers the life flushed cheeks of each as well as if they were now present and speaking, were ruthlessly butchered in their home yard. Just beyond, further west, a band of Euchees [Yuchis], of the Creek Nation, fought a large band of Pawnee Picts in open field fight on Duck Creek prairie,[3] defeating the Pawnees and capturing the war standard of the war chief of the Pawnee Picts.

2. Coweta tribal town was on the north side of the Arkansas between Muskogee and Tulsa.
3. South of present-day Bixby, Oklahoma.

On Tiger Creek, now in Oklahoma,[4] during the fall of 1859, Long Tiger, Tiger Bone and a crippled brother of theirs—three alone, fought a war party of Comanches, who were in alliance with a war party of the Pawnee Picts. These three Tiger brothers whipped the Comanches and Pawnee Picts, killing seven of them. Tiger Bone's horse was shot from under him. Other similar contests extended along the entire western frontiers of the Creek Nation, which was advanced out into Old Oklahoma of today, and beyond the parallel of the Cherokee frontier, and in line with the Seminole and Chickasaw western frontiers. These troubles lasted forty years, with Fort Gibson garrisoned with walking pop guns, followed by Fort Arbuckle, with like conditions.

The last blood shed was by a Creek lighthorse company under Capt. Lesley Haynes, an uncle of Hon. S. J. Haynes, now of Okmulgee, and a party of Caddoes, in 1866. Then the noble red chief of the Caddoes—George Washington—and that illustrious Christian nobleman, Samuel Checotah, then chief of the Creeks, made a permanent peace between the Creeks and the allied tribes that had so long and manfully contended for this land that the United States government had sold to the Creeks. As we mourn the red splashes of blood where the wild lily gave bloom, that the hummingbird and wild bees abhorred, the Muskogees will not say one word of discredit of their old foes. They are too brave and noble—after these old chiefs had clasped their hands in friendship—to do so. It was on a principle of justice that is human the Christian world over, that impelled these wild men of the prairies to hostile acts. They were brave enough to demand, in their manner, what the highest courts of America have termed "a legal right."

1901

Traditions of the Creeks: Story of Their Trek from Mexico More Than Three Centuries Ago

The history of the Creek or Muskogee Indians is yet unwritten, but their traditions have been better preserved and handed down from generation

4. Gregory is mistaken. Tiger Creek was in the Seminole Nation, now Seminole County, Oklahoma. Fort Gibson, indicated below, was in the Cherokee Nation and Fort Arbuckle in the Chickasaw Nation.

to generation, perhaps, than have those of any other Indian tribe. They know that they are of Aztec origin and that their ancestors were in Mexico at the time of the Spanish invasion under Cortes.[1]

At that time they were not known as Creeks, but as "Muskogees," a sonorous Aztec name they still love. The name "Creek" has never been to their liking, but they have accepted it as a necessary part of their vicissitudes and as a result of the disastrous fortunes of war.

According to their traditions they left Mexico about the year 1520. In all probabilities, however, their exodus from that country was several years after this date, as the Spanish subjugation of Mexico was not complete before 1525. There are old stories of the unavailing valor of the Muskogees against the invaders who they say came in ships from across the great waters. They tell of the enslavement and degradation of the Aztecs, but the Muskogees were neither to be enslaved nor degraded. They antedated the Boers in treking by more than two centuries. According to their legends, some priests of the Toltec faith came with them but these had disappeared, as well as all the forms and ceremonies of that faith, when next they come in contact with the white race during the eighteenth century.

Muskogee traditions are rich in stories of a thousand battles as the tribe fought its way to the northeast, seeking to get as far away as it could from the land it was leaving. The Muskogees, as far as can be gathered from these traditions, inhabited a part of Mexico somewhere in the vicinity of what is now the city of Vera Cruz. The sea and the seashore appear as parts of their panoramic history, and in their wanderings they appear never to have got far away from the gulf. They numbered many fighting men, and, if their traditions are to be believed, they prevailed against all the enemies coming up against them, including the warlike Comanches, then numerous in all the southwest; the Natchez, the Alabama Indians and other once powerful tribes. Tradition seems to be borne out by the fact that they did finally establish themselves in Alabama and Georgia, driving out the tribes then inhabiting that country. They set up their Toltec altars and altar fires, but that fervid tropical faith, it seems, could not long survive a change of latitude, for tradition soon becomes silent as gods and sacrifices, and the Muskogees became creatures of their new environments, caring nothing for sacrifices and ceremonies and having for their religion a vague apprehension of a "Great Spirit" and a "Happy Hunting Ground."

1. Muscogee informants agree on the eastward migration of their ancestors but do not agree with Gregory's theory of Aztec and Toltec origins. They were already in the Southeast when the Spanish arrived.

It was in this condition that the white man found the Muskogees when he came again. The white man gave the tribe the name of "Creeks" because of their propensity for a well-watered country. He found them and their neighbors, the Seminoles, more troublesome than any of the other tribes of the Southeast. This may have been, and doubtless was the result of hereditary bitterness and distrust, surviving for three centuries, and moving them to accept death as a welcome alternative of what they feared was to be slavery in the event of their subjugation. General [Andrew] Jackson, who led one campaign against them, is on record with the saying that "They fought like devils." Desultory warfare, directed against the white man, continued until 1832, when the treaty was made under which the Creeks or Muskogees now hold their present homes in the Indian Territory.

What is not tradition in Creek history is a number of illustrious names. All of the full-bloods, including "Crazy Snake" [Chitto Harjo] and his deluded followers, have inheritance in the glory of Charchachee of Tustennuggee. This was one of the great warrior chiefs of the tribe. His glory is not recorded on any printed page, but it is enshrined in the hearts of his tribesmen. And it is not a matter of tradition, merely, for he appeared in that warlike time when the Creek was a dangerous antagonist for even such a warrior as Andrew Jackson. In that time the tribe held a position against the assaults of the United States troops, under the command of Jackson himself until 600 of the Indians were killed. It was a defeat, but the Creeks cherish the memory of such a battle. Charchachee left a long line of descendants in the tribe and much of his blood flows today in Creek veins. Little of it is found among the half or quarter castes, for theirs is an aristocracy in the tribe which has sought to keep itself unspotted from the world, and the descendants of Charchachee are in it and of it. And perhaps there can be found nowhere in the world a prouder or more exclusive aristocracy than this. Even when the most impoverished and ignorant, as it sometimes is, it asserts itself imperiously.

Thluco, or Weatherford, is another historic name in Creek genealogy. His descendants are numerous among the full-bloods and some of them are to be found among those not wholly of the Indian strain.[2] For the most part, however, the descendants of the great have kept themselves free from contamination. This is particularly true of those of the old Chief Menewa, who lived a century ago, but whose memory is cherished

2. William Weatherford, who fought on the side of the Red Sticks, was less than half Muscogee. Gregory suggests by "contamination" in the next sentence that some of Weatherford's descendants mixed with people of African descent.

and whose posterity delight in honoring it. They are compelled to acknowledge, however, that some of the names which add luster to Creek history are not of Indian sound or origin. McGillivary is suggestive of the canny Scot,[3] who cast his fortunes with the tribe, and whose diplomatic talents assisted in the formation of some of the treaties which have brought the tribe great advantages in dealing with the U. S. government. The descendants of McGillivary are not as sand from the sea shore for multitude, but they are to be found, if not wholly among the full-bloods, then among the half breeds, or quarter bloods, and they, as a rule, display the qualities which made their paternal ancestry the children of McIntosh whose name is equally suggestive of the fine art of getting the best of a bargain, an accomplishment upon the possession of which, in their dealings with the government, the Creeks have of late years found many reasons to congratulate themselves. The half-breed has, in truth, cut considerable of a figure in Creek history during the last half century.

But perhaps there is no more illustrious half-breed in Creek history than Paddy Carr. His father was an Irishman, and his mother one of the fairest of the Creek women. Paddy has left no diplomatic legacy to the tribe, and none of the treaties in which Uncle Sam was given the worst of it are to be credited to him. But in border foray, and leading the Creek van in all their battles with hostile tribes, he gave new luster to the Creek name. If all this could be forgotten in these "weak piping times of peace," the story of his house would still survive in the lingering recollections of the beauty of his famous twin daughters, Ari and Adne. Ari and Adne, tradition has it, were peerless even among the women of the quarter bloods, and one who has seen the perfect loveliness of many of the young fourth caste women of this Indian country will understand the superlative degree of comparison. Mrs. Paddy Carr was the flower of that tribe, when the valor and wit of the half-breed Paddy broke down the exclusiveness of the full-blood caste of that day, and the first fruit of the union was Ari and Adne, with as high a place among the Creek immortals as belongs to warriors or statesmen. It may be added that such an immortality means something in a land where handsome young women are by no means rare.

1901

3. Gregory refers to the descendants of half-Scot, quarter-French, quarter-Muscogee Alexander McGillivray (not McGillivary) and below the half-Scot, half-Coweta William McIntosh.

Alexander Lawrence Posey

MUSCOGEE

(1873–1908)

Alexander Lawrence Posey was the first Native American to receive national attention as a lyric poet and as a humorist. A
member of Tuskegee tribal town, Posey was born in the Creek
Nation, the son of Lewis H. and Nancy Posey. His mother was
Creek-Chickasaw and his father, though white, had been reared
in the Creek Nation and was an enrolled member of Broken
Arrow town from early childhood on. The younger Posey was
educated at the Creek National boarding school at Eufaula and
at Bacone Indian University, which he attended until 1894. In
1895 he entered national politics, winning a seat in the national
council's House of Warriors as a representative from Tuskegee.
From then until 1901 he held various government posts: superintendent of the Creek orphan asylum, superintendent of schools
for the Creek Nation, and superintendent of the boarding
schools at Eufaula and Wetumka. Posey began to write for publication during his Bacone days. Though he wrote some prose, his
primary productions were romantic, lyrical poems, most of
which he published under his pen name Chinnubbie Harjo. In
1899 and 1900 his poems appeared in U. S. newspapers, and,
though he received accolades and encouragement to write more,
he dropped poetry as a literary form and became a journalist. In
early 1902 he bought the *Indian Journal*, a weekly newspaper at
Eufaula and published it until 1903. During that time he distinguished himself by his lively journalistic style and established
himself as a dialect humorist, whose Indian dialect letters were
frequently compared to those of contemporary American dialect
humorists. Posey's Fus Fixico letters, which he began in the *Journal* in 1902, were reprinted widely in newspapers throughout the

Indian Territory and in the United States. Posey sold the *Indian Journal* in 1903 and worked briefly for the *Muskogee Evening Times* before going to work in 1904 for the Dawes Commission, enrolling Creeks for allotments. After the tribal rolls were completed in 1907, he became a real estate agent, working at that until once again becoming editor of his old newspaper shortly before his death in 1908.

Though he was widely known as a journalist, wrote more than 250 poems, and published a number of prose works, Posey's greatest achievement was the Fus Fixico letters, in which Fus Fixico, a fullblood, reports in dialect the conversations and musings of Hotgun, a Creek medicine man, and his fullblood companions, Tookpofka Micco, Wolf Warrior, and Kono Harjo. The quartet were Snake Indians, followers of Chitto Harjo, who opposed allotment and dissolution of the tribal government. The letters reprinted here reflect the perspective they assumed on the rapid changes being wrought by the government's allotment policy and reflect the humor they found in the activities of the whites around them. Posey especially liked to poke fun at local folk who made much out of their petty offices and who fawned before national dignitaries, whose names the fullbloods mispronounced in meaningful ways. The last letter reprinted below, for example, was the result of a brief visit to Muskogee by President Theodore Roosevelt, who stopped for only a few minutes on his way to hunt in Oklahoma Territory and Colorado. He was met by Clarence Douglas, a local editor, Chief Pleasant Porter of the Creeks, Charles Gibson the Creek writer, and Alice M. Robertson, the local postmaster, whose "dee-light" and sense of importance contrast humorously with the brevity of the visit and its apparent insignificance to Roosevelt. The poems reprinted here reflect Posey's favorite subjects—the people and landscapes of the Indian Territory, especially the Tulledega Hills west of Eufaula where he was born.

Fancy

Why do trees along the river
   Lean so far out o'er the tide?
Cold reason tells me why, but
   I am never satisfied.

And so I keep my fancy still
    That trees lean out to save
The drowning from the clutches of
    The cold remorseless wave.

1897

Tulledega

My choice of all choice spots in Indian lands!
Hedged in, shut up by walls of purple hills
That swell clear cut against our sunset sky;
Hedged in, shut up and hidden from the world,
As though it said, "I have no words for you;
I'm not a part of you; your ways aren't mine";
Hedged in, shut up with low log cabins built—
How snugly!—in the quaint old-fashioned way,
With fields of yellow maize, so small that you
Might hide them with your palm while gazing on
Them from the hills around them, high and blue.
Hedged in, shut up with long forgotten ways,
And stories handed down from sire to son;
Hedged in, shut up with broad Okataha,[1] like
A flash of glory curled among the hills!
How it sweeps away toward the morning,
Deepened here and yonder by the beetling
Craig, the music of its dashings mingling
With the screams of eagles whirling over,
With its spendid tribute to the ocean!
And this spot, this nook is Tulledega,
Hedged in, shut up, I say, by walls of hills,
Like tents stretched on the borders of the day,
As blue as yonder op'ning in the clouds!

1897

---

1. Literally, "sand," a short-form reference to the North Canadian River, which Posey called Oktahutchee; it flows eastward through the hills and joins the Canadian River near Eufaula, Oklahoma.

Coyote

A few days more, and then
There'll be no secret glen,
Or hollow, deep and dim,
To hide or shelter him.

And on the prairies far,
Beneath the beacon star
On Evening's dark'ning shore,
I'll hear him nevermore.

For where the teepee smoke
Curled up of yore, the stroke
Of hammers rings all day,
And grim Doom shouts, "Make way!"

The immemorial hush
Is broken by the rush
Of man, his enemy
Unto the utmost sea.

1899

Ode to Sequoyah

The names of Watie and Boudinot—[1]
    The valiant warrior and gifted sage—
And other Cherokees, may be forgot,
    But thy name shall descend to every age;
The mysteries enshrouding Cadmus' name
Cannot obscure thy claim to fame.

1. Stand Watie and Elias Boudinot, Cherokee brothers. Watie was a Confederate general in the Civil War, and Boudinot was the first editor of the *Cherokee Phoenix*, founded in 1828.

The people's language cannot perish—nay!
  When from the face of this great continent
Inevitable doom hath swept away
  The last memorial—the last fragment
Of tribes, some scholar learned shall pore
Upon thy letters, seeking ancient lore.

Some bard shall lift a voice in praise of thee,
  In moving numbers tell the world how men
Scoffed thee, hissed thee, charged with lunacy!
  And who could not give 'nough honor when
At length, in spite of jeers, of want and need,
Thy genius shaped a dream into a deed.

By cloud-capped summits in the boundless west,
  Or mighty river rolling to the sea,
Where'er thy footsteps led thee on that quest,
  Unknown, rest thee, illustrious Cherokee!

1899

Hotgun on the Death of Yadeka Harjo

"Well, so," Hotgun he say,
  "My ol'-time frien', Yadeka Harjo, he
Was died the other day,
  An' they was no ol'-timer left but me.

Hotulk Emathla he
  Was go to be good Injun long time 'go
An' Woxie Harjoche
  Been dead ten years or twenty, maybe so.

All had to die at las';
  I live long time, but now my days was few;
'Fore long, poke weeds and grass
  Be growin' all aroun' my grave house, too."

Wolf Warrior listen close
   An' Kono Harjo pay close 'tention, too.
Tookpafka Micco he almos'
   Let his pipe go out a time or two.

1908

Fus Fixico's Letter

"Well, so," Hotgun he say, "the Injin he sell land and sell land, and the white man he give whiskey and give whiskey and put his arm around the Injin's neck and they was good friends like two Elks out for a time."

"Well, maybe so," Tookpafka Micco he say, "the white man was cut it out when the Injun was all in."

Then Hotgun he make the smoke b'il out a his pipe good and answer Tookpafka Micco, "Well, so the Injin was had to go up against it to learn and, maybe so, after while he catch on, same like the white man and go to Mexico and bunco the greaser."

Then Hotgun he take another puff and go on and say, "Well, so like I start to say history was repeat itself. The Injin he sell his land in the old country (Alabama) and he sell his land in Injin Territory and was had a good time out here like back there in olden times. But back in old country he was live different, 'cause he was sit on a long chair like a fence rail—but he was no mugwump. Now the Injin was sit on a chair that was had fore legs and hind legs too, like a oxen, and also a cushion soft like moss. He was got civilized and called the old chair a bench. He wear a white shirt now and black clothes and shoes that was look like a ripe musk melon. Then he was buy bon bons for his papoose and drop-stitch stocking for his squaw and part his name in the middle, J. Little Bear.

"Then the white man he tell the Injin, 'Well so your wagon was out of date and you better buy you a fine buggy; or, maybe so, a fine surrey.' The Injin he grunt and say, 'Well, so let's see um.' Then the white man he say, 'Well, so I sell it cheap like stealing it—sell it to Injun the fine buggy and harness and all for hundred and fifty dollars. That was cheap, 'cause Injun he was sell land and got it lots a money and was out of date riding on two horse wagon.' Then the Injin he look at fine buggy a long time and make good judgment and buy um. His little pony mare team look mighty weak and woolly and got colt, but they was pulled the fine buggy home all right. Then when the Injin was got home he was put the fine buggy under a tree to look at like fine painting."

(Tookpafka Micco and Wolf Warrior and Kono Harjo they was look in the fire and spit in the ashes and pay close attention like they was interested.)

Then Hotgun he go on and say, "Well, maybe so about three years from now the starch was go out a the Injin's white shirt and make it limber like a dish rag, and his black suit was fade like the last rose a summer and his breeches was get slack like a gunny sack, and his big toe was stick through his tan shoes like a snag in Deep Fork, and his fine buggy was tied together with baling wire and his old fillies was made good crow bait pulling the fine buggy to stomp dances." Then, Hotgun he go on and say, "Maybe so the Injin was awakened up to his sense a duty and earn his bread by the sweat a his brow like a good republican or maybe so a democrat."

And Tookpafka Micco he say, "Well, maybe so he be a middle of the roader."

Then Hotgun he say, "Well, so they was only two sides to a clapboard and it's the same way in politics. The Injin couldn't cut any ice or raise any sofky sitting on top a the rail looking at the crabgrass."

(Then Tookpafka Micco and Wolf Warrior and Kono Harjo they was grunt and spit in the ashes again and say, "Well, so we vote it straight.")

1904

Fus Fixico's Letter

Well, so, while the young warriors was played Injun ball and gobbled at one another, like in olden times, last Sunday, at the Weogufky square ground,[1] Hotgun and Tookpafka Micco and Wolf Warrior and Kono

1. Weogufky tribal town was on the south side of the North Canadian River west of present-day Eufaula. The square ground was the place where town business was conducted and where the annual Green Corn Ceremony occurred. The square was a means of indicating general location; the ball game took place on a playing field nearby.

Harjo they was go off to theyselves under the brush arbor where it was cool and no flies buzzing 'round and talked over they pipes and made lots a strong smoke rise up.

"Well, so," Hotgun he say, "this neighborhood wasn't incorporated and they was no policeman standing on the corner with a big sixshooter to throw down on you for being absent from Sunday school."

(Tookpafka Micco and Wolf Warrior and Kono Harjo put on a dry grin and chew the pipe stem and listen right close, like they was like to hear it.)

"Well, so," Hotgun he go on and say, "we was had something yet to be thankful for to the federal judge. We could turn the old work filley out on the grass Sunday morning and, maybe so, shoulder the rusty grubbing hoe and go off down towards the creek and enjoy the sunshine and scenery, while the line was slack in the water. That beat holding down a bench with a straight back to it and no dash board to rest your feet on in the amen corner, where the last Sunday air was musty and the people remember the Lord once a week to be in style.

"The best place," Hotgun he go on and say, "to be sorry for grafting and to get close to the Great Spirit was out in the woods, where you couldn't had any temptation except to feel like swearing when something was stole your bait, or maybe so when a seed tick try to strike up acquaintance with you. That way you could catch mudcat and bass, or maybe so pluck a bouquet, and live and enjoy life.

"Well, so all the same," Hotgun he say, "the butcher was had to kill the frying chicken for 'em and the family horse was had to stand up in the stable and eat dry hay so he could take the Christians sight seeing."

"Well, so," Tookpafka Micco he say, "that sound like good philosophy, but maybe so it was not good policy."

(Wolf Warrior and Kono Harjo was paid close attention.)

Then Hotgun he tell Tookpafka Micco, "Well, so, that's what's the matter with the country now—they was too much policy used. So if a man was talked common horse sense and tried to rake some facts out a the dark so the sun could shine on it you was lost lots a trade by it. So if you was a store keeper, or maybe so a politician, or maybe so a deacon in the church, you was compelled to had a good stock a policy to stay at business. You couldn't let your light so shine, or maybe so show your hand, 'cause policy was the key to prosperity.

"But," Hotgun he go on and say, "philosophy was like the treasure laid up in heaven, and rain couldn't rust it and the flies couldn't corrupt it and was all you could be remembered by. If you was laid up a big roll a greenback in the bank, or maybe so a fine dress suit in the clothes press, you needn't need 'em in your business when you was dead and your tombstone leaning to one side."

(Wolf Warrior and Kono Harjo they was grunt big and approved it.)

1904

Fus Fixico's Letter

"Well, so," Hotgun he say, "Colonel Clarence B. Duglast, he was dee-lighted and Chief P. Porter, he was dee-lighted, and Charley Gibson he was dee-lighted, and Alice M. Lobbysome she was dee-lighted too."

And Tookpafka Micco he was look down his old pipe-stem and say, "Well, so what for?"

And Hotgun he go on and say, "Well, so 'cause the Great White Father from Washington was suffered 'em to go unto 'im on the grand stand, while he was showing his teeth and shaking the Big Stick before the multitude up to Muskogee."

Then Tookpafka Micco he spit out in the yard and say, "Well, so what kind of a thing's the Big Stick, anyhow?"

And Hotgun he look wise, like the supreme court, and explain it, "Well so the Big Stick was the symbol of power, like a policeman's billy. In the jungles of Afriky it was called a war-club; and in the islands a the sea, like Australia, it was called a boomer-rang; and among us full-blood In-jins we call it a ball-stick; and if it was fall in the hands a the women folks, it was called a rolling-pin, or maybe so, a broom-handle. It was had lots a different names, like breakfast food. Over in Europe a king was had precious stones put in it, to make it more ornamental than use-ful, and call it a scepter. The brass-knucks was the latest improvement on it. In olden time Samson was had a Big Stick made out of a jaw-bone of a ass, and was made a great hit with it among the Philistines. Same way when the Great White Father was want to show his influence all he had to do was to flourish the Big Stick and everybody was get out from under it."

(Wolf Warrior and Kono Harjo they was grunt and Tookpafka Micco he was pay close attention and spit out in the yard again.)

Then Hotgun he smoke slow and go on and say, "Well, so, like I first start to say, Colonel Clarence B. Duglast he was dee-lighted and Chief P. Porter he was dee-lighted, and Charley Gibson he was dee-lighted and Alice M. Lobbysome she was dee-lighted too. They was all butt in before the reception committee could see if they badges was on straight. They was put the Great White Father on they shoulders and histed 'im upon the grand stand, and he was made a talk to the multitude. He say, 'Well, so I was mighty glad to see you all and hope you was all well. I couldn't complain and I was left Secretary Itscocked[1] enjoying good health. (Big cheers and somebody out in the crowd say, Bully for Itscocked!) Look like you all was had a fine country down here. You all ought to had statehood and let Oklahoma show you how to run it. (Colonel Clarence B. Duglast, he pay close attention and listen for some word 'bout 'imself.) I want everybody to had a square deal down here. (Lots more big cheers and everybody smiling but the Snake Injin.) You all was had a fine town here too. You could run flat boats up to it from Fort Smith, and deliver the goods over lots of railroads, and pump out oil, and develop salt-licks and float bee-courses. But I didn't had time to talk any more, 'cause I couldn't stop here but two minutes and I have been here put near five. So long.'

"Then the special train was kick up a cloud of dust and hide behind it, and the multitude was climb down off the houses and telegraph poles and go tell they neighbors 'bout it. Colonel Clarence B. Duglast he go and tell his friends the President think he was ten cents straight, and Chief P. Porter he go and tell his friends the President say he was the greatest living Injin, and Charley Gibson he go and write a 'Rifle Shot' 'bout giving the President a fan made out of tame turkey feathers instead of eagle plumes, and Alice M. Lobbysome she go and buy the platform the President stood on for a souvenir. Maybe so she was made a bedstead out of it and distribute the sawdust and shavings among the full-bloods to look at."

And Tookpafka Micco he say, "Well, so I might need some kindling next winter and the keepsakes was come in handy."

(Wolf Warrior and Kono Harjo they was give another big grunt.)

Then Hotgun he go on and say, "Well, so the next stop the Great

---

1. Ethan Allen Hitchcock, Secretary of the Interior.

White Father make was out in Oklahoma in a big pasture, where they was a lots of cayotes. He was got after one a horseback and crowd it over the prairies till he was get good results and captured it alive. He was had lots of fun with it before he was run it down. The President was a great hunter and was kill big game well as a cayote or jackrabbit. So he was go on to the Rocky Mountains to beard the bear and lion in they den."

And Tookpafka Micco he say, "Well, so this time the Lord better help the grizzly."

1905

The Passing of Hot Gun

Hot Gun, whose Indian name was Mitchka Hiyah, one of the most famous of Creek medicine men, and a character who figured prominently in the Fus Fixico letters, satirical Creek logic upon the political administration of Indian affairs by the white man, died yesterday at his home in the forest between Eufaula and Wetumka, at the age of 60 years. He was seized by that disease so fatal to Indians, pneumonia, and lived but a short time.

Hot Gun was a genius. He was an Indian tinkerer of great fame. It was said that he could make anything. His inventive genius was remarkable. He was a philosopher, carpenter, blacksmith, fiddler, clockmaker, worker in metals and a maker of medicines. Out of scraps of iron and wood, old wire springs and small wheels that he had collected, he set to work and made a clock that kept excellent time. It was a crude affair, but it was faithful. In the early days when the government paid a blacksmith to do the work for the Indians when they needed any, Hot Gun was the government blacksmith. Near his old home there stands the same old blacksmith shop, and until he died he worked when so inclined in his old shop.

Among the Snake Indians, to which faction he belonged, he was the most highly regarded medicine man, and it was said of him that he could cure gunshot wounds better than any white doctor. In this he seemed to be especially skilled. He used medicines of his own manufacture and kept his formulas secret. His practice was a strange mixture of modern ideas and the old-time witchery. While he used medicines, he also chanted over his patients, looked into clear, deep water for advice and guidance and did many other strange things to obtain wisdom.

Hot Gun, Wolf Warrior, Kono Harjo, and Fus Fixico were a quartet of Creek philosophers who used to spend much time together, and criticisms became as proverbs among their fellow Indians. Hot Gun was a Snake Indian, and at the time the government decided that the Snakes must be subdued, Hot Gun was at the big camp making medicine for them. He was taken along with a lot of leaders among the rebellious Indians and thrown into the "bull pen" at Muskogee that served for a jail and kept there for several months. His long hair, of which the Snakes are so proud, was cropped close, and this Hot Gun regarded as the one shameful incident of his life.

On an eminence in the deep timber stands Hot Gun's house. He has lived there since the civil war. The government allotted the land to him without his knowledge or consent, but allotted his wife land elsewhere, and neither she nor her husband know or care where it is. The house is a little log cabin without windows. Out the back door leading down to a magnificent spring there is a path that is worn a foot deep in the soil by constant use.

The spring used to be a stopping place for travelers along the old trail leading west from Eufaula. Hot Gun levied tribute on all persons who camped there and used his spring. When the government sent field parties out to survey and appraise the land they located a camp at this spring. Hot Gun went down to levy tribute upon them, and when the government men flatly refused to pay, he threatened to overrun their camp with tarantulas and rattlesnakes, using his power as a medicine man to call them forth. But Hot Gun was up against civilization this time and he had to let the camp remain without getting his usual tribute. That was one of the bitterest experiences of his life, for he hated the government and the policy of allotting lands to the Indians.

1908

Pleasant Porter

Muscogee

(1840–1907)

Pleasant Porter, the last elected chief of the Creek Nation before
Oklahoma statehood, was the son of Benjamin Edward and
Phoebe Porter. After five years' education at Tullahassee Mission
near his home in the Creek Nation, Porter worked as a store
clerk and cattle drover. During the Civil War, he served in the
Confederate Creek army, after which he entered the service of
his nation, first as head of the school system and then as Creek
delegate to Washington, leader of the Creek lighthorse policemen in the so-called "Sands Rebellion," member of the House
of Warriors in the national council, and commander of the constitutional warriors in the Green Peach War of 1882–83. Porter
ran unsuccessfully for election as chief in 1895 but won the post
four years later. He was reelected in 1903 and still held the office
when he died. During his chieftaincy, Porter oversaw the dissolution of the Creek Nation, the allotment of Creek lands, and the
initial steps toward Oklahoma statehood. He had served as a
member of the Creek commission to negotiate with the Dawes
Commission and had sought his nation's highest office because
he accepted the inevitability of change for the Creek people and
urged them to make the best of their unfortunate situation. He
supported one last major effort to salvage some political autonomy for the Indian peoples of the Indian Territory by chairing
the Sequoyah Convention, which in 1905 drafted a constitution
for the proposed State of Sequoyah. The constitution failed of
consideration in Congress, which in 1906 passed a bill to combine Indian Territory and Oklahoma Territory as a single state.
Porter's latter days were clouded by accusations of his involve-
ment in graft in Creek land deals and claims that he supported

separate statehood because of his political ambitions. Be that as it may, the essay reprinted here presents Porter's—and many other Indian leaders'—arguments in favor of admitting the Indian Territory to the Union as a separate Indian state.

What Is Best for the Indian

Much has been said and talked in the newspaper columns suggesting single and separate statehood for Oklahoma and Indian Territory. A bill has passed the lower House of Congress granting statehood to Arizona, New Mexico and Oklahoma, and is pending in the Senate for consideration at the coming session of Congress. Bills have been introduced in both branches of Congress proposing territorial government for the Indian Territory—among others the Moon Bill, which has been favorably reported in the House of Representatives. Conventions have been held in the Territory proposing some law providing for the annexation of Indian reservations to Oklahoma when such Indian tribe or nation shall, through its Council, assent to it. Some disposition will have to be made of the question as to whether separate statehood will be given the Indian Territory by act of Congress or annexation to Oklahoma.

The thought suggests itself that in order to give identity as to the form of states of all the territories within the confines of the United States, it will be fitting and proper to propose an amendment to what is termed the Omnibus Bill granting statehood to Arizona, New Mexico and Oklahoma, providing an enabling act giving statehood to Indian Territory to take effect under the dissolution of tribal government March, 1906. This would settle the question and remove the necessity of a separate statehood act for the Indian Territory to be passed sometime within the next two or three years, and would give ample time for the general government to complete the distribution of the lands to the Indian tribes owning the Territory and would give general satisfaction to the people inhabiting the Indian Territory.

The annexation to Oklahoma of the Territory, either as a whole or piece-meal, as has been suggested by conventions held at different places in the Territory, would only add another factor to the complex problem that is now being wrought out in the Territory, that is, the transformation

of the Indian people from their tribal institutions to that of a more enlarged system of government, that of United States citizenship and statehood, including common holding of property to individual tenure.

It may be well to look into the reasons underlying separate organization of pacific territory into statehood. It will be found that states have
been organized with boundaries and including territory within which pacific rights have been accorded to or won by the prowess of its inhabitants; so it will be seen that the rights of persons was the principle upon
which they have been organized, and the sentiment should not be lost
sight of in the accession of new states or territories by the United States.

The country, upon the older maps denominated the Indian Territory,
was set apart by the United States out of a portion of what has been
commonly called the Louisiana purchase. Since it was set apart, portions
of it have been segregated and organized into states, namely, Kansas,
Nebraska, Colorado, and latterly the Territory of Oklahoma. Now, in
the same manner, the Northwest Territory was organized into the states
of Ohio, Indiana, Illinois and Kentucky by grant of the old state of Virginia, and by some others. This is mentioned to show that the uniform
principle in the organization of states has never been varied since the
foundation of the government to the present time.

Now, when the last portion of the territory, which was granted in per-
petuity to the Indian people for a perpetual home, has to be organized,
the same principle and sentiment under which the older states were organized, having separate history with separate rights and institutions, there
is no reason why this time-honored custom should be violated.

The people of the Territory, acceding to the demands of progress westward, have not demurred to releasing portions of their territory when
conditions had changed and the country was occupied by invading armies of self-governing people from the East and South. All of this magnificent territory out of which states have been born, has passed from the
conditions of the first grant to the people of the Indian Territory. Now,
when it is proposed to induct into statehood all the remaining territory
within the confines of the United States, the Territory has the right to
insist that its identity be not lost or submerged for any economical reason
or any reason advanced as to the symmetrical portion of statehood which
seems to be desired.

Would it not be more consistent with the principles upon which all the
states have been organized to let the identity of the Territory remain?
And when organized, give it perpetual identity by giving to it separate

statehood. The last virgin territory in the United States which, by the unbiased judgment of the people of all the states and travelers from all nations, is denominated the richest and most beautiful portion of the United States, with the finest climate and its productive capacity equal to that of the richest state growing the staples, corn, wheat and cotton, and the best fruits of any of the states, should not be subjected to a lower estate than that of the other states that have been inducted into the sisterhood of states. The Territory should not be compelled to accept a position of concubinage to Oklahoma when brought into statehood. The fairest and youngest should be given equal honor with the older and less attractive. And it is improbable that Uncle Sam will deign to ask the virgin state to accept the entry into statehood on a lower plane than the other states.

1902

Charles Gibson

MUSCOGEE

(1846–1923)

Born near Eufaula, Creek Nation, on March 20, 1846, Charles
Gibson was the son of John C. Gibson and a niece of Opothleyo-
holo, a noted Creek chief. He was largely self-educated, although
he attended the Creek common schools and Asbury Mission
school. Gibson worked as chief clerk and buyer for Grayson
Brothers store until 1896, when he opened his own grocery in
Eufaula. After 1900, he wrote extensively for Indian Territory
newspapers and journals. He began a long association with the
Indian Journal in 1900, writing a feature column called "Gibson's Rifle Shots" for that Eufaula newspaper until 1910. Many
of his pieces were published in other newspapers, Indian school
journals, and popular magazines. His works include philosophi-
cal pieces on Indian history and speculation on the place of Native Americans in American society. Many of his articles carried
the identifiers "Horse Sense" and "Humor," which are good in-
dications of their content. From time to time he also published
Indian Territory folklore. Gibson was at his best offering witty
observations on the current scene.

The Passing of the Indian

It will not be long now when the old people that were little children in
Alabama will be no more. Now and then we see him come to a railroad

town and sit him down and look at the work the white man has done. He is very quiet as he gazes at the improvements on his once wild country. He hardly realizes the change. He wonders in a curious way how a white man can accomplish this work; he admits that the white man is a great wonder to him. The great rocks which he thought were of no use, and the red sand banks, have been and are being converted into square blocks and are making beautiful homes for the white man and his family. He wonders now what the Indian was created for; he is no account, he is in the way of advancement, he sits and wonders at his littleness in the make-up of the world.

Yet he is here, but not to stay. Yet a little while, say 50 or 75 years, and his mother earth will receive him, the last of the red race. He will be known in little sketches of history only. He was once the happiest man on the face of the earth; not so today, the hands of all men seem to be against him. Some would speak a good word for him, some would like to help this fallen brother, but this man with his sympathy has nothing else that will stay the hand of the Indian's enemy. Sympathy is good, when it is widespread but they who are in sympathy with the Indian are very few, and are people who have nothing else to offer for the Indian's good. This sweet sympathy is found without the halls of congress where it wastes its sweetness on the desert air. His true friends in congress have long deserted him and left him to his fate. Have they given him a fair show at civilization before pulling him? Does not the white man's history tell us that it has taken them thousands of years to reach the standard which they now occupy?

The Indian is being hurried into civilization, and also to his doom. He has not had the time to attain the polish of the white man, yet he is expected to gulp down civilization at once. This looks hard, but maybe 100 years hence the Indian will be forgotten, likewise his troubles.

And it will still be a puzzle to the world to know just his mission on this earth, as he has nothing to show to the world of his accomplishments. He has tackled all the paths of fortune of the white man and he has made a botch of all of it. He has been as complete a failure as was ever gotten up. The Indian has been willing, and lots of them have tried to follow the beaten paths of fortune, but were not a success. This would look like he was not built right for the times he now lives in. He seems to be a misfit.

But they are fast fading off of the earth and will soon be gone. White man, spare the Indian; he will not be in your way long, the little Indian infant at the breast today will live but a short life at best and he is about the last generation of the North American Indian. One hundred years from this, the 1st day of January, 1902, an Indian of North America will be the grandest curiosity of the age. White man, stop and think who has brought this upon this poor ignorant race, if not directly, then indirectly. You say the red devils are treacherous. How came him so? Did he not meet William Penn with outstretched arms? How was it with him? They loved this white man, William Penn. Why? He treated them like men as they were. Then treat him today as Penn did and you will not meet a manlier man than the Indian of North America. The Indian does not ask to be pitied or fed by alms; he is not begging for mercy; he is not asking to be put at the head of society; he is not a pauper; all he asks is justice, right, and to be treated like a man, that is all. He wants the great officers at Washington City to carry out their promises. He does not ask the government to go out of her way to please the Indian. No, no! It is to carry out these sacred promises that have been given them from the powerful voice of the United States, whose voice is heard and obeyed to the ends of the world, that is all and no more.

God made man in his own image; is not an Indian built like other men? Then why ignore his appeals for justice and his rights? Does not the white race own there is a God? Then why be a Pharaoh again? This is not a bluff, it is a little comparison in reading the white man's Bible. Does it look good where Moses begged for his people? No. The good Christian will say it did not look good in Pharaoh to do as he did. Then don't oppress the Indians any more than can be helped. He is now hemmed up so that he is as harmless as a dove. His race is run, speak gently to the Indian. It will be but a short while when he may be an angel. He is some of God's people. The white man is the conqueror, his Indian-fighting days are over. The Indian is trying in his simple way to obey the commands of his great father at Washington yet a little while and he may hear the voice from the Great Throne in the happy hunting grounds asking him how he was treated by his stronger brother, the white man, and how shall he answer that he was treated, like a man and a brother, or otherwise?

We have the reading put us to ponder over this great problem—who is right and who is wrong—and if there is or has been a mistake made, who is mistaken.

1902

The Indian—His Present

He is like a stray horse—every body is wanting to use him. There is no Indian today, but what is attractive and full of interest. All eyes are turned on him. Why is it? He is not a solon, nor a railroad magnate, nor a merchant prince, nor a John Pierpont Morgan. He is not a great evangelist, nor a person of royal rank, nor a high official of the United States government. He is only a poor lo. Yet, in popular parlance, he seems to be of a great lot of consequence. Well, the reason of his popularity is because he is land poor. This is what is the matter with him. He has more land than he knows what to do with. He is living at the top of the pot. But friendly strangers have sought abode with him, volunteering to take care of his surplus domain; and in the shuffle the Indian has been caught up in the whirl of an everlasting picnic. Thus is carried out the old sayings, come easy, go easy; let each day provide for itself. His money is all in large bills and he has to mortgage twenty dollars to get fifty cents worth of change. He is patted on the back and told to go in and blow himself. He is put next to the fact that not every man in the United States can boast of 60 acres of terra firma; that there will be lots of land left after he is done with; that it is no use to be a hale fellow well met unless one is a hell of a fellow.

The Indian long ago cared but very little for money. He could do without and not feel inconvenienced. But the Indian of this enlightened age, being more civilized, has learned that the rattle of silver in one's jeans commands respect. So he lets go of a few acres of land and is happy. Nothing like putting on appearances. It is American to do so. Why can't he, the most genuine and uncompromising American.

The Indian will hold his head up and stay in the front push as long as his land holds out. He will live easy though he dies a hard death.

There are a few Indians who are holdbacks—that is, not selling any land and depriving themselves of high living. They seemed to have forgotten that they are liable to drop off any minute; that there is but one life to live on this earth.

Now, in regard to the picnic hereinbefore mentioned, a great many talk like this: You will sell all of your lands and be paupers within a few years.

This sort of talk may be all right, but we are not heeding it, because we are also told that there will be plenty of land left when we are dead and gone. So we are taking the money offered for our land and having a good time, for tomorrow we may die and leave a lot of land for our poor kinfolks to wrangle over in the courts, causing the legal fraternity no end of bother.

With these few remarks on the present of the Indian we will proceed to join the picnickers and shout, on with the dance! Let joy be unconfined!

1902

The Indian—His Past

He was monarch of all he surveyed. He wanted for nothing. Food was at his disposal. He had the pick and choice of such game as his appetite craved. In short, he subsisted on the fat of the land. Having a boundless country to roam over and stretch his tepee where he pleased, he knew nothing of confinement. He owned the earth and enjoyed the freedom thereof. He was a man and rejoiced in his physical strength. He was not savage when his rights were respected. He was even humane; especially in the matter of killing game. He did not destroy game wantonly. What game he destroyed was for food, not for the sport of it. The twang of his bowstring did not make the game wild. He could approach a bear or deer without scaring it out of the country. He did not have the quality termed "game hog" of nowadays. When he sent an arrow home in one deer, he did not look for a whack at another. He took his split cane and proceeded to cut the hide loose from the legs, breast, etc., oblivious to what went on about him. He was very careful not to give the living deer a scare. He hunted only when he needed food and killed no more game than was actually necessary. When he thought he needed a change of meat, he poisoned the streams in the summer for fish. The sport was free to all, likewise the fish. The poisoning of the stream did not shorten the fish crop.

In his simple happiness, he adored the Giver and gave thanks for fruits—strawberries, blackberries and so forth.

With the ripening of the corn came his annual festivity. This event was celebrated with great pomp. He looked upon the corn as being over half of his living. The festival season was religiously observed by his entire tribe for eight or ten days. There was no hypocrisy, only pure simple religion.

During this festival all lost property found was displayed for identification. Such trivial effects as handkerchiefs, ropes, bells, bows and arrows were hung up and a talk made notifying all present that this or that was lost property subject to claim by the owner. Stray horses and hogs were described and located and the owners thereof went and got their stock without a cent of cost to themselves. One of the headmen was always delegated to make a long talk to the young men, admonishing them to lead up-right lives. There was, also, a renewal of good friendship and brotherly love. The camps were filled with rejoicing. Now and then a tear was shed for some dead leader of the dance, or singer, or medicine man, or fire maker. The widows and orphans were special guests at the festival. The sympathy of the tribe was extended to them. Their relatives were admonished to look after them and make them comfortable.

The young men on these occasions were called up before the elders and given their war names. The Creeks were all known by their clans. For instance, a young man of the deer clan was called and when he came up before the namers he would probably be named Echo Micco, or King Deer. Each was called and named according to his clan. He was presented with a piece of tobacco duly cured and wrapped in pawpaw or hickory bark. The young men so named discarded their old names forever. There was no hunching, no laughing, no foolishness. The ceremonies were conducted as sacredly as in any church.

"Don't get mad enough at your neighbor" said the old man to the young men, "to kill him. He that will not take this advice is bilious, sickly and a woman in temper.

"Don't take from your fellowman the worth of an arrow without first asking his consent.

"Don't talk too freely to your neighbor's wife; it might cause your neighbor to lose his friendship for you.

"Above all listen to the advice of your elders."

These are some of the rules of conduct the young Indians of the past were taught to live and die by.

1902

The Indian—His Future

Looking back we see him despised because he is a savage and a shade darker than the pale face. He is not given to work, cares little for progress and is without love for money. Is he to be blamed? For all these faults, if faults they be, he believes that the One looking over him did not intend that he should work; that had the pale face stayed on his own side he would today be happy.

Not so. He has been driven from one reservation to another until he should be a worse savage today than he was five hundred years ago.

On the shore of the Atlantic he stood a giant. The little waves came and went, but came oftener and higher as he stood till finally the giant was forced to retreat from them, seeking safety on the banks. But the waves followed him there and he retreated still further. He climbed the mountains, but the waves sought him out, submerging the mountains. Then the giant set his face unto the setting sun and climbed higher, yet did the waters follow him. Weakened finally by his march, the giant stopped and tried to stand his ground, but stumbled in the effort by selling a piece of American soil to William Penn. Then one stumble followed another until he was swept along with no landing in sight. He struggled in vain to get away from the waves. He became disgusted with his own weakness and man's inhumanity to man. He saw nothing to encourage him to another effort. Meanwhile the waves rose higher.

One of these waves is called the Penn treaty, another the sale of Alabama, another the Georgia squabble, another the emigration west of the Mississippi, another the war of the rebellion whereby the giant lost most of his property, and yet another the misinterpretation of a treaty in 1866, giving the negro about one-third of the giant's country without the consideration of one dime.

The giant, or hero, of our fable has been oppressed more than any other being on the face of the earth.

Did you ever stop to think over this case of our hero? Well, about one-half of our hero's countrymen served as soldiers during the late war. How much of the rebellion they put down is not recorded, but we find many old pensioners among the people of the giant. Now, the giant gets no credit for his loyalty to the union, although the war swept away about a third of his last and only lands.

The last wave which will close over the life of the giant, which is not worth living nohow, will be the winding up of tribal affairs. The wave is already here.

The old Indian, who came from Alabama, has told his young people, "Even the children of the pale face will call you bad names, kick you out and not see that you have your rights. You will only be Indians, the hated and despised people. If you are liked, it will be only while your land lasts. Then you will be a vagabond the balance of your miserable life."

Such is the prophecy of the old Indian, who concluded thus: "The white man will say to you, who have sold your land and are begging food and shelter, 'you are stout and able to work'. The white man's religion teaches him that by the sweat of his brow shall he eat bread."

So will the noble red man of Cooper go down into his grave, if he has any, unhonored and unsung. So will pass one of the honestest, truthfulest, kindest, most charitable, hospitable, humblest, most religious, most wronged, most patient, forbearing, but most revengeful race of people that ever inhabited the earth.

1902

The Way of the Spokogee

When he flourished and was in his glory, he enjoyed his rounds of pleasure and led a simple life. The medicine man was his high priest and not the Secretary of the Interior.

With the first fruits of the season, the high priest, or medicine man, called the Spokogees together at the square ground. The annual festivities began with an all-night dance, after which the lieutenants of the high priest announced when the feast would begin. The time appointed was usually about strawberry and blackberry time.

At these all-night preliminary dances there were fixed up little bundles of split cane, called "nitta kuchka" (loss of time or days) which were distributed among the tribe. The little bundles were taken home and the splits of cane thrown away at the rate of one a day. When but one or two splinters remained in the bundle, the family then made ready to be on their way to the busk ground, where a good time was in store.

The busk or square ground was so arranged that each clan had its respective corner. The visitors were provided with seats to themselves and were treated with the utmost respect. The high priest, who sat apart, had active young men to deliver his communications to the assembly. They were his mouth-pieces, as it were.

There were so many ceremonies connected with the annual busk that we will confine ourselves to the green corn celebration only.

After striking camps, all were subject to the orders of the high priest. His camp was headquarters. At the beginning of the festivities, he dressed up in his wild regalia and went into the square house, where he was waited upon. All the necessary medicine jars were carried to him so he could concoct the proper medicines for the occasion. He sat facing the east upon a stool made especially for him. Under his feet was spread a deer hide. He was isolated from the world, as no one was allowed to go near him. Holding a hollow reed about three feet long, he proceeded to sing certain songs, leaving off after a time and blowing through the reed into the earthen jars containing water and herbs. When he was done the medicine was closely guarded until the lieutenants, as we have called them, announced to the men of the tribe that all was ready. Whereupon all went to their respective stations in the square house and were served with the decoction in gourds. In olden times, back in the south country, they used cocoanut shells, but later resorted to the use of gourds. Everybody of the male persuasion was supposed to drink the medicine. The medicine caused the drinker to vomit freely and thoroughly and was believed to cleanse the system of impurities. At dark all partook of a food called white sofky. Disobedience of the law was punishable by a fine of not less than the last shirt on the offender's back or more than his entire assets. Then came the day of feasting, the bill of fare being new corn, honey, dried venison, bear and buffalo meats, and a different brand of sofky. Then the high priest made the new and sacred fire which was taken home by each member of the tribe and not allowed to go out until the next ripening of fruits.

The high priest, or medicine man, was the greatest among the Spokogees. His crop was worked and kept clean of weeds by his people and he made medicine every full moon for them to drink and so ward off sickness.

Since discarding these old time customs, the Indian has dwindled to a mere dwarf. He is not strong and robust as he was then. The copper color the pale face gave him is lacking. He is darker and looks bilious. It seems the customs of the pale face have been too much for him. He seems doomed because he has forsaken his own customs.

1902

Wild Cat's Long Swim

History is a little silent on the capture of the notorious Seminole warrior, Wild Cat, and seven of his warriors and does the Napoleon act on them, but, tradition, or whatever you might call it, tells us that once upon a time the crafty chief and seven of his followers were captured, taken to an island and dropped there to become quiet citizens before they would be allowed to return to the everglades of Florida.

Tradition has the island of Cuba as the stopping place. After going such a distance by boat and being dumped out on an island, it was supposed that Wild Cat was "done for." Not so. After staying on the island a few months, and being by that time thoroughly disgusted with his lot, he began to look up some scheme whereby he could make his escape. He told his comrades that he believed he would make as good looking drowned Seminole warrior as a Seminole warrior in captivity, and his comrades agreed with him.

Finally, they agreed to try their fortunes over the waves with hand and feet—in other words to swim back to America.

By this time their captors felt secure as to Wild Cat's safety and thought they had converted him and his seven followers into good quiet Seminoles, so the captives were not watched very closely. Thus it happened that at the close of a certain day Wild Cat and his followers were resting alone under the friendly shade of a palm tree.

Said the great warrior, "I've a good notion to save up my rations," (which were very scant,) "and breast the ocean for a few days and land either in America or at the bottom of the ocean."

Immediately his friends jumped at the idea. So they saved up what they thought would last them eight days. When the time came the night was clear and bright with many stars. Wild Cat and his men bundled up and went down to the water's edge. Wild Cat being a great woodsman told his men what star to follow on the route. Each warrior stripped himself of his clothing and in some way fastened his rations on his head.

When all were ready and standing at the water's edge, Wild Cat cheered his men and told them it was better to go to the bottom of the ocean free men than to be slaves to their enemies the rest of their lives. He told his men that he believed the Great Spirit would give them a resting place for their feet now and then and help them back to their native land.

Whereupon Wild Cat, without uttering another word, went to his comrades and shook hands with them and they followed his example. When the solemn hand shaking was over, Wild Cat nodded his head and started on his long swim, his friends following.

They waded out some distance and then began the swim for life and liberty.

The captors had learned the habits of their prisoners somewhat, and knew that the Indians were inclined to stay away from their captors as much as possible, so their absence at first did not cause any alarm. So, unknown to his enemies, Wild Cat swam on and on, feeling his way for a resting place when his limbs grew too tired to go farther. Sometimes he found it, sometimes he did not, but he kept his course day and night. Just when his followers would begin to think they could go no farther but would have to let the waves close over them, Wild Cat would find a resting place for them.

This was continued for eight days and nights. When the eighth night was far spent matters still looked hopeless, but Wild Cat nothing daunted began to sing a war song. He had found a resting place for his feet, and soon the others came swimming up to him. Wild Cat solemnly began shaking hands with them. They thought he had given up to die in the ocean, but Wild Cat said:

"Look my friends, under our guiding star. Methinks I see a great tree, where I have rested with my warriors when I had come back with blood on my beaded belt after killing and scalping my enemy."

The warriors gazed, low down, with their chins resting on the waves, and sure enough they saw the tree tops! Then they rejoiced and Wild Cat inquired about their provisions. They all looked among their bundles and found that among all of them there was only one banana left! Wild Cat took this and broke it into eight pieces, each piece making but a small mouthful for each warrior. But Wild Cat cheerfully remarked as he swallowed his bite that when they reached home they would play football with bananas, oranges, and the like! He cheered them by saying that the sun would be very young where they would "Yar-kee" on their own soil. Then they shook hands and struck out to finish their swim.

Just as the sun was peeping over their brown shoulders they struck wading water and waded into the Everglades and formed themselves into a circle. Then how the old woods rang with the yar-keeing of the old warrior and his little band of brave followers!

To this day, Wild Cat's captors don't know how he and his followers made their escape.

1902

Why the Lion Eats His Meat Raw

Once upon a time, when there were no white, red or black men living, all animals were people, and communed with each other. The little Fice was the wisest of them all, and was called the King of the animals. On a certain day he called a council, and every body was present at roll call. The Rabbit and Fox were nominated for clerk. When the votes were cast, the Fox got the majority, and became clerk of the council.

All subjects were freely discussed. At last the King spoke up and said, "We could be more civilized, I think, if we did not eat our meat raw." He gave this subject to the people for discussion. There was a great deal said on the question for and against, and it was finally decided that if the King knew how it was possible to cook their meat that he be asked to tell the council.

The King said, "Now, we live in this country that we have not named, and as for myself, I am not posted as to who lives across this large river, but it may be that some one of this council has been across the stream, and, if so, may have got acquainted on the other side. I hear there are people living there who cook their meals. If there be one in the council who has been over there, please speak up."

At that, the Rabbit spoke. Now, the Rabbit was known to be the biggest liar of all people. The Rabbit said, "I have been over there; there are many families over there; they are large people and they call themselves lions, tigers and elephants, but it is a very difficult matter to find the way to this land. This river you speak of is very small at the end, and there is where these people live. They are very fierce, and kill and cook their meat over a red substance which they claim is a part of the sun, and are very cautious about letting it go out, and watch it very closely. A large family called Lions are the custodians of the piece of the sun, and are very dangerous people."

So saying, the Rabbit sat down. The King recommended a delegation to that country to contract, or in some way to get a piece of the sun from these people. A vote was taken, and it was ordered that the Rabbit be a committee of one to look after the matter.

Rabbit went to work and made him some new arrows, and departed on his journey. He landed, after traveling a long time, and met all the big families, and tried to negotiate for a piece of the sun, but it was no go.

At last he sprung a plan to steal a piece of the sun, so he went to the house of the Lion that was custodian of the piece of sun. All the others were ordered to extinguish their piece of sun for the night, but the Lion was supposed to watch by his coal of sun, or fire, all night, and to build it up just before dawn by adding more fuel, and then divide it up with all the families.

As we have said before, Rabbit was a great liar. So he began to tell the Lion great stories and kept this up till late at night, when the old Lion became very sleepy. The more the Lion yawned, the more the Rabbit lied to him. At last the Lion began to snore very loud—he was sound asleep. Here was Rabbit's chance, so he snatched up the coal of fire and started out of the house, but the coal was very hot to his hand. However, Rabbit was no fool—he had an over-cup acorn cap with a slate brim; so he just raised the coal and lay it on the brim of his cap, and scampering out of the house, he was off and away.

The Lion awoke and took the Rabbit's trail, making pretty good time, but the Rabbit, knowing how cross the Lion family was, took great precaution to dodge him. Rabbit swam the little stream a great many times, until it became very wide, and yet he swam it. The Lion also swam it many times until it became very wide, and until his strength was about given out. About this time Lion came upon a little animal that he took to be Mr. Rabbit, and caught and killed him, but there was no fire to be found. The Lion knowing that water would destroy fire, decided that after swimming the river so many times, the Rabbit must forever have lost his coal of sun. He returned to his people and reported the loss of the piece of sun. Ever since that time the Lion has had to eat his meat raw.

Mr. Rabbit came back with his little spark of fire, all right, though, and built up a fire for his people. But the little coal of fire was so hot in transit that it burned through his cap a little, and burned the fur a little on his forehead. That is why Mr. Rabbit has a little white spot on his forehead.

No one took to the new way of eating their meat cooked except the King. That is why a dog always likes his meat cooked better than raw.

1903

William McCombs

MUSCOGEE

(1844–1929)

William McCombs was born at Fort Gibson, Indian Territory, on July 22, 1844, the son of Samuel and Susie McCombs. A member of Cheyaha tribal town, he lived most of his life near Eufaula in the Creek Nation. During the Civil War, McCombs fought for the Confederacy in the First Creek Regiment under D. N. McIntosh. After the war, he was elected to the House of Warriors, the lower house of the Creek national council. He subsequently served a term on the Nation's Supreme Court, after which he became superintendent of the Creek public school system. McCombs was the superintendent of Eufaula High School and national interpreter for Chief Pleasant Porter. In 1868, Tuskegee Indian Baptist Church ordained him a minister. McCombs preached in the Muscogee language right up to his death in 1929. "An Eloquent Oration" looks at the past, present, and future of Indian Territory. McCombs recalls the advance of the white culture on the Indian one and looks at the subsequent changes. He urges all Americans, "red, white, and black" in his words, to work together against poverty, ignorance, and superstition. Such presentations earned McCombs the reputation as one of the best orators of the Creek Nation.

An Eloquent Oration

We, the representatives of a once powerful race on the American continent are met here today to play our part on the stage of life and government.

As I stand before you a vision rises before me in which I see the past, the present and the future. The picture unrolls out of the dim and traditional past showing the untutored fathers, mothers and children of our race basking in the sunshine and uncorrupted happiness and health of that romantic and poetic time when as God's children guided by wisdom handed down in song and story and by the lights hung out in the skies and the lessons read from the book of nature laying open before them, they lived and died with the pure light of the morning, the generous warmth of the meridian and the red glow of the setting sun prompting to love and marriage, the chase and the dance. Then came the white man with the civilization and the push and dash and commercial enterprise born of conditions existing beyond the changing plains of the ever rolling sea. With pure hearts, free from suspicion and guilt the red man hailed the coming of the white man as a gracious gift from the Great Spirit, and welcomed his white brother with open arms to the fairest lands laying beneath the circling blue of heaven's canopy; took him by the hand and led him through the pathless forest, along the singing brooks beside the gentle flowing rivers to the mountain tops from whence he could feed his enraptured vision upon broad plains, where the tall prairie grass bending and swaying in music waves before the gentle breeze stretching far away toward the home of the setting sun.

He took him by the hand and led him to his wigwam; fed him upon the sweet and nutritious bread baked of the hand-ground meal of the Indian corn; spread before him the meat of the deer, the elk and the buffalo; made his bed of the aromatic and elastic twigs and branches of the pine, the balsam and the sassafras, covered by the rich and now priceless furs captured in the hunt and the chase; gave him his fairest star-eyed daughters to wed, and countless broad acres for his home, and thus was the door opened through which we passed from the innocent, guiltless, happy past to this eager, madly rushing strenuous present.

Looking about us today we stand entranced as we contemplate the wonderous metamorphosis, the vast and almost indescribable changes brought by the hand of man since the white man first rapped at the door of the red man. Countless hamlets, villages, towns and cities now dot the land once owned and completely dominated by the Indians. Endless stretches of steel rails now bind the Atlantic to the Pacific ocean, the tropical sunlit gulf to the Arctic regions. The demon locomotive with puffs and ear-splitting scream, rushes madly from city to city, from ocean to ocean, the smoke of numberless forges, foundries and factories now mount the ethereal starways of the skies; the schools, the colleges, the churches and the cathedrals are training the mind and comforting the souls of many millions, red, white and black of the sons and daughters of men. And here we stand in the midst of this animate scene of life, enterprise and human energy. Nothing stands still either in nature or among man, everything moves either upward, onward or downward. Confronted by these conditions, by this environment, what is our duty?

Every consideration of expediency, of duty, of right demands of us that we meet the emergencies of the hour; that we step into the front rank of the moving millions of this glorious land of ours; that we buckle on the armor of valiant Americans and armed with the sword of American citizenship cut our way through the ranks of poverty, ignorance and superstition with their concomitant attendants of wants and misery, sheltered by the starry banner of our common country, proclaim ourselves active members and earnest workers in this government of the people and for the people.

1903

Ben H. Colbert

CHICKASAW

(1873–?)

Ben H. Colbert was born at Colbert Station, Chickasaw Nation, and attended Chickasaw common schools, Baptist Academy at Atoka, business college at Denison, Texas, and Baylor University. During the Spanish-American War, he was private secretary to Theodore Roosevelt, and by virtue of his affiliation to the future president and the Republican Party, he received a number of political appointments. He was U. S. marshal for the southern district of Indian Territory (1900–04), held positions in the Bureau of Indian Affairs (1921–23) and the Internal Revenue Service, and was clerk for Congressman Ulysses S. Stone of Oklahoma (1929–31). Between appointments he made his living as a livestock grower near Tishomingo and was known as a grower of champion Poland China hogs. In the early 1940s he moved to Henryetta and became a newspaper distributor. He had enlisted in World War I at age forty-five, and after America entered World War II, he worked in the defense industry, overhauling airplanes at the Spartan School of Aeronautics in Tulsa. During his early life, Colbert had witnessed the dissolution of his tribal nation. He had served as a member of the Chickasaw Commission that drafted the supplemental treaty between the Chickasaws and Choctaws and the United States in 1902. In the essay reprinted below, he assesses the difficult path followed by the five large Indian republics of the Indian Territory, and, like many Indians of his generation on the eve of Oklahoma statehood, he accepted the changes and envisioned a future with promise.

Events of Three Generations

Three generations ago the Federal government of the United States consummated through its commission, assisted in a great many instances by its soldiery, one of the largest land deals of history with the Five Civilized tribes, dealing with each tribe separately. The idea was to acquire dominion over a more centralized body of land. The Choctaws, Chickasaws, Creeks, Seminoles, and Cherokees were herded like so many cattle from their homes and farms and the more uncivilized from their hunting grounds, in what is now the southern states, composing North and South Carolina, Georgia, Alabama, Mississippi, Tennessee and Florida, to the state now known as Oklahoma.

The Cherokees claim that a reputed discovery of gold in Georgia was one cause of the removal; at any rate after many destructive wars and conferences with a frontier soldiery who were as ruthless as medieval barbarians, who laid waste to towns and appropriated property from the tribes for their own, and expected in return therefore humane treatment, the removal was accomplished.

It was all right to murder a few ignorant squaws and papooses, but when one of their white women happened to fall by their frontier home, the country would cry for an awful vengeance. Be that as it may, millions of acres of Indian land was exchanged for thousands of the white man's. At that time the Indian Territory, then a part of the territory of Louisiana, was nothing but wilderness and plains, and was not so entirely wholesome looking to the tribe from beyond the Father of waters. It was the home of the buffalo, elk, antelope, wolf, coyote, bear, panther and cat. Its only human beings were a few skulking Comanches and Apaches, raiding swiftly up from the southwest, and the whole was a trackless, unmarked, unexplored wilderness.

At the time of treating, each and every tribe was negotiated with as a separate sovereign power, and was considered independent of all foreign tribute and alliance. Their property was guaranteed to them in Holy conscious treaty to be theirs forever, free from all encumbrances and obligations, and each tribe, free and independent.

But time wore along. The white man became more civilized. Rudyard Kipling wrote "The White Man's Burden,"[1] and the American republic

---

1. Kipling's poem was widely published in the United States in 1899. Indian Territory

meekly took up the job of taking the Indian Territory away from its rightful owners. The term of savage had long since passed as an application to these people, many of them were part, or wholly white, so it was rather a hard proposition to entirely eliminate the Indians, and perchance we pass through another period of commissioners and treaty making instead of a perfunctory warfare, by which a hundred thousand citizens would have been disposed. Today shorn of their tribal power and independence, reduced by disease and famine and war from probably half a million in the old home east of the Mississippi, to a scant hundred thousand they stand with segregated lands where [George] Crook and [Nelson A.] Miles and [George Armstrong] Custer and [Oliver O.] Howard campaigned, ready for statehood.

Where Geronimo leaped from the tall grass along the Canadian with a thousand braves, today you see the peaceful farmer invading the wheat fields with binders and threshers. Where the buffalo thundered and the antelope startled his visitor with a surprised snort, is heard the lowing of the domestic cow and the grunt of the fat and lazy pig. Where the coyote howled and the bob cat yelled, you may now hear the cackle of the hen disturbed from her nest and the screech of the startled guinea, as the thrifty housewife gathers her eggs for the noonday meal of the hungry, thirsty farmer.

With nearly two million of people, wealth, stock, lands in cultivation, towns, railroads and mines, the new state will be the greatest ever admitted to the Union. In ten years the new state will be greater in agriculture, mines, marble, oil and gas than nine-tenths of the present states of the Union. In twenty years it will be greater in population, stock and wealth. With proper care by the agricultural class, profiting by the lessons of the farmer in the older states and tilling their land scientifically and raising such crops as are suited and in rotation; by properly stocking their farms with productive, profitable strains of stock and with a reasonable amount of care on the part of the law bodies, in fifty years it could easily be the greatest state in the Union, considering the enviable position the state has at the time of its admittance, and considering the wonderful advance in ten years.

1906

readers found its ethnocentrism amusing, and writers—including DeWitt Clinton Duncan (Cherokee), J. C. Duncan (Cherokee), and Alexander Posey (Muscogee)—found it easy to parody.

David C. McCurtain

CHOCTAW

(1873–?)

Son of the last elected chief of the Choctaw Nation, Green Mc-
Curtain, and Martha Ainsley McCurtain, David C. McCurtain
was born at Skullyville, Indian Territory, on January 29, 1873.
He attended schools in the Choctaw Nation and was recognized
as a superior student. With support from the Choctaw Nation,
he attended school at Roanoke College in Virginia, Kemper Military Academy in Missouri, and the University of Missouri. He
then studied law at the Columbian (now George Washington)
University at Washington, D.C. He was admitted to the bar in
1903. McCurtain had held political offices in the Choctaw Nation and continued to serve the Choctaw Nation after Oklahoma
statehood. McCurtain was general attorney for the Choctaw Nation from 1908 to 1912 and for the next two years was mayor
of McAlester, Oklahoma. He served as LeFlore County Attorney
for 1919–1923 and as County Judge from 1923 to 1925. In
1925 he became a district judge and served for ten years. McCurtain was also assistant attorney in the Title Division of the U. S.
Department of the Interior. In 1937, he was appointed a trial
examiner of the Bituminous Coal Divison at Interior and served
until 1943. He then became a hearing officer of the National
War Labor Board, 8th Region, at Dallas, Texas, until his retirement in 1944. As a member of one of the most politically active
families in the Choctaw Nation, McCurtain was familiar with
the Choctaws' staunch opposition to the provisions of the Treaty
of 1866, giving former slaves and free blacks of the Choctaw
Nation a share in the tribal domain. The Choctaws' resentment
is evident in the essay below. Allotment was carried out under
Republican administrations. McCurtain uses that to urge Indi-

ans to vote Democratic in upcoming elections of delegates to the Oklahoma state constitutional convention. The Democrats made race the central issue of their campaign. When the election was held, the Indian Territory voted overwhelmingly Democratic.

Indian Treaties Were Ruthlessly Broken

The history of the Republican party's treatment of the Indian people contains nothing that would justify the Indians allying themselves with that party. We do not have to turn many pages back in the history of the government's relationship to the Indians to get a correct line on the Republican party's regard for the Indian and his rights. Take the treaty of 1866, and there is found recorded as discreditable an act as was ever perpetrated by a great political party in the name of the government. It was in this treaty that the Choctaws and Chickasaws were required by the national government, then in control of the Republican party as now, to give to the negroes, former slaves and their descendants of the Choctaw and Chickasaw people, forty acres of land each. The Choctaws and Chickasaws had to agree to, provide for the negroes before the government of the United States would even consent to make a treaty with them recognizing their rights as tribes.

D. N. Cooley, commissioner of Indian affairs, and a Republican, said to the Indians at Fort Smith in September, 1866, "you have by making treaties with the enemies of the United States (Confederate states) forfeited all rights to annuities, lands, and protection by the United States." Think of it! The Indians were to have their lands declared forfeited because they made treaties with the Confederate states, when, as a matter of fact, no such course was ever pursued or even mentioned against the Confederate states themselves, the very enemies of the United States with whom the Indians had made treaties and for which they were to be so sorely penalized. Mr. Cooley nor any other Republican officer ever said to the citizens of the Confederate states that "you by your allegiance to the enemies of the United States have forfeited all rights to your lands and other property." Then why should they declare or threaten to declare forfeited the Indians' property for doing no more than other people of the south had done? "What was sauce for the gander should have been sauce for the goose." The Indians were under no obligation to the United States government for their lands, much less to the Republican party; they owned these lands and more by a God-given right, and not by the graces of the Republican party. What right, then, had the Republican party to treat the Indian lands as forfeited?

Commissioner Cooley further said to the Indians that one of the conditions which the United States government would insist upon in the treaty was that the Indians would have to incorporate their former negro slaves into their tribes on an equal footing with the original members, or suitably provide for them. Here is a fair sample of Republicanism as applied to the Indians. The Republican party, the boasted friend (?) of the Indian people, would and did take the Indians' property without compensation and give it to the negroes, and all this they did in the name of the United States government. Did the United States government under the control of the Republican party ever do so much for the white people as it has done for the negro? Did the United States government ever provide homes for the white people in the Indian Territory as it has for the negro? Not only that, did the United States government under Republican rule exact of the other slave owners the same requirements it exacted of the Indians? Were the people of Arkansas, Texas, Mississippi and the other slave owning states required to provide for their negro slaves as were the Indian? All these might be embarrassing questions to bring up at this late day, but they are all within the record; besides, this is the first time we have had a chance to bring them up, and from hence forward they will be like Banquo's ghost; they will not down.

In the year 1902 congress ratified an agreement with the Choctaw and Chickasaw tribes whereby in the allotment of lands the Choctaw and Chickasaw freedmen were each to receive land equal in value to forty acres of the average allottable lands of the Choctaw and Chickasaw nations. At the same time it provided that the citizens should receive allotments equal in value to three hundred and twenty acres of the average allottable land of the Choctaw and Chickasaw nations. Under the terms of this agreement the citizen who took the best grade of land would get only one hundred and sixty acres and the freedmen who took the best grade would get only twenty acres. But the Republican party, ever watchful of its own, at the last congress provided that the freedmen should be allowed to buy at its present appraised value and sufficient to increase his allotment in acreage to forty acres; so that the freedman who got only twenty acres by reason of having selected the best land is now permitted to buy twenty acres more at a very low price. How about the Indian or intermarried white citizen allottee who received only one hundred and sixty acres by reason of having selected the best grade of land, shall he be permitted to buy enough land to increase his allotment to three hundred and twenty acres? It seems not. The Indian or intermarried white citizens did not present the proper color scheme to interest a Republican congress.

It is reported and not denied that the Republican administration at Washington has directed the local authorities here to receive applications for the enrollment of negro children, that is Choctaw and Chickasaw freedmen children, born since September 25, 1902, and up to March 1, 1906. It is not claimed that there is any law for enrolling this class of freedmen, but I suppose it is the intention of the Republican administration to receive the application while they have time, and pass a law to enroll them later. Has there ever been a case where the Republican administration has directed the enrollment, or the receiving of an application of an Indian for enrollment in the total absence of a law authorizing it? This is a sort of special dispensation, it seems, for the exclusive benefit of the negro.

All these things sticking out so plain, I cannot for the life of me see how an Indian can bring himself to support the Republican party, a party that is so closely connected with the negro and so strongly committed to his interests as if by some magic power that cannot be shaken off, especially when this close relation to and strong attachment for the negro and his interest has so many times come into play against the Indians and their interests. I am for the Indian as against the negro, and am, therefore, not a Republican.

1906

Ora V. Eddleman Reed

CHEROKEE

(1880–1968)

Ora Veralyn Eddleman Reed's writing career started early, when she was still a teen-ager. Born on a ranch near Denton, Texas, in 1880, Ora moved with her family to Muskogee, Indian Territory, when she was fourteen. She attended school there, including Henry Kendall College, later the University of Tulsa. Her education was greatly complemented, however, in 1897 when her family bought the *Muskogee Daily Times*, for which newspaper the young woman became proofreader, telegraph editor, and reporter, filling in with other publishing tasks as needed. When her sister and brother-in-law started *Twin Territories: The Indian Magazine* in 1898, Ora became chief contributor and later editor and publisher. Eddleman wrote fiction for *Twin Territories* under the pen name Mignon Schreiber and articles on Indian history and biography, mainly concerning herself with the Five Civilized Tribes. As editor, she solicited the work of other Native American writers such as Charles Gibson and Alex Posey. In 1904, *Twin Territories* ceased publication and Eddleman was recruited to write for and edit the "Indian Department" of *Sturm's Oklahoma Magazine* through 1905 and 1906. After that, she raised her family, moving often with her husband, Charles Reed, who was in the oil exploration business. In the 1920s Ora Reed wrote for a Casper, Wyoming newspaper and had a radio program there. In later years she wrote scattered articles for Oklahoma newspapers and magazines until her death in Tulsa in June, 1968. Reed wrote about what she knew best, the inhabitants of Indian Territory at the end of the territorial period. The selections here are representative of her work. "Billy Bearclaws, Aid to Cupid" is a typical example of Reed's romantic fiction, drawing as it does from the juxtaposition of two cultures. This was a prominent theme in *Twin Territories* and *Sturm's Oklahoma Magazine*. "Indian Tales Between Pipes," a series of anecdotes on the sagacity of full-bloods, shows us the sophisticated and ascerbic wit that Reed often displayed.

Father of 90,000 Indians

One of the most unique, it might be said stupendous, positions authorized by the United States Government is that occupied by the man who supervises the 90,000 Indian inhabitants of Indian Territory. These Indians are the members of the Five Civilized Tribes, viz., Cherokees, Creeks, Choctaws, Chickasaws and Seminoles, who, by treaty stipulations with the United States early in the nineteenth century, relinquished their rights to soil in Alabama, Georgia, Tennessee, North and South Carolina and Mississippi and accepted some twenty million acres of land in what now comprises Indian Territory.

Mr. J. George Wright, United States Indian Inspector for the Indian Territory, is the man who holds the peculiar position of father for 90,000 Indians, and his authority is found in section 27 of the act of June 28, 1898 (30 stat., 495), which reads:

> That the Secretary of the Interior is authorized to locate one Indian inspector in Indian Territory, who may, under his authority and direction, perform any duties required by the Secretary of the Interior by law, relating to affairs therein.

The inspector reviews and transmits to the Secretary of the Interior all reports of the agent in charge of Union Agency, the superintendent and supervisors of schools, revenue inspectors, mining trustees of the Choctaw and Chickasaw nations and supervising engineer of townsites—in fact he recommends just what is best for Poor Lo and administers to his wants accordingly.

The individual Indian, however, hardly knows that there is such a man as the inspector. Almost the first English words the full-blood learned in Indian Territory were "the agent," and they come to him for their every want as does a small boy to his father. The agent is really "the man behind the gun" and is greater than the president of the United States in the eyes of the red man.

In truth, the agent is the right hand man of the inspector and upon him falls the brunt of the work of administering to nearly one hundred thousand Indian citizens, ranging from fullblood to $1/128$ Indian by blood. Mr. Dana H. Kelsey, agent in charge of Union Agency, therefore in reality is the foster father, or rather federal guardian, of the Five Civilized Tribes of Indians in Indian Territory, the largest Indian agency in the United States.

To enumerate the different branches of the work of the Indian agent would require much more space than this article can devote. Briefly, he manages all affairs pertaining to the Indian, handles his money, builds his houses, pays his debts, sells his land and sees that he gets the highest market price for it, or if some greedy white man has taken "squatter's" rights, the agent must escort him out of the territory—in fact he is the red man's guardian.

The agent receives and disburses more than three million dollars each year. A large per cent of this money is derived from royalties on coal, asphalt and other minerals, oil and gas, tribal taxes and through the sale of lots in government townsites. In addition to this money the agent is required to make from time to time special payments to the Indians, ranging from a few thousand to nearly a million dollars. One of these was recently finished in which he paid $600,000 to the so-called "loyal Creeks," these being, as one would imply from the term, the Creek Indians and their descendants who were loyal to the United States during the civil war. Another payment to the Choctaw allottees of $900,000 is just being completed, while still another of about the same sum is being prepared.

The Indian agent has under his direct employ one hundred persons (not including field men or Indian police). Eight of these are Indians by blood, three of whom are high grade stenographers. More than 150,000 letters are received by the agent each year and there is mailed from his office 250,000.

When one considers the peculiar conditions of this Indian country and the individuality of the territory—there never was another like it in the world—it is easier to comprehend or realize in a way the difficulties which one man must encounter in administering to the inhabitants. In the first place Indian Territory has never been nor is it now an organized territory; no local government exists except in incorporated towns, and no taxes other than for municipal purposes and the different tribal laws are imposed, which latter are enforced by the Secretary of the Interior. It has neither counties nor political status, and with the exception of certain tribal laws, all laws are made by congress, and the territory has no representative in that body. The administration of certain other federal statutes applicable to the territory, are enforced through the United States courts, divided into four judicial districts.

As the situation and laws pertaining to each tribe are different, Indian Territory is in fact five distinct Indian reservations, and the man who occupies the position of agent must fully understand the peculiar and particular needs of each tribe.

And the most peculiar phase of the unique situation is that every Indian in Indian Territory is a citizen of the United States (Act of March 3, 1901, 31 stat., L., 1447).

It is interesting to spend a few hours in the office of the Indian agent. At all times during the day can be found a line of Indians waiting their turn to see "the agent." The first may be a fullblood Cherokee, who, through an interpreter, asks how much royalty he is to receive for the month. He is informed $1,400 (this amount being the average monthly royalty received by some four or five Cherokees, while many others receive as much as $1,000 each month). The agent tells him that the money is on deposit in one of the United States depositories for this purpose, whereupon the lucky Indian endeavors by every story possible to get possession of it. He can build him a home to cost every cent of the money to his credit and the agent, after ascertaining that he has received "a square deal," will pay the cost; or he may purchase stock and farming implements and have his land improved or make any other judicious investment with the approval of the agent, but he cannot handle his money. He is incompetent as a child in money matters.

The next in line is a Creek woman with a dozen scared youngsters clinging to her skirts. She has a grievance. A white man has taken possession of her land and will pay her nothing for the use of it. The "intruder" is called in and after vainly endeavoring to prove that possession is nine points of the law, is turned over to a squad of swarthy Indian policemen, who march him and his cattle across the Kansas line.

A handsome young Choctaw, in a neat business suit, then demands the attention of the agent and asks that the restrictions upon the alienation of his surplus allotment be removed. He is questioned under oath relative to his education, intelligence, business capacity, etc., to the satisfaction of the agent, who duly makes a favorable report to the Secretary of the Interior through the inspector and the commissioner of Indian affairs. If the secretary approves the agent's findings the applicant is free to use his land (other than that portion designated as his homestead) in any manner he may choose.

The Creek Indians can list their surplus land for sale with the agent without having the restrictions removed. He secretly appraises the tract which the Indian wishes to sell, and for sixty days advertises the land in the daily papers. The bids are then opened and the highest bidder (if his price be above the appraised value) gets the plum.

There are every day dozens of each of the above specified matters, as well as hundreds of others of different nature, reviewed and reported upon by the agent.

In less than another year tribal governments and affairs will be dissolved in the Indian Territory. The present is the period of transition. Titles are passing to the occupants of town lots; the allotments are practically completed (a fair per cent of which are alienable under certain conditions). Congress is working overtime in the endeavor to legislate for the territory and the red man, and the Indian agent and Poor Lo will mutually be happy when the strenuous life is over.

1906

Indian Tales Between Pipes

Many are the amusing stories told by the field parties of the Dawes Commission relative to their experiences with the full blood Indian. A party of these boys recently met at a corn dance down in the Hickory Grove district, and "swapped" experiences as they sat around the fire and smoked their pipes. In some of these stories it was evident that the ignorant (?) full blood got the best of the white man, and demonstrates that his native wit and shrewdness to a large extent compensates his lack of learning acquired from school books.

Mr. H. Van Smith, for several years disbursing clerk for the Commission, came in for a goodly share of the narratives, and said that more than once he was "bested" in an argument with a red man.

Mr. Smith was sent down in Mississippi a year ago to bring to the Territory the few remaining Choctaws who had successfully evaded former officials. After beating the brush for several weeks he succeeded in getting together sixty-four of the natives, and by promising to give them almost anything from a cap pistol to an upright piano, got their promise to be at the railroad station on a certain date. Everything appeared to be moving lovely and according to schedule until the day before the trip to the Territory was to take place. On this day a hungry looking wearer of the blanket approached Smith and after inspecting him for a few minutes said: "Maybe so, Injun take him dog." Smith was preoccupied and merely answered, "all right, take your dog if you want to." However, the Indian was not fully satisfied, and again said, this time with more emphasis "Maybe so, Injun take him dog." Smith replied with like emphasis that as far as he was concerned he could take all the dogs he wanted to, and then promptly dismissed the matter from his mind.

The next day Smith was detained in the town until nearly train time. When he arrived at the depot, however, he understood why his full blood friend had been so persistent on the day previous, for lo and behold—sixty-four Indians and sixty-five dogs. A dog for each Indian, and they had thoughtfully brought an extra one for Smith.

On another occasion a stalwart full blood, laboring under a fair load of Peruna, or some other similar beverage that gives a man nerve to face a visit from his mother-in-law, entered one of the departments and without further ceremony announced that he wanted to file for his twenty-four children. As the applicant appeared scarcely more than thirty years of age himself, the clerk in charge told him there must be some mistake; that he surely did not have twenty-four children. The Indian insisted, and the clerk told him to go home and think it over a few days, then to come back when he felt better, and they would talk it over.

The Indian evidently recognized that he was properly equipped with that which cheers, for he promptly replied: "No, talk it over today. Maybe so come back when I feel better and I no talk any."

Realizing it was best to hear him out, the clerk told him to go ahead and explain it to him. The Indian did so in this manner: "Maybe so I have four children, and squaw she die. I take another squaw with eight children. Then her children mine, maybe so?" The clerk agreed that when he married a widow with eight children, the children were then his. This pleased the Indian and he continued:

"Well so, my children hers, maybe so?"

The clerk also agreed that his new wife would be the mother of his own children. The Indian then promptly closed the argument with, "well so, she have twelve children, hers and mine, and I have twelve children, mine and hers. Maybe so you give land for twenty-four children."

A delegation had come in from the Eucha district to protest to the agent against a white man who would not keep his hogs fenced up, and consequently they were creating havoc with the crops being planted by the Indians. Some of the Creek Indians are great on oratory, and in this delegation was one of this kind—an old white headed King of the town. The younger members explained their mission and endeavored to demonstrate how very necessary it was that immediate steps be taken to compel this white man to pen up his hogs. The old King kept shaking his head in a dissatisfied manner, and finally demanded that he be heard. The younger members respectfully withdrew and the old fellow advanced to the center of the floor, pulled a bandana handkerchief of about the dimensions of an ordinary tablecloth from his pocket, deliberately wiped his mouth and hands, and striking a pose, commenced: "You young fellows don't know what you is talking about. You explanations you'se'f about as clear as mud. Talk about hogs! why you don't know the first principle of a hog. Mr. Agent, let a man talk who has been raised among hogs."

It is needless to say the remainder of his speech was lost, owing to the office force being convulsed with laughter.

I. N. Ury, a Kansas politician, an Indian Territory investor, a resident of Muskogee, and an all around good fellow, has also had some dealings with the full blood. Mr. Ury is gentleness itself wherever the weaker sex is concerned, but he is apt to lose patience when dealing with men, and especially if his feeding has not been up to the standard required by an active politician.

On one occasion Mr. Ury was driving overland in the Creek Nation with a party of friends. When they reached the north fork of the Canadian river, they found the water too high to ford with safety, so drove several miles up the river before crossing. Consequently, they lost their way and drove about aimlessly until sundown, when they pitched camp, relit their pipes for supper, and discussed their predicament. In the morning they tried another smoke for breakfast, and started out in the hope that they would soon meet someone who would direct them to their intended destination. They passed a number of houses, but being in the full blood settlement, the Indian women, according custom in the absence of their husbands, grabbed their children and made for the brush.

Along about high noon the party was overjoyed by seeing a wagon, drawn by two fine mules, approaching them. Mr. Ury hailed the driver, who stopped his mules and politely waited. Ury asked him several questions, but was answered each time with "ugh," and the dull Indian shake of the head.

Finally Ury lost what little patience remained and began swearing, (and being a politician he has a fair "cussing" vocabulary, by the way). He cussed every Indian within the bounds of Indian Territory, then jumped from the Atlantic to the Pacific coast from Canada to the Gulf of Mexico and back. It is difficult to state just where he would have ended had he not exhausted his breath and stopped for a moment.

During this time the Indian had been sitting in his wagon, watching Ury with all interest possible. When the swearing ceased, he asked in excellent English and with the most bland manner, "what is the name of the town you gentlemen are desirous of reaching?"

He then directed them on their journey, which happily was of short duration, as they were within two miles of their desired destination. Ury, however, he who had fought many political campaigns to a finish, had bought and sold land of Freedmen, had met the Indian Territory lawyer on equal ground and been victorious,—Ury was the most subdued one of the party. Since then he has become wary of the "dull" full blood.

1906

Billy Bearclaws, Aid to Cupid

Little Eagle Tom sat by the roadside and dug his brown toes into the sand. Before him stretched the billowy Oklahoma prairie; behind him, more prairie, and to the eastward loomed the grim, gray buildings of the government Indian school. As Little Eagle glanced toward them, he twisted his small brown features into an expression of contempt.

Little Eagle was a truant—just a disgusted little Indian truant. He had tired of the white man's civilization which for several months had been administered to him in regular doses by the big, mustached school superintendent. Little Eagle had tired of it all—the daily routine in the boarding school, the lessons and other duties imposed upon these wards of the government in Uncle Sam's well-meant effort to lead them out of the paths of savagery. Little Eagle didn't want to be civilized, so he decided to run away to where he could live out his life in idle enjoyment.

It hadn't been a difficult matter to come thus far—but then he had come only a few miles from the big school buildings. He was resting until he could continue his journey under cover of darkness. He had it all very nicely planned. They wouldn't miss him for an hour or so yet—not till all the boys and girls filed into the big dining room for supper at 6:30. Then they wouldn't investigate before morning; it was too frequent an occurrence to cause alarm. The superintendent would think he had merely gone home to his parents, as all the boys did when they ran away. He would send, or go himself, in the morning, to bring him back. And his parents would compel him to come back, too. Aye, that was where Little Eagle planned to foil them. He was not going home!

Among the teachers at the government school was the young and rarely beautiful daughter of the superintendent. Little Eagle was in her classes, and to him she was—he expressed it in a very musical Indian word—"The One To Be Adored." Ever since that day when he came to school for the first time and she had led him, a shy little brown boy, to the classes, she had held the supreme place in his childish heart. Indeed, but for her, he would long ago have forsaken the paths of learning. Now, as Little Eagle was only twelve years old, and pretty Betty Merwin was twenty, his love was without alloy; it even extended to and included those she loved, instead of harboring jealousy, as might have been the case with an older lover. For instance, Little Eagle concealed—the word is used advisedly, as all emotions were faithfully concealed by this little stoic— the deepest respect and profoundest admiration for a certain well-to-do young ranchman, Martin Strong, who stood high in the affections of Miss Merwin.

Perhaps no one but Little Eagle knew just how well the ranchman stood in Miss Betty's estimation, since her father had forbidden him to come to the school to see his daughter. But Little Eagle knew. Miss Betty took frequent walks alone, and Little Eagle, feeling she needed protection, skulked along behind in the dusk, like a faithful dog, until Martin Strong stepped forth to meet her. Once Mr. Strong had observed him, and tossed him a dollar with the hand that was not holding Miss Betty's. "Vamoose," he had said, adding, "and keep mum."

"He will, never fear," Miss Betty had said, smiling at him brightly. And forty government superintendents couldn't have dragged her secret between Little Eagle's close-set lips.

Little Eagle's plan was to go to Mr. Strong's ranch for a few months, until the superintendent gave up the search for him. He believed the ranchman would keep his secret as he had kept his; also, he thought that in keeping close to the ranchman, he would not always be very far from Miss Betty. He felt, too, that he could trust Mr. Strong—he could do no more than "keep mum" if Little Eagle asked it.

As darkness gathered, Little Eagle thought he heard a horse galloping far off. The sounds came nearer, and soon the horse and rider came into view. Behind some scrubby bushes Little Eagle darted, until the rider's face was discernible, then he crawled out and uttered a sound something between a friendly salutation and a grunt. The man pulled his horse to a standstill and peered down into the boy's face.

"What the—why, Little Bearclaws, or whatever's-your-name, what are you doing here—running away?"

Little Eagle assented gravely. Then he quietly and evenly explained, in as dignified English as he could command. The young ranchman laughed and took off his hat to him.

"You young schemer!" he exclaimed. "And yet they say the Indian is dull. You've led me into a pretty trap. If I refuse to take you, you'll have to go back to school eventually, and might very effectually put my dream o' love to an end by telling the old man of our meetings. If I take you, I may get arrested for harboring an outlaw. But you wait here till I come back in about an hour, and I reckon you can jump on behind and go with me. Poor little devil," he added as he turned into the road again, "I was savage enough myself once to hate 'rithmetic and g'ography.'"

Little Eagle retreated to the clump of bushes to wait. When he had waited about an hour and a half, he sleepily concluded that this must have been Miss Betty's evening to go for a walk.

"Well, Billikins, hop on," said a voice, and Little Eagle rubbed his eyes. In a jiffy he was sitting behind Mr. Strong on the wiry little pony. Not another word was spoken on the ten-mile ride, until, as they turned in at the big gate, the ranchman said, seriously, "Sonny, you're Billy Bearclaws now, for diplomatic reasons, and you never saw a government school. The boys here may jibe you at first, but, as I've said before, keep mum."

Billy Bearclaws grunted and slid off to shut the gate.

For many days the Boss had been worried. The boys had noticed it, for where heretofore he had "jollied" and made merry with them, he now sat apart and smoked and looked glum.

"Sick, Boss?" asked "Long Jim," sympathetically. But Martin shook his head.

"Not very, I guess," he replied; and the cowboy walked away. To the others he said, "Cain't imagine what it is. Things wuz never in better shape—cleaned up a cool thousand last shipment. Cain't be money matters as troubles him. He must be sick." The other boys shook their heads, as if the problem was too deep for them.

Billy Bearclaws watched the Boss narrowly with those beady little jet eyes of his. Being somewhat on the inside of Mr. Strong's personal affairs, he thought he held the solution to his trouble. Something was wrong concerning Miss Betty—of that much he was certain. But what? He waited. He observed that the Boss did not leave the ranch often and then not long at a time. Consequently, he did not go to meet Miss Betty any more. And why? Was Miss Betty sick, dead—these thoughts harassed him as he idled around the ranch. His staying there had been accepted with little comment. "The Boss had picked the Injun up somewhere," was what the boys said, and as strangers came seldom, no one recognized in him the former school boy, Little Eagle, for he had cast away his government clothes and donned Indian togs before he was five miles from the school buildings. The ranch hands had ceased to wonder about him, and he amused himself happily all through the long days. The first cloud in his new existence was now enveloping him.

The Boss was not one to be questioned, nor Billy Bearclaws one to question. So matters drifted gloomily along, until at last Billy could stand it no longer. He arose one morning with the fire of determination in his eyes. No one else was up on the ranch, for it was quite early. Stealthily, the little Indian crept to the big barn and began to bridle one of the cow ponies. He was wrestling with an obstinate buckle, when he heard the Boss's voice.

"What are you doing, Bearclaws?" he asked sternly. The boy turned quickly.

"Goin' back to guv'ment school," he answered promptly.

The Boss chuckled. "Are you? And going on one of my best ponies? And slipping away without saying goodbye? I guess that is what we might call 'Indian leave,' eh? Take the bridle off, Billy, and wait till after breakfast," he added kindly.

Billy stood silent, while the Boss came close and laid his hand on the child's shoulder.

"Poor little kiddie; are you tired of us here? Tell me, honest Injun—where were you going?"

Billy Bearclaws threw his head back dramatically, and the fire of oratory, which is the heritage of every Indian, burned in his whole expression. "I go," he began, "for you an' Miss Betty. The Sweet-Angel-of-Light, The-One-To-Be-Adored, The-Bright-One-Of-Your-Heart. I see you, yesterday, today, tomorrow, silent and unhappy. I know something wrong. I go to see. To prepare place for you. I return back again." He finished with a flourish of his hands, having glibly mixed his Bible knowledge with his small stock of ready English. The Boss sat down on a box, and when he raised his head presently, his cheeks were wet—that they were tears of mirth, Bearclaws never knew.

"Well, well, Billy you're all right," he said. "I'm no end obliged to you, old chap. Sit down here, and let's have a talk. I believe a fellow could trust you, all right. Now, tell me, what possible good could your going back to the school do for me? If you are properly penitent for running away, and want to go back, why, that's well and good, and I'll send you over any time. But I don't see how that could help me and Miss Betty."

Bearclaws had no answer. Evidently his one object had been to satisfy himself that Miss Betty was well and safe, and to return when he could, with the news for the ranchman.

"You see, Billy," continued the boss, almost as if reasoning with himself, "the superintendent has forbidden her seeing me any more, and has even made it impossible for us to meet as we've been doing. No letter I send her is delivered, and she believes me untrue to my word to see her and write to her. It is a sad predicament, and I wouldn't stand for it one minute—I'd tear up the earth or go to her—except," his voice grew wistful, "I've thought maybe—maybe the old man's about right. I'm not much for a pretty girl like Betty. She loves me, but maybe she'd forget me if she didn't see me any more. Her father has notified me that as soon as this term of school is closed she is to return to an aunt in Washington and be married to one of those high-up, rich ducks, and she'll be about the same as Queen somebody, and can do the society stunt every day in the year. Who am I to stand in her way to better herself? What could I offer her to equal all that? She'd be almost the same as buried here on the ranch, just plain Mrs. Strong, and only a lot of cow punchers to kowtow to her. So I've just made up my mind not to see her again. I won't stand in her way. It's about to kill me to do this, but maybe when I know she's gone away and I'll never see her again—"

The words were like an electric shock to Billy. "No, no," he cried, springing up; "You go get her. She loves you and me."

"Oh, come," said the Boss half angry that he had said so much to a mere Indian boy. "Clear out now and go to breakfast. And keep mum—do you hear?"

But Billy clung to him. "Why you not steal her from the super'ntendent?" he insisted.

"It seems the idea of stealing always appeals to an Indian," muttered the Boss, turning away.

At breakfast everybody was silent. The Boss rode away soon after the meal was over, the men went to their duties, and Billy Bearclaws was left to himself. Nothing amused him this morning—he was doing some deep thinking. Suddenly a plan of action evolved in his active brain, and he darted to the barn. One little pony stood in a stall munching hay. Billy led him out, jumped on his back and was off like someone suddenly gone mad.

By noon he drew rein in front of Big Elk Joe's grass house. The huge Indian greeted him pompously.

"Greeting to you, Little-Boy-From-Spirit-Land," he said. "You have been mourned as dead. First the big superintendent send to your father's house to find truant Indian boy. He no find you there. Then send here, there, everywhere. He offer reward. Nobody get that reward. Little Eagle Tom dead, then. Indians make big cry. Now here you come from happy hunting ground. Tell me, what must Big Elk do for spirit boy?"

Since the belief that he was dead evidently had been generally accepted, Little Eagle Tom, alias Bearclaws, lost no time in dispute or explanation. He slid off the tired pony and began a serious conference with the big Indian. An hour they talked together, Billy apparently explaining, the man nodding and grunting comprehendingly. After a while Big Elk called two others to his side. They were brave braves indeed, in their gorgeous trappings, and when introduced to Billy as the "Returned-Spirit-Boy," gave no evidence of fear or surprise. Big Elk spoke a few words to them, and they nodded, going away presently. Billy, after eating with Big Elk, went out to the little mustang, removed his halter, and with a waving motion of his arms, frightened the animal off the premises. With a dreamy expression in his pathetic dark eyes, he watched the pony loping, riderless, toward the ranch.

The afternoon was drawing to a close, and at the government school the Indian boys were busy with their various chores. The superintendent, stern looking, yet kind withal, was among them, giving suggestions and help when necessary. Glancing down the big road leading to the school, he noticed three Indians riding single file. They rode into the yard and the superintendent went to greet them.

"Come in, Big Elk," he called, and nodded to the others. But Big Elk shook his head gravely, and motioned to the boys all about them.

"Do you want to see me alone?" asked the superintendent. The Indian nodded.

"Then tie your horse and come into the office." The three Indians followed him into the house.

"Now then," said the superintendent, seating himself and speaking pleasantly, not knowing exactly what to expect, since these Indians often came to him with troubles of one kind or another. "What is it, Big Elk?"

"Little Eagle Tom, he want come back to school," calmly announced Big Elk.

"Little Eagle Tom! Why, sir, the boy is dead, isn't he? At least you Indians all reported such to me. The agent and I have kept a pretty faithful watch for him, and I am quite positive that his own father and mother think he is dead. His name has even been entered on the roll of deceased Indians—he is bound to be dead!"

But Big Elk stolidly shook his head. "Little Eagle Tom not dead. He come back today from spirit land. He say to me he will come back to super'ntendent's school."

"Oh, all right then; of course, I am very glad to know he is alive and certainly the thing is to get him back into school. But it's really too bad he's got onto that deceased roll. I suppose you've come to know if that reward is still good. Well, bring the boy to me tomorrow, and the reward is yours." He closed the roll top desk and rose, as if to end the conference. But Big Elk's head was again shaking solemnly.

"We come not for reward. Little Eagle very sorry he run away. He love you and your school and your daughter, his teacher. He now very ill in my grass house. Tomorrow he may go again to spirit land." Big Elk paused, as Miss Betty, passing in the hall, heard his words and came in and stood beside her father. Then he continued, very impressively,

"Little Eagle does not forget the teaching of The-One-To-Be-Adored. In his sickness he talks of her, he calls for her. If she will come to him, he will return to school as soon as he is able. 'Will she come quick?' he ask, through me."

The big Indian folded his arms. He had delivered his message. He awaited its effect. Miss Betty's blue eyes opened wide, and she turned from the solemn-visaged Indian to her father.

"Is it true, father? Is the poor little fellow sick, and asking for me? Oh, it must be, or Big Elk would not say so," she added, casting a quick glance at the Indian, who nodded.

"Yes, I suppose it is true, Betty," responded her father; "the little rascal has probably been in hiding till he's sorry of his action and will be glad enough to come back to us. Of course, our duty is to get him back into school, where he can be properly cared for."

"He ask only for Miss Betty," put in Big Elk. "For her he call to see before he died again."

"Oh, I must go to him, father—may I not?"

"I hardly think it advisable," began the superintendent, frowning.

"Oh, but surely it is our duty to look after him—mine as much as yours; he was my pupil and so loyal to me," she faltered, almost tearfully. "Father, surely you can trust me with Big Elk—he has been such a faithful friend to you. He would take me safely there."

"Yes," assented the Indian.

"I cannot allow you to go alone, Betty," said her father firmly, and Big Elk saw that he had failed in his errand. "Tomorrow we will drive to Big Elk's house—as early in the morning as we can start. Go back, Big Elk and tell Little Eagle we rejoice to know he is alive, but regret his illness. Tell him I will bring Miss Betty to see him tomorrow morning and if possible he shall return with us here. See that he is well taken care of through tonight."

The Indians bowed and went out. And with her father's decision Betty had to be content, yet there were ill forebodings in her tender heart, for she feared the boy might die before she reached him. Also, why had he left the ranch—for she had known all along where he was concealed. Was Martin Strong really so heartless as to turn the child out, even as he had apparently so ruthlessly banished her from his heart? Oh, if the boy only lived for her to see him and ask him one little word concerning Martin—these were her harassing thoughts as she lay awake that night.

The following day being Saturday there were no classes, and Betty was ready early to accompany her father to Big Elk's house. Just as they were starting, however, the mail was delivered, and some of it proved to be so urgent that at the last moment the superintendent decided he would remain at home to attend to it, and send one of the boys with her.

"These letters are extremely important—I can't afford to delay them so much as a day. John Makes Brave can take you over. It isn't far—you can drive it in an hour and a half. Don't stay too long. Take some food with you. See if Little Eagle is able to be moved. Find out all about the case. Big Elk assured me it was nothing contagious. I'll send the agency physician over, if you think it's necessary."

With these hurried instructions he went back to his desk and Betty drove off with the solemn John Makes Brave.

On a rug in one corner of Big Elk's grass house lay Little Eagle Tom. When Miss Betty bent over him, he smiled shyly. The medicine man had been there, and some concoction of his had almost made Little Eagle sick, but his black eyes were bright enough. While Miss Betty was talking to him in low, gentle tones, and noting inwardly that for a sick boy he was looking unusually well, some one entered the grass house—someone tall and erect and handsome. When he spoke, Miss Betty's heart almost stopped beating, and Little Eagle turned eagerly. It was Martin Strong, and he came quickly to Miss Betty's side.

"Betty, dear!" was all he could say, and with the words the tired look that had recently come to his eyes disappeared. Betty crept close to him and laid her hand on his arm. Big Elk walked outside. Little Eagle lay quite still. In the dim light of the grass house it seemed to him he could discern but one figure, so close-clasped were the lovers. Presently he coughed cautiously. Betty turned quickly.

"Oh, Martin, how shameful of us! The poor little fellow is quite, quite ill, and we selfish people almost forgot him. What shall we do for him? Father said I must bring him back with me to the school, if he was able to be moved. I wonder—"

Little Eagle blinked at the ranchman appealingly.

"Wait, Betty mine, let me talk to this boy. You may be able to teach this little rascal to read and write, but when it comes to really understanding him, I believe I have you bested. Billy Bearclaws, look at me!" he commanded, turning to Little Eagle. The boy gazed back at him through half-shut lids.

"Are you sick, kiddie?" The boy shook his head.

"You ran off from my ranch, on one of my ponies. You came here and pretended sickness to Big Elk. You sent after Miss Betty. You then sent word to me to come here this morning. Isn't it all so?"

Again the boy nodded, and the small brown face was almost permitted to show signs of smiling.

"You see, Betty, dear," continued Martin Strong, "the best friend you and I have in all the world is Billy Bearclaws, once Little Eagle. He is sort of partner of Cupid—looks after Cupid's affairs out west here; he is an—"

"He is an angel!" exclaimed Miss Betty rapturously, as she realized Little Eagle's maneuverings to bring her to her lover. But instantly her face clouded.

"What good will it do, Martin, after all?" she asked, the big tears very near the surface in her wide blue eyes. "I must return to the school, and Little Eagle must go, too. And after that you know how hard it is for me to see you."

"Betty," said Martin Strong firmly, taking both her hands into his own. "I have you now, and I don't intend you shall ever leave me. I have given your father every opportunity to treat me well, and at least the chance to investigate my character before he utterly condemned me. He will do neither. Now I shall simply take matters into my own hands. For a while I had almost decided to try to give you up, for I thought he might be right—you might not be happy out here with me—and I wanted to do the thing that would give you the greatest happiness. I will not always be a ranchman, but I want to make good out here, and it seemed a selfish thing to ask a girl to stay with a man like me, not specially good nor interesting, when she might choose a richer man and live a life of pleasure and ease. So I hesitated to ask you to take the step, when I found your father had made such dazzling plans for you. But now, Betty, I ask you to make the decision—do you love me well enough to live with me in obscurity and share, it may be, a life of hardship?"

And Miss Betty answered bravely and unhesitatingly, "Yes, Martin." He drew her closely to him. When they turned presently, guiltily, to Little Eagle's couch, he was no longer there. They found him sitting with Big Elk outside.

"Well, little sick boy," called Martin Strong, "jump into the buggy there. Miss Betty and I will take you back to school." Little Eagle looked dazed and hurt. Betty turned inquiring eyes on her lover.

"Surely, Martin, I thought—"

"I am going with you, certainly, Betty. Didn't I say you were not to leave me any more? Your driver may ride my horse. I will take his place in the buggy with you."

"But father—"

"That is why I am going with you, dear child. I would carry you off with me instead, this very minute, but—I will steal no man's property—it would be a bad example to set for Billy here," he added whimsically. "Besides, I must see your father regarding our immediate marriage."

Betty said no more, except to coax Little Eagle to go with them. He finally got into the buggy, but he wasn't very buoyant about it.

When the stern and dignified superintendent saw the returning buggy, he went out to meet it pleasantly enough; but his expression changed to anger when he recognized Martin Strong. He gruffly ordered Betty to go into the house, but Martin Strong put his hand on her arm.

"I ask your pardon, Mr. Merwin, but I cannot allow Betty to leave me. I found her, through no arrangement of hers, at the bedside of this little sick chap here. I have loved your daughter ever since I first saw her, and she loves me. Two people who love as we do can never be happy apart, no matter how much they would like to consider other people's wishes. So Betty and I will be married this evening at six o'clock, at Rev. Bryson's, over at the agency. I suppose you realize that we could have gone on over there without telling you anything about it, but we want to treat you fair and square. I do not forget that she is your daughter; it honestly makes me rather like you, when I think of it. And please don't forget that she is my affianced wife."

He was quite calm, while the superintendent was growing white with rage.

"You—you—" he stammered wrathfully.

"Martin Strong is my name," supplied that young man promptly. "And it might interest you to know that my father is James M. Strong, the copper miner of Montana; that my family connection is the equal of yours, and that your daughter is not exactly marrying a pauper. I never told you these things before, for I don't thrust my credentials in every man's face; and I like to stand on my own worth. But you seemed to take me for a rascal from the first. The facts may make a difference in your opinion of me, but that doesn't count with me now. I like to remember that Betty accepted me for myself alone."

With a movement of the reins he started the horse. Betty looked back at her father, standing there alone, and her heart ached for him. After all, he was getting old, and he had tried to be father and mother both, for all his harsh, stern way. Tears came into her eyes, and she leaned close to the one man she loved better than her father. "Dear," she said, and her voice trembled, "when we are married, won't you bring me back to him—tonight—for his forgiveness and blessing? He will like you now— and remember, he's my father."

Martin Strong bent over her and kissed her tenderly. "You dear little girl," he murmured. "Yes, we will drive back tonight if you wish, child. Your happiness is my law."

And Billy Bearclaws, little brown-faced aid to Cupid, slipped down onto his knees in front of the dashboard, picked up the fallen reins, and guided the tired horses along the prairie road.

1909

Royal Roger Eubanks

CHEROKEE

(1879–?)

Royal Roger Eubanks—teacher, artist, and writer—was born at Tahlequah, Cherokee Nation, the son of William and Eliza Thompson Eubanks. The younger Eubanks was educated in the Cherokee schools, graduating from the Cherokee Male Seminary in 1897. After graduation he taught school at Braggs, Cherokee Nation, and at the Cherokee Orphan Asylum before returning to the Seminary as a teacher in 1901. By 1905 he had become superintendent. While teaching, Eubanks had also pursued a career in art and had published a number of political cartoons in Cherokee Nation newspapers. He moved to Chicago where he worked for a cartoon syndicate, the Star Cartoonist Company, but returned a few years later to resume his career in teaching and commercial art. He also began to write. He produced dialect tales and short stories, some of which are reprinted here, as well as historical sketches, all of which had to do with Cherokee culture and history and all of which he illustrated. In 1920 he illustrated the dialect stories *Tales of the Bark Lodges* by Hen-toh (Wyandot). Later, he moved to Berryville, Arkansas, where he continued to work as a teacher and commercial artist. Eubanks's story "The Middle Man" portrays the way real estate speculators systematically used the Indians' ignorance of the American legal system to divest them of their land allotments. The animal tales reflect his propensity for humor, and they fit into the literary tradition of dialect humor written by American Indians. They also clearly relate to the style of story cycles produced by Joel Chandler Harris, especially *Nights with Uncle Remus*.

The Middle Man

Kent walked briskly into his office, sauntered over to his desk at the farther end, tipped his little green hat to the back of his head, lighted a cigar and sat down.

McNeil, his partner, sat at the large table in the center of the room. In his left hand, with his fingers as a book-mark, he held a roll-book, and he perused abstractly an open plat-book which lay upon the table. The roll-book contained the names, ages, sexes and degrees of blood of the citizens of the Five Civilized Tribes, and the plat-book contained township maps of that part of Oklahoma which was formerly the Cherokee Nation and which was allotted to the members of the Cherokee tribe. Each township occupied a full page in this large book and showed each individual allotment, on which was printed the name and roll number of the allottee. These two books were, by far, the most necessary pieces of furniture in an office similar to that of Kent & McNeil Realty Co.

Kent turned about in his swivel chair, placed his feet upon the table, glanced at the uncovered typewriter and asked:

"Hasn't Miss Reed gotten here yet?"

"Oh, yes. She has gone over to the Agency to look up that stuff we were talking about last night. She ought to be back by this time." McNeil had hardly finished speaking when Miss Reed, the stenographer, with note-books and pencils came in at the open door.

Kent was impatient and jumpy, and forever keyed to high tension. He glared at the young lady as she slowly unpinned her hat.

"Well?" he snapped, his voice querulous.

"Well," she began, referring to her notes, "I found an approved lease on everything except the Nancy Keycatcher stuff. I got a cross reference but found nothing against it. There had been a lease given to the Puritan Oil Co., but it was disapproved. The description of the land shows it to be forty acres in Section 6, 27, 13."[1]

Kent sprang to his feet, snatched his cigar from his mouth and went over to examine the notes.

"Why, Thunder, Miss Reed! The piece in 27, 13 can't be clear, surely."

"That's what the records at the Indian agency show," said Miss Reed, between humility and sarcasm.

1. That is, Section 6, Range 27 East of the Indian Meridian, Township 13 North—the legal description of the land in question.

"Maybe she's married or dead," observed Kent, looking at McNeil.

"What does the roll-book show her age to be?" McNeil turned the leaves of the plat-book until it was opened at 27, 13. He ran his fingers over Section 6 until he found the little square on which was printed the name, Nancy Keycatcher, and the number 25,640.

"Twenty-five, six, forty," he sang to himself as he turned to the roll-book. Nancy Keycatcher, female, three-quarters,[2] sixty-three years old."

"She's dead," said Kent, as he ran his hands down deep into his pockets and looked out of the window.

"Where is 'Chick'? He ought to know this old girl," suggested McNeil.

"Chick" was a quarter blood Cherokee with few scruples and no inclination to work, and was consequently one of a number of hangers-on who loafed about the streets of Muskogee and loitered about land dealers' offices, ready at all times to act as a tool in "getting a deal through" between an Indian and a real estate agent. "Boosters," they are called. "Chick" was doubly valuable because of his wide acquaintance and because of his ability to speak the Cherokee language.

Kent leaned over on the table with his elbows and scrutinized closely the forty-acre tract shown on the map.

"Is 27, 13, good?" Miss Reed ventured to ask.

"I should say, yes," fairly snorted Kent, without lifting his eyes from the map.

"If that's her surplus," explained McNeil, "she can sell it, she being only three-quarters."

Kent looked sharply on the map for the little "h" which designated "homestead," but it was not there.

"Why, that's so. She can sell it, can't she," he said, becoming excited, "and this is her surplus."

"There must be something wrong," said McNeil, becoming pessimistic, "that's too good a piece of stuff to not be taken in before now. I'll go and see if I can find 'Chick.' " With this he indolently unfolded himself out of the chair and strolled into the hall.

Kent paced nervously about the room, then stopped for a moment to look at 27, 13 as shown on the Oil Map which hung on the wall. Dots, indicating oil wells, were on adjoining allotments and on all four sides of

2. That is, three-quarters Cherokee blood quantum, an important factor to land dealers. Each allottee received a homestead allotment and a surplus allotment. Indians of more than half blood could not sell their homestead allotments but could sell the surplus, as indicated below.

the piece in question. This was not necessary, however, for Kent, because he knew as well as every one else in the business that township 27, 13 was in the very heart of the oil belt. He looked at his watch and went hurriedly out of the door to help in the search for "Chick." On reaching the stairway, however, he found McNeil with the big quarter-blood hurrying up the steps. The three men huddled together in the hall.

" 'Chick' knows her all right," began McNeil, becoming enthusiastic and breathing audibly from the exertion of trotting up the stairs, "and he says she's not dead, not married, nor sold unless she has done one or all in the last two weeks."

"Now you want to be sure about this, 'Chick,' " said Kent feigning nonchalance, "because—"

"Oh, I'm giving you straight goods, all right," "Chick" interrupted, "I helped R. G. Smith get a oil lease on some of her land up clost to Bartlesville. She's a kind of old woman. She lives up clost to Stillwell an' talks all Injun. She's a full-blood—"

"She may be a full-blood," put in McNeil, "but the roll-book says she's three-quarters and what the roll-book says, goes." They walked leisurely down the hall back to the office door and stopped. Kent turned around and said:

"See here, 'Chick,' you show up here at the office this afternoon at six o'clock, you and I may have to go to Stillwell tonight."

"All right, good," "Chick" answered eagerly.

"All right," repeated McNeil, "and keep everything under your hat, old man, and we'll see you at six." "Chick" seemed to have assimilated some of the enthusiasm now at its height in the other two men, and he walked away jauntily whistling.

Kent put in a long distance telephone call for the Washington County Abstract Company. With dire exasperation and feverish suspense the entire day was consumed in getting connections, giving the order and receiving the report, but it was worth the suffering because the report was that the Nancy Keycatcher stuff was clear—clear except for an oil lease which was evidently the one written for the Puritan Oil Co. by R. G. Smith, and which Miss Reed had found to be disapproved.

It was now five o'clock. The Dawes Commission gong sounded in their offices across the court, Miss Reed adjusted her hat, took up her parasol and hurried out into the hall to join the bevy of stenographers and office girls chattering down the stairs.

Kent arose from his chair, walked over to the door, closed it, turned the thumb latch and sat down again. McNeil was the first to speak.

"Damn my cats, old man; that's a dickens of a good piece of oil; that stuff is worth $150 an acre!"

Kent moved over to the desk telephone, laid his cigar down carefully so that the fire end extended from the edge of the desk.

"What do you say to my calling up old man Connors at Bartlesville and putting it up to him at $150?"

"That's the right dope," McNeil acquiesced.

When Kent hung up the receiver he said:

"He says he'll take her up if we can deliver the goods. He knows the stuff; was out there to-day; you know he has leases all over that section. He said to put the deed and abstract in the Muskogee National Bank and he'd wire the 'mazuma.' 'Chick' and I can get out of here on the M. O. & G. at 6:30."

When the Kansas City Southern north bound passenger train stopped at the Stillwell station it was just breaking day. Only two passengers alighted. One, a man of medium build walked with a firm energetic step; his neck was short and his eyes had a downward tilt; he bore all the marks of the shrewd, the crafty. His dress would be designated in slang vocabulary as "loud." His companion was tall and massive in build; his skin dark and his hair and eyes black; his shoulders were high and square and he walked with the erectness of the dare-devil—the brazen.

The first was Ernest Kent, the other was "Chick" Glory.

Both bore evidences of having made it convenient to run across the state line on the Missouri Pacific to Fort Smith to make connections with the Kansas City Southern instead of at Sallisaw, and had evidently "improved each shining hour" of the four "wee sma'" ones spent in a saloon town.

The Keycatcher home was eight miles from Stillwell on the Little Sallisaw; one of those old-fashioned double log houses with a porch in front and a detached kitchen in the back yard; an old, unused spinning wheel sat on the end of the porch—a relic of former days; a mortar and pestle sat near the chimney.

The boys were out somewhere in the woods. Little Quatie moved noiselessly about in the kitchen, washing the breakfast dishes, and old lady Keycatcher, the grandmother and matriarch of this humble household, sat out in the yard in the shadow of the house stringing beans for the midday meal. It was thus that Kent and "Chick" found her when they drove up to the gate.

They diplomatically shook her hand; "Chick" helped himself to two chairs on the porch, which he placed near her, and they sat down. Little Quatie brought from the spring a bucket of pure, sparkling water in which a gourd dipper wabbled like an anchored canoe.

"Chick" talked jocularly in Cherokee, though his tongue seemed thick, and Kent sat silently trying to appear interested in a conversation no word of which he understood. When the commonplace conversation between "Chick" and the old lady had subsided, Kent asked "Chick" to say to her that the company which had leased her land in the prairie country for oil had made an error in the papers and that he, Kent, was representing the company and desired her to accompany him and "Chick" back to Stillwell and go before a Notary Public that the error might be corrected. That it would take but a minute. That he would pay her for her trouble and that he would send her back in a buggy. "Chick" interpreted this to her and she declared her willingness to aid in straightening out any error that might have been made.

"It would have surprised you how easy it was!" Kent afterwards told McNeil.

After reaching Stillwell they drove directly to the little office of J. K. Haines, Notary. Haines, always in need of an extra fifty cents, dropped his feet from the table, crumpled up the local paper he was reading, and gave his only chair to Mrs. Keycatcher.

"Just a little paper," explained Kent, as he nervously took from his pocket an innocent looking instrument and spread it upon the table. It was a warranty deed neatly filled in even to the signature, Nancy Keycatcher, in a bold running hand.

"Has she signed it?" Haines asked, as he reached for his seal on the shelf.

"No," answered Kent, "she only makes her mark." He helped himself to a pen, dipped it into ink, and tested its metal on a piece of paper.

"Tell her to touch the pen," he said to "Chick," as he held it out to Mrs. Keycatcher. The interpretation was unnecessary, however, because the old lady, innocently and mechanically, reached out and touched the pen.

It was a matter of but a minute for Kent to make a cross between Nancy and Keycatcher and write above and below "her" and "mark," respectively; for Haines to fill in the Notary's blank and affix his seal, and for "Chick" and Kent to sign as witnesses.

Kent threw a fifty cent piece upon the table for Haines, and magnanimously (?) slipped old Mrs. Keycatcher a ten dollar note.

"Chick" was walking down Broadway in Muskogee with Kent when remembering an item he had seen in the morning's Phoenix he said:

"I see they have got Roy Gardner for forging a deed on a nigger." Kent looked the picture of disgust and almost snarled as he said:

"I don't see why, in God's name, a man wants to do that kind of underhanded work when there is so much legitimate business!" And when Connors & Cane had wired $6,000 to the Muskogee National Bank to be credited to Kent & McNeil; when he had waited on the outside until Kent went into the bank and came out to count $25 into his large, brown palm in payment for his services on the Stillwell trip, "Chick" Glory was perfectly oblivious to the fact that the Nancy Keycatcher stuff had been bought legitimately by Kent & McNeil for $10 and sold to Connors & Cane for $6,000.

1909

Nights with Uncle Ti-ault-ly: The Ball Game of the Birds and Animals

Uncle Ti-ault-ly would never attempt to speak English, in fact he never spoke to anyone on the farm except father, who spoke Cherokee fluently and with him he had many a lengthy and animated conversation, but with the little boy who tagged after him in his work, he made an exception after a few weeks' acquaintance and talked English when he was sure no one else could hear him. They became great chums and it was many a romp they had together in the woods and by the river, hunting and fishing, and it was many an evening they spent together in the cabin back of the big house, the old man telling the tales of long ago with the earnestness of an eye witness and the little boy listening with eagerness and wild-eyed wonder.

It was raining a slow, drizzling rain, Uncle Ti-ault-ly and the little boy sat by the light of the oil lamp, the one smoking and looking vacantly out of the open cabin door into the gathering darkness, the other watching his companion almost envious of the pleasure he seemed to get out of his old clay pipe and anxious for a story. A bat flew in at the door and went around and around and then deliberately went to the middle of the ceiling, caught a claw in a small crack and hanged with head downward.

"Huh!" observed Uncle Ti-ault-ly with all seriousness, "funny bird, stick tail in crack an' hang down he hade." In the dim light it looked even so and when he saw that his remark had had the desired effect, he laughed his peculiar little cackling ha-ha-ha and said: "It's no bird, it's *Tla-meha*, a bat," and then he began.

"Way lon' time 'go when animals an' birds could talk an' nobody lived here but Injuns, they animals match game o' ball with birds. They leaders fix day an' fix it place; they animals on grass place smooth like table an' birds in top o' trees. Bear, he's leader the animals; he's big leg, big arm, heap stron' he t'row down everybody. All 'lon' road to ball play he was t'row big log, big rock, show he heap stron' an' he all brag what he do to birds in ball play. Talapin too—not little one like same we see now— big one, them long," here he measured out as far as he could reach with both hands. "He shell hard like a iron. He stan' on him hind leg an' fall on ground hard, brag them way he mash it birds in ball play. Deer, too, he run fastest like wirlwind. Eagle, he leader the birds, an' he an' Hawk, *Tla-nuwa*, all heap stron' an' fastest flyin' like lightnings but they was leetle 'fraid animals beat 'em.

"The dance was done an' the birds was fixin' they feathers an' wait for leader to give the word and here come two leetle thin's, lee-tle like rats, crawl up tree where Eagle, he set, crawl out limb to where Eagle set and say: 'We want play in ball play.' Eagle he look clost he see they have four foot an' no wing and he say: 'Why you no go to animal side like you were belong to?' And they say: 'We go and animals make fun 'cause we leetle and no let us play.' Eagle he sorry, he want them play, but he no see how they play on bird side when they no got no wings. Eagle, Hawk, *Tla-nuwa* and some more bird they together and so they 'cide we make wings these leetle fellow. They think and think and talk and talk how they was make it them wings and bymby Owl he heap know everythings, he say: 'Take it ground-hog skin off that drum we use in dance.' Well, so they take it skin off drum, cut it same like wings, stretch on pieces cane and fasten on fore legs one leetle animal. They call him *Tla-meha*, the Bat. An' so they was t'row they ball to him and he dodge twistnin, circulin' roun in air and no let it fall ground 'tall. An' so they was know he heap good man. Well, so they was used up all ground-hog skin to make wings for Bat and they was no somethings to make wings that other leetle animal. Well so Owl 'g'in he say: 'Maybeso we make wings from stretch he own skin out on sides.' An' so Crow and Buzzard and some more bird heap stron' bill ketch hold skin on each side and pull and pull and stretch skin 'tween fore legs and hind legs on both sides and they was call him *Tewa*, Flying Squirrel. They was t'row ball to him and he ketch in he teeth and take it t'rough air to tree put near cross ground. And so they was know he was good man, too.

"Well, so they was already for ball play and when word was give and ball play was started, Flying Squirrel ketch ball, take up tree, t'row to birds and they was keep it in air lon' time but let drop on ground. Old Bear run to get it but Martin swoop down, t'row to Bat who flyin' clost to ground and he dodgin' and turnin' and twistnin' and circulin' even Deer, he no katch him and he t'row ball t'rough 'tween posts and the birds was the win the ball play.

"Old Bear and Old Talapin who aletime brag, no got it chanct even tetch it ball. 'Cause Martin, he save it ball when drop on ground, they birds give him gourd for to build nest in and he has it same yet."

1910

Nights with Uncle Ti-ault-ly: How the Terrapin Beat the Rabbit

Uncle Ti-ault-ly always prefaced his narratives with: "Way lon' time 'go when all kinds animal and birds and trees could talk an' nobody lived here but Injuns."

And this time he went on and, between long and deep draws at his old clay pipe, told the following:

"Eve body know old Rabbit he run it fastest. Old Rabbit he knowed it too an' he aletime brag. An' when he come it cross Talapin he make it fun 'cause he heap slow.

"One day he come it cross Talapin an' he jump it him plum over, then run it roun' fastest, jump it over big log heap high, jump it high everthin' an' run it roun' fast like whirlwin' then he come back to Talapin heap grin an' laugh an' he say: 'Say, Talapin, you ever get it hot box, you slide it on ground so fast?'

"Talapin he know Rabbit make it fun. He get mad. He spit it tobacco juce an' look way off. Rabbit he see Talapin chaw tobacco an' he say: 'Say, Talapin, one day me run it roun' tree so fastest me stick it nose in hip pocket an' take it chaw tobacco.'

"Talapin he know he tell it heap big lie. He look it Rabbit straight in eye an' turn it up lip an' he say: 'Shuck! You think you run fastest? Huh! You no run it fastest. Me run it heap fastest.'

"Rabbit he put it han' to nose to keep it back laughin' then he look it solumn, take it out pipe, knock it out ash an' he say: 'Sho' 'nough you run it fastest?'

"Talapin he heap mad yet, he red in face. He say: 'Me run it fastest like a lightnings, me beat it deer, me beat it everthin', me beat it *YOU* ever-days-in-a weeks.'

"Rabbit he say: 'Maybeso you run it me race?'

"Talapin he say: 'Me run it you race when you get it ready yourself! Me meet it you here nex' Choosday this place, we run it over them four ridges, the one cross last ridge fust is the win.'

"Rabbit he say: 'Ah, Talapin, you heap much mad an' heap big fool. You old shell game, you know you no can run. Me give it you fust ridge, then you run it t'ree ridge, me run it four ridge. Me beat you.'

"Talapin he say: 'Al'ight, me meet it you here nex' Choosday this place.'

"An' he went it crawl it off home. He call it in all he flens an' he tell it flens 'bout race an' he tell it flens: 'Me want you help me. Me know me no can run it fastest like it Rabbit, but me want it stop he aletime brag.' Then he talk it low an' tell it plan an' he flens say: 'We help you.'

"When Choosday come all kinds animal come to see it race an' ol' Rabbit he there already an' Talapin he gone on close to top fust ridge, just see it head in grass.

"Crow he give it word t'ree time, *Caw, Caw, Caw.* Way went it Rabbit like it lightnings, heap fastest up side the hill an' Talapin he crawl it on top an' over on other side. Rabbit he get it on top an' look all round, he no see it Talapin. He run on down side it hill an' heap fast up nex' an' when he look up he see Talapin ahead just go over top.

"Now he run it fastest, heap high jump, heap long jump, an' when he get it top he see Talapin way head going over nex' ridge.

"Now Rabbit he heap tired, he breathe hard like steam kear and when he get it top he see Talapin go over top last ridge, an' he knows Talapin's the win. Rabbit give plum up fellen in the weed, an' say, *wi, wi, wi, wi,* like he do now when he no can run some more.

"Everybody no see how Talapin win, but Talapin he no tell. It wuz heap slick trick, like it White Man's. Talapin's flens all look same like him and he hide it one on fust hill, two hill, t'ree hill all close to top an' when Rabbit come where he see him he crawl it over top an' hide it in weed. Rabbit he think Talapin gone on head, he see nex' one he think it same one.

"The same talapin he make the race, he on last hill to be come out end heself."

1910

Elias McLeod Landrum

CHEROKEE

(1866–?)

Elias M. Landrum was born in Texas, where his parents, David
Dixon and Susan Crutchfield Landrum, were Confederate refu-
gees from the Cherokee Nation during the Civil War. Shortly
after his birth the family returned to the Cherokee Nation, where
Landrum attended Cherokee public schools and Worcester
Academy at Vinita, graduating in 1885. He then attended Emory
College and graduated in 1890. Back in the Cherokee Nation,
he taught school, farmed, and held various political offices, including judge of his home district, senator in the national council, and city councilman and city clerk in Tahlequah, the Cherokee capital. There he worked as a bookkeeper before establishing
his own jeweler's firm. After Oklahoma statehood, he served as
senator in the first three legislatures. Landrum believed that the
concerns of Indian peoples might be lost in the transition to
statehood. Thus he used his public position to foster projects and
pursue issues that involved them: the erection of a statue of Sequoyah in Washington, D. C.; establishment of a normal school,
now Northeastern Oklahoma University, at Tahlequah; restoration of lands to Indian orphans; printing of public laws in Indian
languages; and, though unsuccessful, an attempt to outlaw the
use of wooden Indians in advertising. Landrum was renowned
for his speaking ability and in his speeches frequently moved
from "proper" English into the dialect of a Cherokee who had
learned English as a second language. He believed that the full-
blood members of his native nation were imbued with a profound wisdom and, though they might appear ignorant to out-
siders, had a clear understanding of the national tragedy that
had beset them in the allotment period. And he keenly appreci-

ated the sense of humor they often displayed as they watched and contemplated the goings on of the Americans around them. He attempted to capture that humor in dialect speeches and letters, the latter published under his own name and a pen name, Bill Kantfraid. In the one reprinted below, he spoofs the confidence schemes of whites who attempted to use the approach of Halley's Comet to frighten the fullbloods into selling their land.

A Cherokee on the Comet

He's come my house, tother day, one fellers, an' he's plumb scared most nigh to death, 'cause he say he's tell 'im, one white mans, he's come this way one these what you call it come at (he's mean a comet), an' he's got tail, long one, an' spec so give it a swipe this old worl' an' knock it sky west and crooked ever'thin', an' he's want sell it land, that Injun feller, an' get it moneys and have it big time spendin' it. He says so, "Well, if he's got to die ever'body can't take it land an' can't take it money, neither, so spec mebby so better jus' sell it land an' git it money an' have it one more bully time, this world 'fore it's all gone ever'thin'."

Well, I seen it this feller he's in middle of a bad fix, so I'm makin' out I don't know nothin' 'bout it no comet, an' I'm axin' him what it is look like it this comet. He say he's like it big one an' got it a tail, great long one, mebby so fifteen or twenty feet long, but that white man's say he's big one, that comet, same alike 'nother one big world flyin' through it space, with head up an' tail up.

"Well," I says, "it's his own tail, spec so he can hold it any way he want to."

He say that white man's tell 'im he's twenty millions and a mile long that tail.

I says then, "Well, what's use fussin' 'bout it little stub tail comet like a that? Shucks, a tail twenty million miles long can't hurt it nothin'. He can't switch it off flies if he's bad kind, with little tail like that, muss less switch it a world outen a jint."

Then he say what for he call it come-at, that white man's. I say I don't [know] 'cept it 'cause he's come at us jist a hellity-scat.

He say I'm jist plum fool, all time make a fun ever'body and ever'thin', that I ought to be for shame to make it fun when a feller's jist plum scart an' got no place to go an' nothin' to do when he gets there.

Well, so it is lots a people's scart of it that comet, and he's want to build it 'fraid holes, some of 'em, an' he's want to sell it land an' ever'-thin' an' spend it money 'fore he's hit us, that comet, an' knocked it out all of the sound out of us. Spec so he's 'fraid it'll all melt, that money, where he spec to go.

I tell you he can't fraid me, that comet. He come foolin' 'long with me I ketch 'im an' jerk a knot in he's tail an' sling out in Jupiter's back yard.

But show 'nough, I'm get it up soon one mornin' 'fore daylight he's begin poppin', an' I'm look way over to'rds where the sun he gits up, an' I'm seen it a pooty one sight.

I seen it a comet, that Halley's, lookin' to'rds the sun an' a long tail of light stretchin' it up the sky more than a half way from it, the horizon to it the zenith, an' I'm think 'bout it how fast it goin'. He's got long ways to go an' I spec so that the reason he rise so early—gets it up 'bout four hours an' fifty cents 'fore sun, an' he's jist a plungin' it along through it eddyin' gulfs of air—guess he's gittin' plenty of it fresh air, ain't it.

Well, I seen it good my friend 'gin an' I'm tell 'im taint look danger at us that comet, he's just what you call it gas that tail an' he can jist wallow in it this world an' taint hurt nothin'. He say, "Well, what for he come an' where he come from?" I tell 'im he's a come that same comet, some-times 74 years, sometimes 79 years, but he's average 'bout 75 years. I know, 'cause last time he come I mark it on it mantleboard, June 30, 1835. It's just like a ground hog day. I'm had pet ground [hog] one time an' I'm watch it, betcher 'bout one hundred times an' he's crawl it out an' look for it shadow ever time on second day February.

1910

Jesse J. McDermott

MUSCOGEE

(1882-?)

Jesse J. McDermott, a member of Hickory Ground tribal town, was the son of Daniel Thompson and Sally McDermott. His father died when he was an infant, and his uncle Paddy Carr raised him and saw to his education. McDermott attended the Creek national boarding school at Eufaula and business college at Fort Smith, Arkansas, where he trained as a stenographer. He became a field worker and interpreter for the Dawes Commission and later was appointed interpreter for Chief Moty Tiger, serving for a number of years. McDermott left public office in 1914 and little is known of him until the 1940s and 1950s, when he worked to settle outstanding Loyal Creek Claims in behalf of the descendants of original claimants who had lost property in the Civil War. For several years after Oklahoma statehood in 1907, McDermott wrote dialect humor for local newspapers, taking for his literary model his well-known fellow Muscogee, Alexander Posey, with whom he had worked for the Dawes Commission.

Legends of the Creeks

During the reign of the Indian laws in the old Indian Territory days, the Creek nation was divided into six judicial districts, namely: Muskogee, Okmulgee, Eufaula, Wewoka, Deep Fork and Coweta. Under the provisions of the law, the national council at its regular assembly was vested with the authority to elect an officer, whose term of office continued two years, to preside over each of the above named districts. He was called a "District Judge."

The duties of a district judge were to preside at hearings in both criminal and civil matters, administer oaths, solemnize the rites of matrimony and consider any other matter that might arise for adjudication within the limits of his jurisdiction.

The judge, of course, was a man of high degree of intelligence and naturally the performance of his duties was in fact an easy task for him so long as the duty of solemnizing a marriage ceremony between a non-citizen couple was not asked of him: then, the task would put on a gloomy appearance with the magistrate.

Here is an example of the difficulty that the judge of Coweta district once experienced during the last days of his incumbency when a non-citizen couple, thinking ten cents per mile by rail to Kansas and return a bit expensive, called on "His Honor" to marry them. The judge arose with a solemn air assumed on such occasions and commanding the blushing couple to join their hands, proceeded with the ceremony, using the following language:

In questioning the groom, the judge said:

"You know it this woman?"

"Yes."

"Is he good woman?"

"Yes."

"You like it this woman?"

"Um huh!"

"You stick to it this woman long as he live?"

"Yes."

"You help it this woman when he sick?"

"Um!"

"You help bury it this woman when he die?"

"Yes."

To the bride he queried:

"You know it this man?"

"Yes."

"Is he good man, you think?"

"Yes."

"You like it this man?"

"Yes."

"You stick it to it this man long as he live?"

"Yes."

"You help it this man when he sick?"

"Yes."

"You help bury it this man when he die?"

"Yes."

"Congratulations! Hope you make it all right."

1910

Oklahoma Justice as Seen by a Fullblood

Whiteman, he kill it man. Sheriff, he arrest it this whiteman. Justice Peace, he try it first this Whiteman for murder. Justice Peace, he say I bind you over to district court on charge murder but if you can make it bond $1,000 you can stay out of it jail. Two men worth maybe $100 apiece sign it bond and prisoner he go free on it.

District court, he call it for trial this Whiteman case but court he find out good witness for state was suffer with bad cold so case continue till next term on old bond. After wait three four years court, he call it this Whiteman case again. After lawyers wrangle over it long time jury, he get empanel and leave courtroom. After deliberate three four days jury, he report "We find it this defendant not a bit guilty" and prisoner, he shake hand with it juries and leave court room free man.

Whitewoman she help kill it her husband. She go through with it same thing as Whiteman and, of course, she get out of it not a bit guilty too.

Whiteman, he get elected for big office where lots money was pile up. After while this Whiteman he get so he think big pile money was all belong to him so he take it and have good time, take long automobile trips and go everywhere. When automobile rubbers begin wear out, some peoples was get notice from this Whiteman office about money that was due when they was already paid it long time ago. When these peoples receive it delinquent notice, they raise big howl about it 'cause they had receipt for it same thing. So when this big howl was come up, a man come from way off and check it up books in this Whiteman office and sure 'nough he find it lots money gone. But this Whiteman was so good 'fore he get elected for big office, these peoples was cease howl and just let him go on with it automobile ride and big banquets 'cause they was all know this Whiteman would get out of it anyhow, and, maybeso go to congress next time.

Injin, he buy it half-pint "Whitemule" or "Sunny Brook." This Injin, he take it pretty good "snort" and go walk down big road and while he was walk maybeso he stumble and thats make him so mad, he just whoop and gobble. Deputy sheriff he rush out and arrest it this Injin. Justice Peace, he try it this Injin and maybeso read it in Manfield's Digest and he say I find you guilty for disturb peace. I sentence you 30 days in jail and fine you $25. and cost. This Injin, he serve it out term in jail and pound it out fine and cost on rock pile.

Some folks calls it Freedman, he break into it somebody chicken coop. Maybeso he play pretty lucky so he get it one-eye rooster. Deputy Sheriff, he chase it down this Freedman with blood hawns [hounds] and capture it. Justice Peace he just call it case against this Freedman and he say you guilty grand larceny. I sentence you six months in county jail.

I know it this is law in Oklahoma 'cause I read it in newspapers all time.

1913

Gabe E. Parker, Sr.

CHOCTAW

(1878–1953)

Born near Fort Towson, Choctaw Nation, on September 19, 1878, Parker was the son of John Day and Eliza Emily Miller Parker. His early years were spent on the family ranch. He graduated from Henry Kendall College (later Tulsa University) in 1899, afterward studying at Kansas State Normal at Emporia, Kansas. He began teaching at Spencer Academy in Indian Territory and was later principal there. When the school was destroyed by fire in 1900, Parker became principal at Armstrong Academy and superintendent in 1904. Parker was a member of the Oklahoma Constitutional Convention in 1906 and devised the great seal of the new state. In 1913, he became register of the U. S. Treasury. He resigned this post to accept an appointment as superintendent of the Five Civilized Tribes, serving in this capacity until 1921. After that, he engaged in farming, stock raising, and banking. Parker died in 1953. Parker was active in the Society of American Indians, whose early agenda included a campaign for American citizenship for all Indians. Parker's address, delivered in 1914 and reprinted here, represents one formulation of the pro-citizenship argument. In later years, the Society would disintegrate, in part, because its members disagreed over what was best for the Indians. In this speech, Parker gives voice to one side of the controversy: that Indians should be removed from all federal control and left to survive in twentieth-century American society through their own efforts.

The Great End: American Citizenship for the Indian

Mr. Chairman, members of the Society of American Indians, ladies and gentlemen: It affords me pleasure to be here on this occasion and to express my approval of the purposes of this Society. It is proper and important for the American Indians to have an organization of this character. Those Indians and our white friends who have given unselfishly of their time and effort to this cause, deserve the credit and co-operation of all Indians and their friends. A Society whose foundation is the principle of mutual helpfulness, and whose activities are in the interest of education and progress, has the splendid opportunity to render valuable service.

I have been requested to speak to you on the subject, "The Great End: American Citizenship for the Indian." The American Indian has occupied a unique position in the life of this nation. He has been independent in his tribal relations, yet dependent upon the government which has surrounded him. He has been regarded as a sovereign, yet treated as a ward. He has been a part of the government, yet not a member of it. He has been subject to the laws of the land, yet often without protection under them, and without the right to participate in their enactment. He has been expected to conform to the ways of civilized life, yet he has been restrained to his tribal relations. Notwithstanding these paradoxical relations, he has made excellent progress; but much remains to be done by him and by the government before the proper relation shall be obtained.

When the Government of the United States confers its citizenship upon an individual, the greatest opportunities and responsibilities of the world are thereby conferred. The opportunities for individual effort and progress are nowhere surpassed, and the responsibilities for preserving, developing and perpetuating our institutions of freedom constitute an infinite honor and a life of devoted service. This government is founded upon the aspirations of Plymouth Rock, inspired by the Declaration of 1776, and preserved by the valor of Yorktown. Truly, this is the "land of the free and the home of the brave." Certainly every resident of such a land should desire to be its citizen, and surely such a land will not deny the worthy.

Statistics show approximately 304,640 Indians by blood in the United

States. Of that number 166,311 are citizens and 138,329 are still without the privileges of citizenship. Nearly one-half the Indians of the United States are not its citizens. The law provides that Indians who sever their tribal relations and adopt the habits and customs of civilized life, those who select allotments, and those who receive patents in fee, thereby become citizens of the United States. It is therefore evident that nearly half our Indians still maintain tribal relations, have not selected allotments, or have not received patents in fee. Since these requirements of law must be met before there can be citizenship for the Indian, the plain duty of all concerned is to remove as rapidly as possible these barriers to the Indian's real chance for progress and independence.

However reluctant the Indian may be to depart from his tribal relations and customs, and with due regard for the fancies of the sentimentalist who believes he is the Indian's best friend, the irresistible fact remains that tribal relations must be abandoned and the responsibilities of American citizenship must be assumed before the Indian can become a self-supporting and contributing factor in this nation.

Standards of life are the result of changes; likewise, changes are often the result of standards. What we are to-day is not what we were yesterday. Everywhere we find progression or retrogression, integration or disintegration. The philosophy of life is the philosophy of change. The important consideration, then, is that out of inevitable change shall come the best and widest sphere of life. How may there be the best? And how may we know it? These are the great questions of life, and probably will not be answered this side of the Great Beyond. But our constant attempts to answer them furnish the means of our advancement and the hope of our reward. The individual or the nation who embodies the best answers to these questions has made the greatest advancement and enjoys the greatest rewards. Each succeeding generation ought to be wiser and better than its predecessor, because it has the successes of the past to impel, the mistakes to deter and the strength to guide.

Upon the foundation of the past rests the condition of the Indian of the present. With few exceptions, a magnificent foundation; with many regrets, and incommensurate consummation. It is true that the self-sacrificing missionary has done much to banish superstition and to inculcate the Gospel of eternal life; that education and environment have joined hands to impart a knowledge of a common language and the skill to earn a living under new conditions, and that our government has exercised a good-intentioned, paternal guardianship. Still, the voice of the past cries out for the thousands who have perished—reminds us that progress has been too slow, and implores us to regard the Indian as a man, with the capabilities and the possibilities of a man.

At the beginning every one must have seen that the inevitable, final result had to be either extermination or assimilation, and the basis of any policy should have been laid accordingly, else the policy would be out of harmony with the inevitable, and a failure in the end. Certainly no one thought of extermination, hence assimilation should have been the basis, and every possible provision made for the Indian to grow into that kind of citizenship to be prescribed and developed in these United States. Every inducement to break away from tribal, clannish relations, to learn the English language, to depend upon individual effort for mainte-nance—in short, to live as and like the white people themselves propose to live—should be offered, and all laws, rules and regulations should make it possible for the Indian to be localized individually, to have pos-session of himself, with the fewest possible restrictions on his initiative, ingenuity and disposition to accommodate himself to the white man's ways.

While the Indian of to-day shows great progress toward thinking and living in the substance of this civilization, still this progress is too often defective in the one vital essential of self-reliance. This is not the Indian's fault, neither from heredity nor from choice. The fundamental fault lies in the construction of the Indian's ownership of land as being only the "right of occupancy." Such a title, if indeed it can be called a real title, has had neither stability nor security; certainly it has not encouraged in-dividual sagacity or industry; in fact, it has been a community restriction which has now passed to the individual where allotments have been made. It is hard to get away from the idea that the Indian has only the "right of occupancy," for, indeed, a restricted individual title is nothing more nor less. We must get away from this idea if the Indian is to make real progress. Give the Indian a real title to some land, with real privileges and responsibilities of his own. Give him what he has been led to believe he will receive in lands and moneys, with restrictions only on those who are determined by personal investigation to be incompetent, those restric-tions to be the fewest possible. There is probably no surer or quicker way to develop self-reliance and individual effort than by making a man earn his own support, and there is probably no surer or quicker way to extin-guish these essential qualities than by giving him something for no effort on his part. Herein lies the difference between success and failure. The moving, ration and expectant systems must cease before individual effort and progress will begin. Quit doing so much for the Indian; permit and require him to do more for himself; give him a real chance. Regard the Indian as a man; think more of his personal development, and remember that competency is the result of performance, not of enunciation. Thereby will the Indian be prepared for American citizenship.

1914

Charles David Carter

CHICKASAW

(1868–1928)

Charles David Carter was born at Boggy Depot, Choctaw Nation, the son of Benjamin W. and Serena Guy Carter and nephew of the poet James Harris Guy. Carter was educated in the Chickasaw common schools and at the Chickasaw Manual Labor School at Tishomingo. He was a ranch hand and store clerk before becoming auditor of the Chickasaw Nation in 1892. After two years as auditor, he served as superintendent of schools (1894–96), a member of the Chickasaw National Council (1897), and mining trustee for the Indian Territory (1900–04). In 1905 he was a founding partner in an insurance firm. With the dissolution of the Chickasaw Nation and approaching Oklahoma statehood, he entered politics, serving as secretary of the first Democratic Executive Committee for the proposed new state in 1906 and the next year was elected one of its first Congressmen. He served in the House of Representatives for the next twenty years. Carter's family on his mother's side had been very active in Chickasaw politics. Thus he was familiar with not only Chickasaw history but also that of the Choctaws, with whom his tribe was closely allied. The article reprinted here was presented at memorial exercises at the grave of Chief Pushmataha at the Congressional Cemetery in Washington, D. C., in 1921, honoring the great Choctaw chief who had died during a diplomatic visit to the nation's capitol in 1824. Congressman Carter had the piece printed in the *Congressional Record*.

Memorable Debate Between Pushmataha and Tecumseh

I will pause only long enough to tell you something of what I believe his own people, the Choctaws, consider one of Pushmataha's greatest achievements. This has to do with the part he took in saving the white man's civilization west of the Alleghenies and specifically his reply to the wonderful address delivered before the Choctaw Council by the great Shawnee orator, Tecumseh. The War of 1812 was impending and the British authorities were doing all in their power to stir up antagonism between the Indians and Americans. The astute Shawnee chief, Tecumseh, was sent on a tour by British agents to organize all Indians west of the Alleghenies with the purpose to expel the white American beyond the mountains. One of the first tribes he visited was the Choctaw. After his mission had been explained to Pushmataha, the wise old chief advised Tecumseh that he was only one of the three chiefs of the Choctaw Nation; that the Choctaws could only take part in any war upon the decision of the general council of the tribe; and that before this was done they would probably desire to consult their kindred tribe and ally, the Chickasaws. Tecumseh then requested that both tribes be called together in order that he might lay his plan before the council. After a consultation with the other two Choctaw chiefs, Masholatubby and Apuckshinubby, and the principal chief of the Chickasaws, a general council of the two tribes was called.

Tecumseh was classed by many of his contemporaries as the most powerful debater of his generation, and this was saying much, for it was during the day of [Henry] Clay, [John C.] Calhoun and [Daniel] Webster. Realizing the full power of his oratory, Tecumseh surmised if he could get to speak to the Choctaw people in general council they would not be able to resist his magnetic logic and eloquence. The council was assembled, and Tecumseh, with his suite of 30 warriors bedecked in panoply of paint and feathers, filed in before the council fire to deliver his address. We must bear in mind that the Shawnees spoke an entirely different language from the Choctaws and Chickasaws, the Shawnees belonging to the Algonquin stock and speaking their dialect, while the Choctaws and Chickasaw are of the Muskogeon stock and spoke the Muskogeon dialect. Therefore it was necessary for each speech to be translated by an interpreter so all might understand.

The great Shawnee chief was thoroughly familiar with past relations between all Indian tribes and the whites, and he began by recounting all the wrongs perpetrated on the Indians by the palefaces since the landing of Columbus. He related how the white man had beguiled the Indians along the Atlantic coast to part with their lands for a few trifling beads and a little fire water, leaving them beggars, vagabonds, peons, and strangers in their own land, to be scorned and despised by their paleface neighbors. He told how the Shawnees and other northern tribes were being stripped of their patrimony. He laid down the principle that the Great Spirit had given the Western hemisphere to all red people in common and that no particular tribe had anything more than the right of possession to any lands, and therefore asserted any relinquishment of title by one tribe to be null and void, because many of the owners had not joined in the transfer. These wrongs discussed, he declared had been made possible by the ingenuity of the whites in attacking only one tribe at a time, but if all Indians would join and combine their forces in one attack at one time, the white man could be driven back over the mountains whence he came; that the golden opportunity was now at hand to join hands with the British and scourge from their revered hunting grounds eternally the hated paleface. He closed his eloquent address with a stirring appeal to the patriotism of the Choctaws and Chickasaws, asking if they would await complete submission or would they now join hands and fight beside the Shawnees and other tribes rather than submit?

Evidently Tecumseh's purpose had been fully accomplished. His magnetic words seemed to arouse every vindictive sentiment within the souls of the Choctaw and Chickasaw warriors; their savage enthusiasm had been stirred to white heat when Pushmataha calmly strode before the council fire and began his wonderful reply to Tecumseh's speech. What a pity that no accurate account of this wonderful debate between these two giant primitive orators was at that time preserved. Lincecum, Pickett, Randall, and other historians have left us brief excerpts, Cushman undertakes to give Pushmataha's speech in full,[1] but his recital does not even faint justice to the original and in no measure conforms to the Choctaws' account of it. For many years it was handed down from generation to generation by tradition to the Choctaws and Chickasaws, but it can be easily understood how that method might fail to preserve all the virile force and eloquence of this wonderful address. I will undertake to give it

1. Historians Gideon Lincecum, Albert J. Pickett, E. O. Randall, and H. B. Cushman.

to you in part as nearly as I remember hearing it told by some of the old Indians many years ago. Pushmataha began his speech as follows:

Pushmataha's Reply to Tecumseh
"Omiske, tushkahoma ho chukma hashche yumma! Anumpa tilofasih ish huklo."

("Attention, my good red warriors! Hear ye my brief remarks.")

"The great Shawnee orator has portrayed in vivid picture the wrongs inflicted on his and other tribes by the ravages of the paleface. The candor and fervor of his eloquent appeal breathe the conviction of truth and sincerity, and, as kindred tribes, naturally we sympathize with the misfortunes of his people. I do not come before you in any disputation either for or against these charges. It is not my purpose to contradict any of these allegations against the white man, but neither am I here to indulge in any indiscreet denunciation of him which might bring down upon my people unnecessary difficulty and embarrassment.

"The distinguished Shawnee sums up his eloquent appeal to us with this direct question:

" 'Will you sit idly by, supinely awaiting complete and abject submission, or will you die fighting beside your brethren, the Shawnees, rather than submit to such ignominy?'

"These are plain words and it is well they have been spoken, for they bring the issue squarely before us. Mistake not, this language means war. And war with whom, pray? War with some band of marauders who have committed these depredations against the Shawnees? War with some alien host seeking the destruction of the Choctaws and Chickasaws? Nay, my fellow tribesmen. None of these are the enemy we will be called on to meet. If we take up arms against the Americans we must of necessity meet in deadly combat our daily neighbors and associates in this part of the country near our homes.

"If Tecumseh's words be true, and we doubt them not, then the Shawnees' experience with the whites has not been the same as that of the Choctaws. These white Americans buy our skins, our corn, our cotton, our surplus game, our baskets, and other wares, and they give us in fair exchange their cloth, their guns, their tools, implements, and other things which the Choctaws need but do not make. It is true we have befriended them, but who will deny that these acts of friendship have been abundantly reciprocated? They have given us cotton gins, which simplify the spinning and sale of our cotton; they have encouraged and helped us in the production of our crops; they have taken many of our wives into their homes to teach them useful things, and pay them for their work while learning; they are teaching our children to read and write from their books. You all remember well the dreadful epidemic visited upon us last winter. During its darkest hours these neighbors whom we are now urged to attack responded generously to our needs. They doctored our sick; they clothed our suffering; they fed our hungry; and where is the Choctaw or Chickasaw delegation who has ever gone to St. Stephens with a worthy cause and been sent away empty handed? So in marked contrast with the experience of the Shawnees, it will be seen that the whites and Indians in this section are living on friendly and mutually beneficial terms.

"Forget not, O Choctaws and Chickasaws, that we are bound in peace to the Great White Father at Washington by a sacred treaty and the Great Spirit will punish those who break their word. The Great White Father has never violated that treaty and the Choctaws have never yet been driven to the necessity of taking up the tomahawk against him or his children. Therefore the question before us tonight is not the avenging of any wrongs perpetrated against us by the whites, for the Choctaws and Chickasaws have no such cause, either real or imaginary, but rather it is a question of carrying on that record of fidelity and justice for which our forefathers ever proudly stood, and doing that which is best calculated to promote the welfare of our own people. Yea, my fellow tribesmen, we are a just people. We do not take up the warpath without a just cause and honest purpose. Have we that just cause against our white neighbors, who have taken nothing from us except by fair bargain and exchange? Is this a just recompense for their assistance to us in our agricultural and other pursuits? Is this to be their gracious reward for teaching our children from their books? Shall this be considered the Choctaws' compensation for feeding our hungry, clothing our needy, and administering to our sick? Have we, O Choctaws and Chickasaws, descended to the low estate of ruthlessly breaking the faith of a sacred treaty? Shall our forefathers look back from the happy hunting grounds only to see their unbroken record for justice, gratitude, and fidelity thus rudely repudiated and abruptly abandoned by an unworthy offspring?

"We Choctaws and Chickasaws are a peaceful people, making our subsistence by honest toil; but mistake not, my Shawnee brethren, we are not afraid of war. Neither are we strangers to war, as those who have undertaken to encroach upon our rights in the past may abundantly testify. We are thoroughly familiar with war in all its details and we know full well all its horrible consequences. It is unnecessary for me to remind you, O Choctaws and Chickasaws, veteran braves of many fierce conflicts in the past, that war is an awful thing. If we go into this war against the Americans, we must be prepared to accept its inevitable results. Not only will it foretoken deadly conflict with neighbors and death to warriors, but it will mean suffering for our women, hunger and starvation for our children, grief for our loved ones, and devastation of our beloved homes. Notwithstanding these difficulties, if the cause be just, we should not hesitate to defend our rights to the last man, but before that fatal step is irrevocably taken, it is well that we fully understand and seriously consider the full portent and consequences of the act.

"Hear me, Choctaws and Chickasaws, for I speak truly for your welfare. It is not the province of your chiefs to settle these important questions. As a people, it is your prerogative to have either peace or war, and as one of your chiefs, it is mine simply to counsel and advise. Therefore, let me admonish you that this critical period is no time to cast aside your wits and let blind impulse sway; be not driven like dumb brutes by the frenzied harangue of this wonderful Shawnee orator; let your good judgment rule and ponder seriously before breaking bonds that have served you well and ere you change conditions which have brought peace and happiness to your wives, your sisters, and your children. I would not undertake to dictate the course of one single Choctaw warrior. Permit me to speak for the moment, not as your chief but as a Choctaw warrior, weighing this question beside you. As such I shall exercise my calm, deliberated judgment in behalf of those most dear to me and dependent on me, and I shall not suffer my reason to be swept away by this eloquent recital of alleged wrongs which I know naught of. I deplore this war, I earnestly hope it may be averted, but if it be forced upon us I shall take my stand with those who have stood by my people in the past and will be found fighting beside our good friends of St. Stephens and surrounding country. I have finished. I call on all Choctaws and Chickasaws indorsing my sentiments to cast their tomahawks on this side of the council fire with me."

The air resounded with the clash of tomahawks cast on the side of the Choctaw chief and only a few warriors seemed still undecided. Tecumseh seeing the purpose of his mission thwarted and thinking Pushmataha could not understand the Shawnee language, spoke to his warriors in his native tongue, saying: "Pushmataha is a coward and the Choctaw and

Chickasaw braves are squaws," but Pushmataha had traveled much and knew a smattering of many Indian dialects. He understood Tecumseh and turning upon the Shawnee with all the fire of his eloquence, he clinched the argument and settled the decision of the few wavering Choctaw braves by saying:

"Halt, Tecumseh! Listen to me. You have come here, as you have often gone elsewhere, with a purpose to involve peaceful people in unnecessary trouble with their neighbors. Our people have had no undue friction with the whites. Why? Because we have had no leaders stirring up strife to serve their selfish, personal ambitions. You heard me say that our people are a peaceful people. They make their way, not by ravages upon their neighbors but by honest toil. In that regard they have nothing in common with you. I know your history well. You are a disturber. You have ever been a trouble maker. When you have found yourself unable to pick a quarrel with the white man, you have stirred up strife between different tribes of your own race. Not only that, you are a monarch and unyielding tyrant within your own domain; every Shawnee man, woman, and child must bow in humble submission to your imperious will. The Choctaws and Chickasaws have no monarchs. Their chieftains do not undertake the mastery of their people, but rather are they the people's servants, elected to serve the will of the majority. The majority has spoken on this question and it has spoken against your contention. Their decision has therefore become the law of the Choctaws and Chickasaws and Pushmataha will see that the will of the majority so recently expressed is rigidly carried out to the letter. If, after this decision, any Choctaw should be so foolish as to follow your imprudent advice and enlist to fight against the Americans, thereby abandoning his own people and turning against the decision of his own council, Pushmataha will see that proper punishment is meted out to him, which is death. You have made your choice; you have elected to fight with the British. The Americans have been our friends and we shall stand by them. We will furnish you safe conduct to the boundaries of this nation as properly befits the dignity of your office. Farewell, Tecumseh. You will see Pushmataha no more until we meet on the fateful warpath."

Obviously those two noble sons of the forest and their tribes had reached "the point where the trail divides." The Choctaws and Chickasaws were persuaded to refuse participation in Tecumseh's conspiracy against the Americans and the action of these two powerful tribes prevented many other Indians from siding with the British. The Choctaws and Chickasaws finally joined hands with the Americans and fought from the early battles of the war to the Battle of New Orleans, and Pushmataha arose to the rank of brigadier general in the American Army. The Shawnees joined forces with the British and Tecumseh was slain while leading a forlorn charge under Procter at the Battle of the Thames.

1926

Will Rogers

Cherokee

(1879–1935)

William Penn Adair Rogers, known to the world simply as Will Rogers, was born at Oolagah, Cherokee Nation, the son of Clement Vann and Mary Schrimpsher Rogers. The elder Rogers, a substantial rancher and well-known Cherokee politician, and his wife, who had been educated at the Cherokee Female Seminary, sent their son beyond Cherokee grammar schools to Willie Halsall College at Vinita and then to Kemper Military Academy in Missouri. After a year at the latter, Will Rogers left in 1898 to become a cattle wrangler in Texas. In 1902 he set out to see the world and in South Africa joined Texas Jack's Wild West Circus, with whom he toured, billing himself as "The Cherokee Kid" and putting to good use the riding and roping skills he had learned on his father's ranch and during his days as a wrangler. Back in the United States in 1904, he soon joined Zack Mulhall's wild west show, which opened the way to his career in show business. He progressed to vaudeville and then to musical shows, joining the *Ziegfeld Follies* in 1916, playing with that production five years between then and 1925. He then went on to lecture circuits and radio shows and finally to the movies, playing in a number of them between 1925 and 1935.

Early on, Rogers' comic routines led him into writing. He began to mingle humorous talk with his rope-tricks performance. As time passed, his commentary turned more and more to current events, and in late 1922 he was convinced to write a weekly syndicated column, which he wrote until his death. He also produced a number of books, including *The Illiterate Digest* (1924), *Letters of a Self-Made Diplomat to His President* (1926), *There's Not a Bathing-Suit in Russia* (1927), and *Ether and Me*

(1929). Rogers' writings made him America's most loved humorist of the twentieth century—perhaps of all time. His success was due in large measure to his style. Because of his conversational tone, purposeful misspellings, ungrammatical statements, slang, coined words, and understatement at times and exaggeration at others, he was embraced by the common folk of America who appreciated his "down-home" style and attacks on highbrows, the rich, pretenders, and politicians. Yet his exposure through print and other media made him known world wide, and he became a kind of roving ambassador for America, flying to all parts of the world. On his last trip, he was killed in a crash at Point Barrow, Alaska, along with his friend, the Oklahoma pilot and flight pioneer, Wiley Post.

Most of Rogers' writing is topical, concerning itself with current events and personalities, many of his weekly columns beginning with his now-famous statement "All I know is what I read in the newspapers," or some variation of it. Because of their topical content, many pieces have lost some relevancy for today's readers. Most, however, with some editorial assistance can be easily read and enjoyed. And some, such as those reprinted here, seem strikingly apropos to the contemporary scene.[1] Such a small sampling as this can in only a small way reflect the range of his subjects and can barely hint at the versatility of his style.

Slipping the Lariat Over

Now, in my more or less checkered career before the more or less checkered Public, I have been asked to publicly endorse everything from Chewing Gum, Face Beautifiers, Patent Cocktail Shakers, Ma Junk Sets, even Corsets, Cigarettes and Chewing Tobacco, all of which I didn't use or know anything about. But I always refused.

You never heard me boosting for anything, for I never saw anything made that the fellow across the street didn't make something just as good.

But, at last, I have found something that I absolutely know no one else

1. Because of the large volume of Rogers' work, the Oklahoma State University Press reprint Series IV, Weekly Articles of Will Rogers, was indispensible in searching for possible articles to include here. Especially useful were volume one (1980), edited by James A. Smallwood, and volume five (1982), edited by Steven K. Gragert. This reprint series, despite some textual errors, makes Rogers' writing easily accessible for contemporary readers.

has something just as good as, for an all-seeing Nature put this where it is and it's the only one he had, and by a coincidence it is located in the Town near the ranch where I was born and raised.

So I hereby and hereon come out unequivocally (I think that's the way you spell it) in favor of a place that has the water that *I know* will cure you. You might ask, cure me of what? Why, cure you of anything—just name your disease and dive in.

Claremore, Oklahoma, is the birthplace of this Aladdin of health waters. Some misguided Soul named it RADIUM WATER, but Radium will never see the day that it is worth mentioning in the same breath as this Magic Water. Why, to the afflicted and to all suffering Humanity, a Jug of this Water is worth a wheelbarrow full of Radium. Still, even under the handicap of a cheap name, this liquid God-send has really cured thousands.

Now you may say, "Oh, you boost it because you live there," but I don't want you to think so little of me that you would think I would misguide a sick person just for the monetary gain of my Home Town. We don't need you that bad. The city is on a self-supporting basis without Patients, just by shipping the Water to Hot Springs, Ark.; Hot Springs, Va.; West Baden, Ind., and Saratoga, N. Y.

Now, as to a few of the ignorant who might still be in the dark as to where the Home of this Fountain of Youth is located, I will tell you. I shouldn't waste my time on such Low Brows, but, unfortunately, they get sick and need assistance the same as the 95 Million others who already know where Claremore is located.

It is located, this Mecca of the ill, about 1,700 miles west of New York (either city or State, depends on whichever one you happen to be in). You bear a little south of west, after leaving New York, till you reach Sol. McClellan's place, which is just on the outskirts of Claremore. Before you get into the City proper, if you remember about 500 miles back, you passed another Town. Well, that was St. Louis, most of which is in Illinois.

Now, if you are in the North, and happen to get something the matter with you, we are 847 and a half miles south by west from Gary, Indiana. We have cured hundreds of people from Chicago, Ill., from Gun Shot wounds inflicted in attempted murders and robberies. There is only one way to avoid being robbed of anything in Chicago and that is not to have anything.

If you are from Minneapolis, our Radium Water guarantees to cure you of everything but your Swedish accent. If you are from St. Paul, we can cure you of anything but your ingrown hatred for Minneapolis.

I will admit that these waters have quite a peculiar odor, as they have a proportion of Sulphur and other unknown ingredients, but visitors from Kansas City, who are used to a Stock Yard breeze, take this wonderful water home as a Perfume.

Approaching this City from the north, don't get it confused with Oolagah, Oklahoma, my original Birthplace, which is 12 miles to the north, as both towns have Post Offices.

From the West, if you are afflicted and you are sure to be or you wouldn't have gone out there, why Claremore is just 1,900 miles due East of Mojave, California, one of the few towns which Los Angeles has not voted into their Cafeteria. You come east till you reach an Oil Station at a road crossing. This oil station is run by a man named St. Clair. You will see a lot of men pitching Horseshoes. Well, that is the Post Office of Tulsa, Oklahoma, and the men are Millionaires pitching Horseshoes for Oil Wells.

You should, by this description, have the place pretty well located in your minds. Now, if you are living in the South and are afflicted with a Cotton Crop under a Republican Administration, or with the Ku Klux Klan, or with the Hook Worm, we guarantee to rid you of either or all of these in a course of 24 Baths.

Claremore is located just 905 miles North of Senator Pat Harrison's Mint Bed in Mississippi. In coming from the Gulf Country some have got off the road and had to pass through Dallas, Texas, but have found out their mistake and got back on the main road at Fort Worth before losing all they had. You easily can tell Fort Worth. A fellow will be standing down in front of the Drug Store making a speech.

Now, before reaching Claremore, you will pass, even though it's in the middle of the day, a place where you think it's night and you won't know what is the matter. Well, that's Muskogee, Oklahoma, and this darkness is caused by the Color scheme of the population, so put on your headlights and go on in. This Muskogee is really a parking space for cars entering Claremore. Of course, if you want to drive on into the Town of Claremore proper, it's only 60 miles through the suburbs from here.

The City is located on Cat Creek, and instead of having a lot of Streets like most Towns and Cities, we have combined on one street. In that way no Street is overlooked.

You might wonder how we discovered this Blarney Stone of Waters.

In the early days, us old-timers there, always considered these Wells more as an Odor than as a Cure. But one day a man come in there who had been raised in Kansas and he had heard in a round-about way of people bathing, although he had never taken one, so, by mistake, he got into this Radium Waters.

He was a one-armed man—he had lost an Arm in a rush to get into a Chautauqua Tent in Kansas to hear [William Jennings] Bryan speak on Man vs. Monkey. Well, he tried this Bath, and it didn't kill him and he noticed that he was beginning to sprout a new arm where he had lost the old one, so he kept on with the Baths and it's to him that we owe the discovery of this wonderful curative Water. Also, he was the Pioneer of Bathers of Kansas, as now they tell me it's no uncommon thing to have a Tub in most of their larger towns.

Now, it has been discovered that you can carry a thing too far and overdo it, so we don't want you there too long. A man came there once entirely legless and stayed a week too long and went away a Centipede.

I want to offer you my personal Testimonial of what it did to me. You see, after this Kansas Guy started it, why, us old-timers moved our bathing from the River into a Tub. Now, at that time, I was practically Tongue Tied and couldn't speak out in private, much less in Public. Well, after 12 baths, I was able to go to New York and make after-dinner speeches. I stopped in Washington on the way and saw how our Government was run and that gave me something funny to speak about.

So, in thanking the Water, I also want to thank the Government for making the whole thing possible. Now, had I taken 24 baths I would have been a Politician, so you see I stopped just in time.

The only thing I get out of this is I have the "Thrown Away Crutch Privilege." If you don't get well and throw away your Invalid Chair or crutches I get nothing out of it, so that is why we give you a square deal. If you are not cured, I don't get your Crutches. There is no other resort in the World that works on that small a margin.

W. J. Bryan drank one drink of this Water and turned against Liquor. Senator [Robert] La Follette drank two drinks of it and turned against everything. So, remember Claremore, The Carlesbad of America, where the Frisco Railroad crosses the Iron Mountain Railroad, not often, but every few days.

1923

Slipping the Lariat Over

Somebody must have seen me out in Public; I think it was Emily Post, for she sent me a Book on Etiquette that she had written herself.

It has 700 pages in it. You wouldn't think there was that much Etiquette, would you? Well, I hadn't read far when I found that I was wrong on most every line of the whole Book.

Now, you wouldn't think a Person could live under fairly civilized conditions (as I imagined I was doing) and be so dumb as to not have at least one of these forms of Etiquette right. Well, when I got through reading it, I felt like I had been a heathen all my life. But after I got to noticing other people I met I didn't feel so bad. Some of them didn't know much more about it than I did.

So I predict that her Book and all the other things you read now on Etiquette are going to fall on fertile soil. Now take, for instance, being introduced, or introducing some one; that is the first thing in the Book. I didn't know up to then that inflection of the voice was such a big factor in introductions.

She says that the prominence of the party being introduced determines the sound of the voice, as she says for instance, "Are you there?" and then on finding out you are there she says, "Is it raining?"

Now the inflection that you use on asking any one if they are there is the same inflection that you are to use in introducing Mr. Gothis, if he is the more prominent of the two. Then for the other person, who Mr. Gothis probably got his from, why, you use the "Is it raining?" inflection.

You see, a fellow has to know a whole lot more than you think he does before he can properly introduce people to each other. First, he has to be up on his Dun and Bradstreet to tell which of the two is the more prominent. Second, he has to be an Elocutionist so he will know just where to bestow the inflection.

Well, I studied on that introduction Chapter till I thought I had it down pat. So I finally got a chance to try it out. My wife had invited a few friends for Dinner, and as she hadn't finished cooking it before they come, I had to meet them and introduce them to each other.

Well, I studied for half an hour before they they come, trying to figure out which one was the most prominent so I could give her the "Are you there?" inflection. It was hard to figure out because any one of them couldn't be very prominent and be coming to our House for Dinner. So I thought, well, I will just give them both the "Is it raining?" inflection.

Then I happened to remember that the Husband of one of them had just bought a Drug Store, so I figured that I better give her the benefit of the "Are you there?" inflection, for if Prohibition stays in effect it's only a matter of days till her Husband will be prominent.

So, when they arrived I was remembering my opening Chapter of my Etiquette on Introductions. When the first one come I was all right; I didn't have to introduce her to any one. I just opened our front door in answer to the Bell, which didn't work. But I was peeping through the Curtains, and as I opened the door to let her in 2 of our Dogs and 4 Cats come in.

Well, while I was shooing them out, apologizing and trying to make her believe it was unusual for them to do such a thing, now there I was! This Emily Post wrote 700 pages on Etiquette, but not a line on what to do in an emergency to remove Dogs and Cats and still be Non Challant.

The second Lady arrived just as this Dog and Cat Pound of ours was emptying. She was the new Prescription Store Owner's Wife and was to get the "Are you there?" inflection. Her name was (I will call her Smith, but that was not her name). She don't want it to get out that she knows us.

Well, I had studied that Book thoroughly but those animals entering our Parlor had kinder upset me. So I said, "Mrs. Smith, Are you there? I want you to meet Mrs. Jones. Is it raining?"

Well, these Women looked at me like I was crazy. It was a silly thing to say. Mrs. Smith was there of course, or I couldn't have introduced her, and asking Mrs. Jones if it was raining was most uncalled for, because I had just looked out myself and, besides, any one that ever lived in California knows it won't rain again till next year.

But that didn't discourage me. I kept right on learning and from now on I am just mangy with Etiquette.

Why, just the other day I heard what I had always considered up to then a well-behaved Woman introduce one Gentleman friend to another and she said, "Allow me to present."

Now anybody that's ever read the first 5 lines in the book knows that the word Present is never used only on formal occasions. You should always say, "May I introduce" on all informal occasions. There was a

Woman who, to look at her, you would never have thought could possibly be so rude and uncultured as to have made a mistake like that.

It just spoiled her for me. I don't care how many nice things she may do in the future, she just don't belong.

Rule 2, Chapter 5—"No Gentleman under any circumstances chews Gum in Public." Now that kinder knocked me for a Goal, for I had been Chewing Gum before some the best families in this Country. But from now on it is out. I am going to live according to the Book.

Chapter 6—"Gentlemen should not walk along the Street with their Cane or Stick striking the picket fence. Such habits should be curbed in the nursery."

Now that rule didn't hit me so hard, for I am not lame and I don't carry a Cane yet, and furthermore, there are no Picket fences in California. If they had enough pickets to make a fence they would take them and build another Bungalow and rent it.

Outside of eating with a sharp Knife, there is no rule in the Book that lays you liable to as much criticism as the following: "Whether in a private Car, a Taxi or a carriage a lady must never sit on a Gentleman's left, because according to European Etiquette a Lady 'on the left' is no Lady."

I thought at first when I read that it was misprint, and meant a Lady should never sit on a Gentleman's Lap, instead of Left. But now I find that it really was Left. So I guess you can go ahead and sit on the lap. It don't say not to. But don't sit on his Left, or you can never hope to enter smart society.

Then it says "the Owner of the car should always occupy the right hand side of the rear seat." No matter how many payments he has to make on it, that is considered his seat.

Chapter 7 is given over entirely to The Opera. What to wear, when to applaud—it tells everything but how to enjoy the thing. The fellow that figures out how to enjoy the Opera in a foreign tongue, without kidding himself or fourflushing, has a fortune in store for him.

Chapter 12 tells how the Butler should dress. You don't know what a relief it was to me to find that news. I never had one, but if I do I will know what to costume him in.

The Book says: "At 6 o'clock the Butler puts on his dress Suit. The Butler's suit differs from that of a Gentleman by having no braid on his trousers."

Now all you Birds that never could tell the Servants from the Guests, except somebody called one of them a Butler and the other a Gentleman, you can't tell them that way. More than likely the Butler is the Gentleman of the two.

But I can tell the Butler. He has no braid on his trousers.

Now, all I got to do is find out how to tell the Gentleman.

If you see people walking around looking down at your trousers, in the future, you will know they are looking to see if the braid is left off.

1923

Wild Movie Titles

All I know is just what I read in the Moving Picture ads and say Boy what an education it is! I thought the underwear ads in the magazines were about the limit in presenting an eyefull, but these Movie ads give you the same thing without the underwear.

Even I myself appeared in a Nightgown in The Connecticut Yankee, so on the billboards it would add a touch of romantic glamor, to say nothing of a smattering of sex appeal.

Mind you you musent let the ad have anything to do with what you see on the insides. You are liable to see the wildest stuff facing you on the billboards, and then go inside and everybody is dressed as esquimos all through the picture. In other words Will Hays big trouble is getting pictures that will live up to the pictures on the ads.[1]

You know in all Latin American countries (I am speaking of authority as I flew over them at an altitude of sometimes as low as ten thousand feet), in those countries, if you put a picture on the boards to advertise what you are having inside or if in your wording you say that Miss Millie De Hokum will entirely disrobe on a tight wire, why on the said night Millie better do a mighty good job of stripping or the cash customers will clothe Millie and her management with some seats and chairs, and any other handy article laying around.

Or if it shows a picture of a bull fight and a Matador being gored, by an unruly ox, why the day of the fight you better have the man gored, or be prepared to be gored yourself. In other words you got to deliver what

---

1. Gragert identifies this man as William H. Hays, head of Motion Picture Producers and Distributors.

you advertise. So the big problem of the Movies now is to deliver up to what the Lithograph makers and ad writers have shown on the outside.

In other words, that branch of the industry has "outstripped" the Production end. We just can't seem to get em as wild as they show em on the outside. We got to get wilder people. A lot of these have been out here for years, and they are getting kinder old and tame. There is an awful lot of us out here that just cant arouse the passions in our public like we ought to. And thats why we keep trying to get new blood into this ART.

Then in the Titles of Pictures, there is where its getting hard. They just cant think up enough suggestive Titles to go around. They bring every big Writer out here from New York and England and have them in an Office just thinking all the time on Titles that will lead you to expect you are going to see on the inside about four of the most prominent Commandments broken, right before your eyes. But there is just so many of those Titles, and every Company is fighting to get em. You take old [p]lays like the "Old Homestead." Now they are just waiting till they can think up some title for that, and then it will go into Production.

A few of the best that have been turned in by the highest priced Writers up to now is "The old Love Nest," "Home In Name Only," "The Birthplace Of Folly," "Devilment Galore among the Honeysuckles," "What Took Place Under The Old Roof," "The Gal Pays The Mortgage With Body And Soul," "The House is Old but the Carryings on is New And Spicy," "The Gangsters Birthplace as Far as We Know."

So you can see that they are right on the edge of getting something that will combine all these, and give you an inkling of what the old roof has seen take place under it, and then they will start in making it.

The word "hell" while generally frowned upon as conversation in the grammer grades, has been literally pounced upon by the movie title manufacturers, and they have just about "helled" everything to death. They have pictured the doorway, the stage entrance, and every part of hell, till hell has just got so it don't mean nothing more anymore but another word in a title. Putting the word hell on the billboards and expecting to scare up any excitement among the prospective victims anymore is just blowed up.

Course my old friend Will Hays still insists that virtue triumphs, but they keep making you more and more doubtful right up to the end, in fact most of them hold back till after the final fade out. And I have seen some of 'em here lately where it looked like it was still in doubt as to whether it triumphed or not.

Thats called "subtelry." All the writers try to be what they call "sophisticated" or "subtelry." That means nobody knows what you are talking about and don't give a D____. Sophistication means talking all day about nothing. You are both bored but you have to do something till somebody mixes another cocktail. We are getting a lot of those kind of talking plays now. Titles that if printed on the old silent screen would have got the "Rawsberry" now are considered smart, for they apply to nothing and mean less.

I saw one the other night called "Kiss And Leave Each Other Flat." It was so subtle that it didnt say whether you can leave 'em flat physically or financially. They call 'em drawing-room plays, women with nothing on their minds eat 'em up, kids hiss 'em, and old men sleep right through 'em.

They had 'em on the stage till they ruined it. So between "Subtelry" and Gangsters we have run the old Cowboy trying to save the Sheriff's daughter, right back to the dairy farm. No modern child would want to learn how to shoot a 45 Colts. He wants to know how to mow 'em down with the old Browning machine gun. But we will live through it, and come out with something worse. We always do. So we better make the most of this while its here.

1931

Educational Frills

Say, any of you that have kids in schools, either grammar, high or College, it dont make any difference, but can any of you parents get head or tail of what they are doing, what they are taking, what they are learning?

This modern education gag has sure got me licked, I cant tell from talking to 'em what its all about.

All the kids I know, either mine or anybodys, none of em can write so you can read it, none of em can spell so you can read it, they cant figure and dont know geography, but they are always taking some of the darndest things, political science, international relations, drama, buck dancing, sciocology, latin, greek art, Oh, Lord, the things they go in for runs on by the hour!

But its as I say, not only our brood, but none of em that I have seen can write, spell, figure or tell you what bounds Corea. Everybody has swimming pools, but nobody has got a plain old geography. Gymnasiums to the right of you, and tennis courts to the left of you, but not a spelling book in a car load of schools.

Then they got another gag they call "Credits." If you do anything thirty minutes twice a week, why you get some certain "Credit." Maby its lamp shade tinting, maby its singing, maby its a thing they call "music appreciation." That used to drive my cowboy son Jim pretty near "nuts." He never could see how that would aid you to rope a calf. They give out these things at schools for anything that any one can think of. Some of em you get more "credits" than for others. If a thing is particularly useless, why it give you more credits. There is none at all for things that we thought constituted "school."

You could write, read, spell, figure, and give the capital of Rhode Island, and they wouldent give you a "credit" in a year. But you can tell where a Latin word was originally located, and how its been manhandled and orphandized down to the present day, and say they will claim that you have the nucleus of a "Thesis," and you are liable to get a horde of "credits." Now who cares about the word, or what it has contributed to the welfare of Nations that never minds to them.

You have got yourself the family tree of a word. Course you cant go out and get a job on it, but these old proffessors value it mighty highly. Some of these days they are going to remove so much of the "Bunk and Hooey" and the thousands of things that the schools have become clogged up with, and we will find that we can educate our broods for about one-tenth the price and learn em something they might accidentally use after they escaped.

But us poor old dumb parents we just string along and do the best we can, and send 'em as long as we are able, because we want them to have the same handicaps the others have. We dont know what its all about. We just have to take the teachers' word.

They all say education is our salvation, but you could turn ten college presidents loose in a forest with nothing to eat, or nothing to get it with, and then ten old so-called "Ignorant" backwoodsmen, and your presidents wouldent last a week.

The smarter a nation gets, the more wars it has. The dumb ones are too smart to fight. Our schools teach us what the other fellow knows, but it dont teach us anything new for ourselves. Everybody is learning just one thing, not because they will know more, but because they have been taught that they wont have to work if they are educated.

Well, we got so many educated now that there is not enough jobs for educated people. Most of our work is skilled and requires practice, and not education.

But none of these big proffessors will come out and tell you that our education might be lacking, that it might be shortened, that it might be improved. They know as it is now that its a "Racket," and they are in on it. You couldent get me to admit that making movies was the bunk either. None of us will talk against our own graft. We all got us our "Rackets" nowadays.

There is just about as much "Hooey" in everything as there is merit. The heathern live with less effort, and less worry.

Trying to live "Past" our parents, and not "Up to Em" is one of our drawbacks. The old Chinese got the right idea along that line, but ever once in awhile some fellow does pop up and declare himself. Look at that college professor in Chicago University. He said our learning system was all haywire.

He is a smart young fellow that guy. I heard him speak at a dinner in Chicago during the Convention. He knew a whole lot more than just where a lot of words "Come From." This education is just like everything else. You got to judge it by results. Here we are better educated (according to educational methods) than we ever were. And we are worse off than we ever were, so its not living up to its "Billing." Its over rated. It's not worth the price.

Its costing us more than its worth. They got to devise some way of giving more for the money. All he is getting out with now is "Credit" and nobody on the outside is cashing em.

1932

Rollie Lynn Riggs

CHEROKEE

(1899–1954)

Born at Claremore in the Cherokee Nation on August 31, 1899,
Lynn Riggs became an important figure in the American theatre.
Riggs was educated in Oklahoma schools, then wrote for newspapers in Chicago, New York City, and Los Angeles. He returned to his early home in 1920 to enroll in the University of
Oklahoma. There he wrote for the school newspaper, contributed poetry to the magazine, and traveled with the Sooner Sing-
ers on a Chatauqua tour. During the twenties Riggs published
poetry in *Poetry*, *The Nation*, and *The Bookman*. He began writing plays in 1923 in Santa Fe, New Mexico, where he had gone
for his health. During 1928 and 1929 he lived in France on a
Guggenheim fellowship. He wrote what he called his "folk play"
there, *Green Grow the Lilacs*, which was later produced as the
hit musical *Oklahoma!* and then as a popular film. Riggs' other
plays, such as *The Cherokee Night* (1933) and *Russet Mantle*
(1936), brought him critical and popular acclaim. During the
1930s Riggs worked for Hollywood studios such as Paramount,
Metro-Goldwyn-Mayer, and Universal on a series of movie
scripts. He continued to work in the stage and to write poetry
until his death. He is now recognized as one of the premier play-
wrights of the twenties and thirties. In many of his plays of this
period, both one-act and longer, Riggs used characters and settings from the Indian Territory, particularly the old Cherokee
Nation, and early Oklahoma. He was among the vanguard of
writers who sought to bring folk themes—especially American
Indian and African-American—into plays and the opera. *Knives
from Syria*, reprinted here, is a sample of his use of the folk mo-
tifs. Reference to the Verdigris River places its setting in the area

where Riggs grew up. Also reprinted is a sample of his poetry. Though he published a collection, *The Iron Dish*, in 1930 and published numerous poems thereafter, he seems at his best when he writes about specific landscapes, such as that of New Mexico in these poems.

Spring Morning—Santa Fe

The first hour was a word the color of dawn.
The second came, and gorgeous poppies stood,
Backs to a wall. The yellow sun rode on.
A mocking bird sang shrilly from a nest of wood.

The water in the acequia came down
At the stroke of nine, and watery clouds were lifting
Their velvet shadows from the little town.
Gold fired the pavement where the leaves were shifting.

At ten, black shawls of women bowed along
The Alameda. Sleepy burros lay
In the heat and lifted up their ears. A song
Wavered upon the wind and died away.

And the great bells rang out a golden tune.
Words grew in the heart and clanged, the color of noon.

1930

Santo Domingo Corn Dance

The Chorus
"Bring rain,
As we bring now
Our gift of dance and song
To You—who dance not, nor sing—
Bring rain!"

The Dancers
Bodies
Reddened, and gourds,
Rain girdles, ornaments,
The skins of foxes—what should please
You more?

Portent
But look!
Where the line whips
Like rain in corn, like clouds
Wind beaten, or like the frown
Upon His brow!

Song of the Bodies
"I am
Naked before
You, High One—look! Hear me!
As I stamp this ground worn smooth
By feet.

"Not as
A supplicant
I shake the doors of earth—
Let the green corn spring to meet
My tread!"

The Clouds
Just now
Across the line
Of these red men there swept—
Like wings of thunder at the sun—
Shadows!

The Koshari
As if
Their feet were struck
With scorn, their hands with pride—

Koshari glide, halt, grimace, grin,
And turn.

The Child Dancer
"But that
I am a child,
I should not notice the branch
Of spruce tied on his arm
In my eyes."

The Orchard
Beyond
The baking roofs,
A barren mountain points
Still higher, though its feet are white
With bloom.

Rain
One drum—
Note more, one voice,
One slant of bodies,
And my tears will fall like rain
Upon this ground.

1930

The Deer

It is a pool of shadow close and blue;
The slant ray of the sun is a golden javelin to run it through
But not to slay.

Three tan deer are nimbly at the cool
Grass nibbling. Their sides are thin,
Each liquid eye a little pool
For javelin.

1930

Knives from Syria

CHARACTERS

MRS. BUSTER, *a widow*
RHODIE, *her daughter*
CHARLEY, *the hired man*
THE SYRIAN PEDLER
Scene: *Oklahoma Farm living-room*
Time: *Present*

The scene is an Oklahoma farm living-room, about eight o'clock of an evening in October. Organ, with a stool, against the right wall. A chair, farther toward the center of the room, is before it. An old bench against the right wall in the corner. In the back wall, center, a door. To its right a window, curtained. To the left of the door, a tall food-cabinet, or "safe," with a lantern hanging from it. A door, left, goes into the bedroom. Down-stage, left, is a table, with two chairs—one at its right, one before it down-stage. On the table, an old red cloth, RHODIE'S *sewing basket and a tall lamp. On the organ, magazines, papers, a Bible, and a pistol. On the walls, cheap prints and crayon enlargments. A few rag rugs on the floor.*

When the curtain rises, MRS. BUSTER *is sitting in the chair, right. She is a gaunt, leathery-faced woman still definitely young. She wears a coarse calico dress drawn in at the waist, and coming out again over wide hips. Over her dress she wears an apron. Her daughter,* RHODIE, *is about eighteen, a creature of the soil, with the quiet power and poise of an animal. Her hair is braided in two long yellow coils like thick ropes, and brought forward in front of her shoulders, and down into her lap. She is sewing before the table, left. Her dress is a coarse print, formless and ugly. She wears flat, slatternly slippers and white stockings.*

MRS. BUSTER (*going to the window and peering out—anxiously*). They ain't a sign of him, Rhodie.

RHODIE. Well, I wisht you'd quit yer worr'in' about him, Maw. He ain't had time to git to Verdigree and back yit. Give him a little time. Ye've been fidgetin' for half a hour.

MRS. BUSTER. Well, I ain't noticed you a-doin' any fidgetin'. 'Pears to me if someone I was *more'n* interested in was out somewhere, and mebbe in danger of his life—

RHODIE (*scornfully*). Danger of his life! Charley's went to Verdigree to git his horse shod, and you expect him back afore he's hardly had time to git there! (*Slyly.*) And the only *real* danger he's in is a-gettin' mixed up with that gal in the grocery store at the Switch—

MRS. BUSTER. They's other dangers. Whut if his horse ud fall down, step in one o' them prairie dog holes? It ud throw Charley off, and mebbe break his neck. And they's hold-up men about, too. One held up a man here on Cat Crick not two weeks ago and near killed him. 'Twas old Bill Wyche hisself. I heerd him tellin' it in at Foster's grocery store Satiddy. (*She goes over and picks up the Bible from the organ.*) Rhodie, I'm a-gonna read a passage frum the Bible t'keep him safe. No tellin' whut harm it'll save him frum. (*She crosses and sits down in the other chair at the table, left. She opens the Bible and reads.*) "And he shall bring the bullock before the congregation of the Lord. And he shall lay his hands on the bullock's head, and he shall kill the bullock before the congregation of the Lord." Rhodie, whut's become of the slip of paper I had in here?

RHODIE. I put it in the back. Why?

MRS. BUSTER. It tells on it whut passage to read to stop the flow of blood. Mebbe I better read that too.

RHODIE (*amused*). But, Maw, whut if Charley ain't a-bleedin'?

MRS. BUSTER. Makes no difference. If he is, this'll stop it. "To stop the flow of blood read Ezekiel, Chapter 16, Verse 6." (*Reading.*) "And when I passed by thee, and saw thee polluted in thine own blood, I said unto thee when thou wast in thy blood, Live; yea, I said unto thee when thou was in thy blood, Live." Now.

RHODIE. Maw, don't it tell somewhere there a passage to read that'll keep Charley frum fallin' in love with that gal?

MRS. BUSTER (*severely*). Now, Rhodie, quit yer mockin'! Ye're a-makin' light of God's word. And ye're sinnin' when ye do it. And if Charley did go and git interested in that gal, it's little *you'd* care!

RHODIE. Why should I care?

MRS. BUSTER. You *ought* to! Ye're a-goin' t'marry him, ain't ye? I've always wanted that and you know it. (*Firmly.*) Ye'll *have* t'marry him, Rhodie.

RHODIE (*wearily*). I reckon so. They don't seem to be no way out of it. But, Maw, why is it ye're so anxious to have me marry him? He's fifteen years older'n me if he's a day—

MRS. BUSTER (*sharply*). Whut's age got to do with it? We've got to have a hand to run the place, Rhodie. Whut good ud us two women be without one? And we can't afford to hire one, you know that as well as me—

RHODIE. But it ain't right, it ain't fair! This marr'in' was all *yore* idee. Looks like I might have a sayso—

MRS. BUSTER. Botheration! Do you think you could do any better?

RHODIE. No, I guess not.

MRS. BUSTER. Who would ye git if ye didn't take Charley?

RHODIE (*hesitating*). Why—why, Maw, no one, I reckon.

MRS. BUSTER. Mebbe ye're a-thinkin' of Earl Baker, him that helped us last year at hayin' time.

RHODIE (*scornfully*). Him? Good fer nothin' fool! That's whut Earl Baker is. All he thinks of is playin' tricks on people.

MRS. BUSTER. Well, if it ain't Earl Baker, it might be old Bill Wyche's boy—

RHODIE. Yes, it might be—but it ain't.

MRS. BUSTER (*suspiciously*). Air ye got yer mind set on marr'in' someone else, Rhodie?

RHODIE. No, Maw. No one. And whut if I did? 'Twouldn't make no difference.

MRS. BUSTER. Ye're a-thinkin' of someone else, Rhodie. Who is it? (*With sudden penetration.*) Rhodie! You ain't thinkin' of the pedler, air ye?

RHODIE. Mebbe I am.

MRS. BUSTER (*incredulous*). That Syrian?

RHODIE (*wistfully*). Mebbe—

MRS. BUSTER. Rhodie Buster! You'd marry that foreigner, that Syrian pedler that'd beat you every day and never have no home to keep ye in?

RHODIE. Course not, Maw. I was jest a-jokin'. Only I could do it if I wanted to.

MRS. BUSTER. *Course* ye could! (*She goes over to the organ, puts the Bible back, and is fumbling among the papers.*) Whut's become of that letter he wrote ye—(*With scorn.*) a-asking ye t'marry him? I put it right here.

RHODIE. I've got it, Maw.

MRS. BUSTER. Where?

RHODIE. Here. (*She takes it out of her dress.* MRS. BUSTER *looks at her in astonishment.*)

MRS. BUSTER (*coming over*). You been wearin' it around?

RHODIE. It—it had a mighty purty *on*velope. And he writes so nice. (*Opening the letter.*) Whut was it he said about the lace cap he sent me?

MRS. BUSTER (*snatching the letter*). Never mind, I'll find it. (*Reading.*) "Put it on at once. You will look like a princess with yore golden hair. And mebbe the prince you have waited for—will come to kiss you into joy." Humph! Fine idees to put in yer head! (*Examining letter.*) He was to be in Claremore on the 9th or 10th and come on out. *This* is the 10th, ain't it, Rhodie? He'll have to be showin' up right away. (*She goes toward the organ.*) I remember the first time we ever seen him—this pedler. It was three years ago, jest after Paw died. Uncle Tom was here—he had that widder from Spiro here to see us. We set out there at the end of the house when he come up. He was twirlin' his mustache, awful smart-alec, and he starts talkin' a blue streak, tellin' jokes, and actin' up.

RHODIE. Yes, and we near died laughin'. After he left we talked about him fer weeks. He kinda livened things up, didn't he?

MRS. BUSTER (*sharply*). Yes. But it's one thing to have him make ye forget yer troubles, and it's another t'marry him. (*She sits down in the chair, right.*) Besides, he's a foreigner who goes traipsin' all over the world.

RHODIE. I know. But it must be nice to travel and see foreign lands.

MRS. BUSTER. Is they anything wrong with the land right here?

RHODIE. It's all right. But it's always the same—always the same. (*With surprising fire.*) I git tired of it. I ain't old, Maw, I'm young. And I ain't never knowed anything but jest right here—

MRS. BUSTER. Well, it's good enough fer you, I reckon, or fer anybody. And besides, if you ain't railly promised to Charley, he kinda understands that you'll marry him come Christmas. Don't this—this Syrian pedler know about Charley?

RHODIE (*wearily*). Yes, he knows. I told him last summer when he was here.

MRS. BUSTER. Then he knows Charley's yore choice?

RHODIE. He knows—I told him I was supposed to marry someone else—

MRS. BUSTER (*with finality*). Well, then—that's settled. (*She goes again to the window. RHODIE, seeing her mother's back is turned, crosses over, secures the letter from the organ, and hides it again in her dress.*)

RHODIE (*turning suddenly*). Whut's that?

MRS. BUSTER (*looking out the window*). It's Charley! Why, his horse is a-runnin'! (*She is alarmed.*) Whut do you suppose has happened? Mebbe his horse is runnin' way? Mebbe he's hurt. No, he's jumpin' off. He ain't hurt, then. He's runnin' in—sumpin's happened to him!

(*There is a great clatter of hoofs, footsteps, then the door is flung open by* CHARLEY, *a tall overalled man about 33, with the red face and hands of the farm laborer. He closes the door hurriedly. He is hatless. His breath comes in short gasps. He sinks into the chair at right of table.*)

CHARLEY. Mrs. Buster! Someone's after me. (MRS. BUSTER *moves nearer, agitated by his fright.*) I was crossin' the hayfield. It was black as pitch. Shorty kept snortin' and wanted to run. And right by that big stack, you know the one, close to the crick, a man jumped out and tried to grab the bridle! Shorty started runnin'! He run all the way home!

MRS. BUSTER. Who was it? Didn't you see? Couldn't ye git a look at him?

CHARLEY. No, it was too dark. But he had a bandanna tied over his mouth. It wasn't white, it was some dark color—red or blue. And while his one hand was grabbin' at the bridle the other one grazed my hand. Look! (*He shows a long bleeding scratch on his hand.*) He had a knife! He woulda killed me!

MRS. BUSTER. Charley! You're hurt!

CHARLEY. Aw, I ain't hurt none. It's jest a scratch. But he'd a-killed me shore, if it hadn't a-been for Shorty. (RHODIE *sits down again, right.* CHARLEY *begins to be a little ashamed of his fright.*) I ain't a-feard of him. I'd meet him anywheres in a fair fight. (*With determination.*) I'm goin' back. I'll show him. (*He is half-way to the door.*)

MRS. BUSTER (*stopping him*). Charley! Charley! You musn't! I'm a-feard fer ye.

CHARLEY (*slowly*). You're a-feard fer me?

MRS. BUSTER. Yes. Promise you won't go back.

CHARLEY. I ain't a-feared of him!

MRS. BUSTER. No. I know ye're not. (*Pleading.*) Ye're not.

CHARLEY. But I'll have to go out again, anyways. I'll have to feed Shorty. I ain't fed him yit. I'd *better* feed him, I reckon. (*He goes to the door and turns.* MRS. BUSTER, *very worried, goes left, back of the table.*) Now don't git worried about it, Mrs. Buster. (*He looks at* RHODIE, *who is re-reading her letter.*) Rhodie ain't. They ain't no harm done. (*Coming down a little.*) You ain't a-feard fer me to leave fer a minute or two, air ye?

MRS. BUSTER. I ain't a-feard to stay here, Charley. But I don't like the idee of yore goin' to the barn. It's a long ways off—

CHARLEY. But I got to feed Shorty, Mrs. Buster. I won't be long.

MRS. BUSTER. Well, then you better take the lantern. (*She goes over toward the cabinet, on which a lantern is hanging.*)

CHARLEY. I better *not* have the lantern, I reckon. But I better have my gun. (*He crosses to the organ and secures a pistol, comes back and is about to open the door.*)

MRS. BUSTER (*coming to him—anxiously*). Ye'll be keerful, won't you, Charley?

CHARLEY (*patting her shoulder*). Yes, I'll be keerful—Martha.

(*He goes out.*)

MRS. BUSTER (MRS. BUSTER'S *tired brown face takes on a new look. She stands a moment without speaking. Then she clasps her hands and moves nervously to the window*). Who could it a-been? Whut if I hadn't a-read the Bible, Rhodie? Now ye see, fer all yer scoffin'. (*She comes down and sits in the chair, right of table.*) O, I hope he won't be gone long! (*She is very nervous and excited still.*)

RHODIE. I wouldn't worry so much, Maw.

MRS. BUSTER. No, *you* wouldn't. He could be killed and butchered up, and you wouldn't be worried.

RHODIE. It don't help him none.

MRS. BUSTER. You ain't human, Rhodie.

RHODIE. I'm human, Maw—but *I* ain't in love with Charley.

MRS. BUSTER. You'd do well to be. If you was, mebbe you'd not only be anxious about him. Mebbe you'd be like folks that have throwed away everything for the sake of someone they loved.

RHODIE (*wonderingly*). Would it be human to do that?

MRS. BUSTER. Love ain't human. It's unhuman. It's a terrible cruel thing.

RHODIE. And whut if someone stands in the way of it?

MRS. BUSTER (*afraid to say more, in her indecision*). Oh, don't ask me! It's hard—hard to know whut to do. It's hard to choose. Who could it a-been tried to git him? He ain't got no enemies—

RHODIE. It coulda been the same one that tried to git him last night—

MRS. BUSTER. Last night!

RHODIE. Yes, at the crossin' a mile up the road.

MRS. BUSTER. Rhodie! At the crossin? Someone tried to git him last night? Why didn't I know?

RHODIE. *You* was *not* to know. Charley told me this mornin'.

MRS. BUSTER. He told you?

RHODIE. Yes.

MRS. BUSTER. Why didn't he want me to know?

RHODIE. He was afeard of havin' you worried about him.

MRS. BUSTER. Why should he keer if I was worried?

RHODIE. I don't know.

MRS. BUSTER (*is silent and thoughtful a moment. Then she goes restlessly to the window and looks out*). Oh, I wish he'd hurry! I wish he'd hurry! (*Turning—thoughtfully.*) Whut if this man followed Charley on home? he must be someone with a grudge agin him. He could be hidin' in the barn while Charley come in here. And Charley's gone out there! He's out there now—and this man is mebbe hid there a-waitin' fer him—a-waitin' so he can—Oh, mebbe this minute he's a—(*There is a noise outside.* MRS. BUSTER *and* RHODIE *are frozen into silence. Then* MRS. BUSTER *rushes to the door.*) Oh, he's back! He's back! (*She stops and turns, doubt on her face.*) No. He ain't had time. Whut if it wouldn't be Charley? Whut if it ud be—him! (*There is a knock.* RHODIE *rises. Then another knock—more imperious.* MRS. BUSTER *and* RHODIE *dare not move. The latch is lifted. The women shrink back in terror. The door is flung open. On the threshold stands a short dark man dressed in an ordinary dark suit. He has a black mustache. Around his neck is a red bandanna. In one hand he holds a heavy grip. It is the Syrian* PEDLER.)

PEDLER (*with a slight accent*). Good evening to you, ladies! (*He bows elaborately, smiles, steps into the room and closes the door.*)

MRS. BUSTER. You! Whut are *you* doin'—

PEDLER. Yes, *I*, at your service. You weren't expecting me?

RHODIE. Why—no, we—well, we thought—

PEDLER (*he seems a little puzzled by his reception.* RHODIE *and* MRS. BUSTER *exchange glances.* MRS. BUSTER *is terror-stricken.* RHODIE *is puzzled and uncertain*). You thought I would not come after—after supper, I guess. (*He sets his suitcase down about center stage, just right of the chair at table.*)

MRS. BUSTER (*excitedly*). Which way did ye come frum? I didn't hear no buggy drive up.

PEDLER. Oh, I walked. It is so little! It is three miles only. They was no buggy to be had. How have you been, Mrs. Buster? You're looking fine, very fine.

MRS. BUSTER. I been fair, I reckon. We—we got your letter. (RHODIE *attempts to silence her. Wait! her eyes ask. But* MRS. BUSTER *goes on,*

nervously.) We got it. And we don't think—we cain't have—(*firmly.*)
Rhodie cain't marry you. (RHODIE *sinks into her chair.*)

PEDLER (*in a low voice*). That is what you think? That is final, Mrs.
Buster?

MRS. BUSTER. Of course it's final! And the sooner ye give up the idee,
the better fer ye.

PEDLER (*to* RHODIE, *appealingly—with dignity*). And you—is this
your answer, too—Rhodie?

RHODIE (*her head droops. She is about to remonstrate. But* MRS.
BUSTER'S *eyes are on her. She cannot ignore their command*). Yes, it's
my answer.

PEDLER (*is about to argue the question, but thinks better of it. He
throws up his hands in a gesture of submission*). All right! (*He says this
jovially, and dropping on his knees, opens one of the bags.*) We won't let
it spoil things, our evening. Let me show you what I've got. (*He begins
taking things out of the case.*)

MRS. BUSTER (*to* RHODIE*).* See! The handkerchief! It's him—he's the
one!

RHODIE. He ain't seen Charley. Be still!

PEDLER (*as he takes them out of the case*). Syrian table cloths, drawn
work from the little villages of Mexico, Dutch caps, beads from the shops
of Paris, Italian colognes. See here, a jacket of many colors from the land
of Egypt. Try it on, Mrs. Buster. (*He throws it over her shoulders. She
draws back. But he goes on.*) Ah, divine! You will keep it? How much
better you look in it than Mrs. Richards at Claremore—you know her,
the doctor's wife. She bought a coat just like it. (*The* PEDLER *goes back
to his suitcase, kneels and takes out a lacquered box.*) Japanese lacquered
box from the cities of the Chong-Chong. Slant-eyed women patting
around in lovely silks. Their hearts are on the sea, I think, with their
lovers. Their jewels are here—in the box. (*He opens the box.*) Rubies,
garnets, old gold, old silver rings. (*He goes over, hands* MRS. BUSTER *a
handful. She handles them gingerly. They glitter in the light. The*
PEDLER *laughs and goes back to the suitcase.*)

MRS. BUSTER (*crossing to him*). I don't want these! I don't want none
of these things! (*She throws the rings and the coat back into the suitcase.
The* PEDLER *has turned over a rose-colored tablecloth.* MRS. BUSTER
starts at what she sees underneath. Pointing—*) Whut's them! Whut's
them things?

PEDLER (*taking them out one by one*). Knives! Knives from Syria! Pearl-handled, 10 inches long. Blades of the very fine steel. Made to cut a hair—or a throat. (MRS. BUSTER *steps back in alarm.*) In my country the robbers carry them in their belts. (*He rises.*) Many a throat is cut, many a good woman widowed by blades like these! They are so *very* sharp. See! (*He runs a hand along a blade, and laughs sardonically, enjoying his histrionism.*) And not only the bandits find them of use, Mrs. Buster. (*Darkly.*) The husband who does not trust his wife, the son mistreated by his father, the lover crossed in his love—When there's two men who want the same girl, Mrs. Buster, it is knives they use to see who gets her—

MRS. BUSTER. You mean—?

PEDLER. Oh, it is so very simple. One kills the other—

MRS. BUSTER. Oh! You'd kill—?

PEDLER. We think not so much about it. One dies anyway—one has to.

MRS. BUSTER. It's murder! You'd do this—You?

PEDLER. I am a Syrian. (*Laughs.*) But here! (*He picks it up.*) This fine rose-colored tablecloth—matchless linen it is. It is for you. For you I got it special in my home land. (*He puts it into her hands. She has shrunk back farther and farther, and is now back of* RHODIE'S *chair.*) Put it on your table. Then though the fare be not so much, and the purse low, the eye will be brighter and the heart lighter for its beauty. (*Change of tone—softly.*) But I have give you nothing, Rhodie. What will you have? Jewels? Linens? An embroidered scarf? Or a bright handkerchief from Slovakia? (*He is back at the suitcase now.*)

RHODIE (*rising*). It don't matter. (*She comes over, and kneels, right of* PEDLER.) Do you really sell things like these?

PEDLER. Oh, yes! People like them. They are beautiful, they are lovely things.

RHODIE. But it must be hard going from farm to farm—

PEDLER. It is hard—(*softly.*) and lonesome, a little. But the people who love beautiful things are very kind. And there is always the sky, and the rich brown earth, and waters flowing, and sunlight everywhere. Always I stop my horse on a high hill that looks into the fertile valley, and I say: "I go now into a new world. And if there is hunger there, and tongues that are mean, and bad dogs—I will come out again soon. It cannot be forever. And there are always more and more hills, and I am free to go to them—whenever I choose!"

RHODIE (*standing up—breathless*). It ud be beautiful!

PEDLER (*softly*). If only you could share it with me—

RHODIE (*she goes over and sinks into the chair in front of the table hopelessly*). If I could!

MRS. BUSTER (*coming down to the* PEDLER—*with decision*). She can. Mebbe it's best. (*She turns, buries her face in her apron.*)

PEDLER. Mrs. Buster! You will let her? She will go with me? (*Angrily.*) You are fooling me?

MRS. BUSTER. No! No!

PEDLER. You mean it?

MRS. BUSTER. Yes—

PEDLER. She will marry me?

MRS. BUSTER (*desperately*). Oh, yes!

PEDLER. You have changed your mind. It is lucky—lucky for me. But you will change again. To-morrow you will say no—

MRS. BUSTER. Oh, I tell you—I'll let her go. She'll go with you.

PEDLER. You say so now. But to-morrow—Oh, if only I could be sure you mean it. Ah! You will swear? You will swear she can go, and then I believe you.

MRS. BUSTER. I tell you she can go.

PEDLER (*persisting*). You will swear—on the Bible! Where is your Bible? Give me the Bible!

MRS. BUSTER (*she gets the Bible, reluctantly, from the organ, and hands it to him.*) Here.

PEDLER. Say it after me: I swear that Rhodie will marry you to-morrow.

MRS. BUSTER. I—I cain't do that. It ain't necessary. I told you I'd changed my mind.

PEDLER. And you will change again. No, Mrs. Buster, you'll have to swear it.

MRS. BUSTER. Ye're makin' me do this. Ye're makin' me. I didn't mean—

PEDLER. Swear, Mrs. Buster.

MRS. BUSTER (*after a frightened glance at* RHODIE, *she puts her hand on the Bible. She is trembling*). I swear that Rhodie will marry you—to-morrow. (*She bursts into tears.*)

PEDLER (*softening*). There, there, Mrs. Buster. I didn't mean to be hard. I only wanted to be sure of her. (*He is about to touch her.*)

MRS. BUSTER (*turning on him*). Oh, she'll go with you. I've swore it. You won't harm no one—*now,* will you?

PEDLER (*genuinely puzzled.*) Why, I wouldn't harm you—or anyone.

MRS. BUSTER. Oh, please! Please go now!

PEDLER (*crossing to* RHODIE. *She rises*). Mebbe I better leave now. I better go. She's upset. I'll be back for you to-morrow—with the preacher. You are sorry, no?

RHODIE. No, I am glad. (*The* PEDLER *takes her hands tenderly*.) I am. Honest!

PEDLER. Well then, good-by. I'll leave the things here until to-morrow. Good-by, then. (*He goes toward the door—softly*.) To-morrow! (*He goes out.* RHODIE *goes toward the door*.)

MRS. BUSTER (*rushing to* RHODIE). He'll come back to-morrow! Oh, whut'll we do then? He made me swear you'd go with him. He *made* me, I tell you! I didn't mean to. It was *him!* He would a-killed Charley; he would a-killed us all. I knowed he was the one when I seen the hankerchief, and then the knives. Oh, I *had* to tell him you'd go!

RHODIE (*shaking her off*). He didn't do it! He didn't do it! And whut if he did?

MRS. BUSTER. But we'll find a way; they must be a way out of it—

RHODIE (*scornfully*). You swore I'd go, didn't you?

MRS. BUSTER. Yes, but they must be a way!—he *made* me swear. I had to! It was to git rid of him I done it.

RHODIE (*sure of herself at last*). You swore—and on the Bible that kept Charley safe. An you cain't go back on that, can you? I'll go then. Don't worry, Maw. Charley's safe, you're safe—you won't be killed.

MRS. BUSTER (*turning away*). You've turned agin me now. I knowed you would. I always knowed you would. But mebbe I won't need help from you—Mebbe—What air we goin' to tell Charley?

RHODIE. I? Tell him what you want to. He won't keer—he'll be glad. (*With fine scorn*.) He'll think whut *you* think—as he always does. I leave him to you.

MRS. BUSTER. You—leave him to me? (*There is a noise outside, and* CHARLEY *bursts into the room. He is dishevelled and excited*.)

CHARLEY (*dramatically*). I got him!

MRS. BUSTER. You got him?

RHODIE. Charley!

MRS. BUSTER. Whut do you mean?

CHARLEY. He won't try a trick like that again!

MRS. BUSTER. You didn't—

CHARLEY (*bragging*). Yes, I did.

RHODIE (*she rushes to him, shakes him frantically*). Charley! Whut have you done? It wasn't him! It wasn't him!

CHARLEY (*shaking her off*). It was *him* all right. Whut's the matter with you?

RHODIE. Oh! Whut've you done! (*Starting toward the door.*) Where is he? Tell me—

MRS. BUSTER. Whut's happened, Charley?

CHARLEY. Well, I went down to the barn and purty soon I heerd a noise a little ways down the crick. I slipped easy-like down there, and who do you suppose I saw?

MRS. BUSTER. Who?

CHARLEY. Earl Baker and that worthless cousin of his! (RHODIE *stops, relieved. She comes down, weakly, and sinks into the chair right of table.*) They was sittin' down by the old spring a-laughin' at the joke Earl played on me. It was Earl tried to grab my horse. He done it last night, too, the same way. When I seen 'em there a-laughin' I jumped out and lit in on him. I licked him good. He won't do sich a trick again. His cousin run away or I'd a-licked him too! (*He looks triumphantly from one to the other.*)

MRS. BUSTER. You licked him—you licked him, Charley? It was him—it was Earl Baker tried to hold you up?

CHARLEY. Yes, it was him.

MRS. BUSTER. Ye're shore?

CHARLEY. 'Course I'm shore! I heerd him sayin' so, I tell you. They ain't no doubt of it.

MRS. BUSTER. Oh! And I thought all the time—

CHARLEY. Whut did you think, Martha? Did you think someone else done it?

MRS. BUSTER. Yes.

CHARLEY. Who?

MRS. BUSTER. It don't matter now. I'm glad it's turned out this way. (*Going to him.*) Oh, Charley, I *am* glad! Only—Rhodie'll hate me now.

RHODIE. Hate you?

MRS. BUSTER. You'll never forgive me fer it—

RHODIE (*picking up her sewing basket from the table*). I won't even think of you. (*She goes toward the bedroom door, left, and turns.*) I won't even remember you and Charley a-slavin' here together. (*Slowly, softly.*) I'll be on the hills *he* told me about. I'll be with *him!* We won't never come back!

CURTAIN

1925   1927

Muriel Hazel Wright

CHOCTAW

(1889–1975)

Honored in later life as an eminent historian and editor, Muriel Hazel Wright was born at Lehigh, Choctaw Nation, into a well-known Choctaw family. Educated in Choctaw Nation schools and at Wheaton College and East Central (Oklahoma) State Normal School, she began her career as a teacher, teaching from 1912 to 1924 with a year off for graduate studies at Columbia University. From 1922 to 1928 she served as secretary of the business committee of the Choctaw Nation, then as researcher in the history of the Five Civilized Tribes for the Oklahoma Historical Society from 1929 to 1931. From 1934 to 1944 she was secretary of the Choctaw Advisory Council. In 1943 she became associate editor of *The Chronicles of Oklahoma*, the scholarly journal of the Oklahoma Historical Society, and assumed the editorship in 1955, serving in that capacity until she retired in 1973. Throughout her career she wrote extensively. Her first major works were *Oklahoma: A History of the State and Its People*, a four-volume collaboration with Joseph B. Thoburn, and *The Story of Oklahoma*, a school textbook, both published in 1929. These works were instrumental in ensuring that school studies of Oklahoma history included the study of Indian history. There followed five major works, including *A Guide to the Indian Tribes of Oklahoma* (1951), still a standard work, and dozens of historical articles. In 1971 the North American Indian Women's Association named her the outstanding Indian woman of this century. Though known primarily for her scholarly works in history, Wright also wrote popular pieces. Reprinted here are two of the latter that heretofore have not been easily accessible, dealing with the ancient and the more recent history of the Choctaws.

Legend of Nanih Wayah

The panther screamed twice this night. Once down the river from afar, came a discordant snarl that rose to the scream of a frightened woman. Unmoved by the wild cry, the Dreamer of the Chahta listened tensely in the darkness by the river. He knew the panther traveled fast. Heavy silence for many minutes forewarned some strange happening. Suddenly, a second scream tore through the night, this time coming from the mountainside a long way up the river. The Dreamer's heart leaped.

"Ah, again! For certain, it is the Big One. My hunt ends at daylight." He almost sang the words, a courage song carrying an ending note of triumph.

This was the third time in the past fortnight the panther had screamed twice in a night—something unusual in one season. During the two weeks, the Dreamer had plotted his hunting, searching out all trails of the mighty beast through the underbrush and the forest, and around the crags of the mountain, even down to the river's edge.

The Dreamer of the Chahta was held in disregard by his people. "The youth only dreams," they said among themselves. "Will he ever become a great warrior?"

But they never taunted him openly, uncertain in their estimate of him, perhaps. It was not necessary for them to tell him their thoughts, and he asked no questions. Sensitive by nature, an inheritance that marked the members of his clan, he reasoned things out for himself. He learned by observation. He also acquired a knowledge of the woods and streams and of birds and animals that no other Chahta youth had. In fact, it was his appearance, rather than any lack of character, which kept him from sharing the first love of every Chahta youth—that prowess in the ball play. The Dreamer was frail looking, tall and thin, almost to gauntness; his hands and feet were slender and graceful.

For a time after the panther's second scream, the Dreamer sat listening. Finally, since it was some hours before the darkest part of night, he left the river bank and traveled several miles through the forest, on up the mountain to a crag around which the panther's beaten trail led to the river. Selecting a spot that he knew commanded a view of the mountainside, he hid by some high rocks just off the trail, knowing the mighty beast would come along early in the morning after slaking its thirst before going to its lair to sleep through the day.

While the youth waited, he visioned a beautiful mantle from the coat of the panther. Once only, he had glimpsed the animal in the sunlight when, disturbed in its lair, it had moved back into the brush out of sight. In that fleeting moment, the tawny color of its back shone like burnished gold; the grayish tinge of its sides, like silver.

In the dusk of the early day, the young hunter was more alert. He kept a close watch for the slightest movement on the mountainside in the growing light of morning. A rustle in the foliage of a tree by the trail below attracted his attention. His eyes remained riveted on the spot. Gradually, a crouched form was outlined on a large limb marking the edge of a glade in the woods. The panther was waiting, too. In the glance that revealed the crouching animal, the hunter's eye caught another movement beyond the glade. A clump of bushes parted and another form crept out into the grass toward the edge of the glade. The form stopped and half arose, revealing itself—a powerful figure! The son of Talking Warrior!

The Dreamer's blood surged hot, but cool reason served him well. He overcame the word upon his lips that would have broken the silence. Hidden by the rocks on the mountain, he quickly shifted to a better position, at the same time placing an arrow in his bow. Having crept on, Talking Warrior's son was now nearing the tree, unaware of the danger ahead. Steadily, the Dreamer braced one end of the bow between two of his toes and drew back the bowstring—

Twang!

With the arrow through its body, the panther clawed the limb beneath. Suddenly, with a frenzied roar, the huge beast sprang toward the Warrior's son, missed his charge and landed on all four feet. Talking Warrior's son, in the instant of warning, had leaped a few steps backward. Ears flat, open mouth snarling and tail lashing in fury, the panther stood gathering strength for the supreme effort of its life,—all at once, went limp and fell full length upon the ground. The Dreamer's first great kill!

The young hunter came down the trail and stood contemplating the motionless panther. Talking Warrior's son looked from one to the other.

Consternation and chagrin mingled in the expression on his face. He had been caught doubly unaware and his resentment doubly flared.

"You bone picker!" he raged. "You steal a prize that rightfully belongs to me—sometime the greatest warrior of the Chahta."

The Dreamer made no reply. He was intent on the beautiful animal stretched at his feet. The other youth divined his thoughts.

"It is well that you admire your kill now," the latter said contemptuously. "Ere the moon passes you will have to adorn the grave of your bone-picker ancestor with the panther's skin to keep the charm. All the good it will do you is lying there.

"Bone picker!" Talking Warrior's son spat out the words. Turning away, he stalked into the forest.

"Bone picker!" The words sank deep in the sensitive soul of the Dreamer. He stooped and felt each one of the panther's feet in turn,—big balls of fur with hidden claws. He lifted the head and looked closely at the massive jaws. He was scarcely able to accomplish his work that day. When at last he spread the panther's skin before him, he marveled at its beauty.

But the Dreamer's heart was heavy. Wearily, he threw himself on the grass. Yet his thoughts gave him no peace. He recalled the contempt and the cold aloofness with which the other Chahta youths had treated him on more than one occasion. Tomorrow he would visit Prophet Chief, the wise old legend keeper of the Chahta. Prophet Chief would be patient with any question and help solve the problem.

The next morning, he found Prophet Chief sitting in the shade of a red elm, scraping and polishing seasoned wood for a bow.

"Do not fret because the Nahullo (One who causes fear)[1] would call us 'bone pickers,' " said Prophet Chief. "Na Foni Aiowah—the Nahullo does not understand, also many of the Chahta who have forgotten the old ways. The thoughts of the ancient Chahta were good.

"Na Foni Aiowah—bone gatherers. They were acquainted with knowledge. Wisely, they gathered up the sacred bones of the dead after the body lying upon its bier—a high scaffold—had been purified by air and wind. Then they washed the bones clean and buried them in the shadow of Nanih Wayah."

Prophet Chief scraped the seasoned wood for his bow with a sharp piece of flint. After a while he stopped and resumed his story.

---

1. Nahullo means "white man" in the Chahta (Choctaw) language [Wright's note].

"The ancient Chahta said that the earth was first a vast plain or quag-mire destitute of hills. One time a Superior Being, a Great Red Man, came down from his home in the sky and began to build up a mound which finally rose as high as a mountain in the center of the wide plain. When the mountain was completed, the Great Red Man called forth the Red People from its midst. After the multitude had come forth, he stamped his feet and these people who were just emerging from the mountain into the light of day perished.

"Turning to the Red People who rested in the sunshine, awaiting his command, the Great Red Man delivered a long speech in which he called the mountain 'Nanih Wayah.' During the course of his address, he proclaimed the laws and instructed the people how to live. He also told them they would live forever, but they asked him to repeat this remark, since they had not listened closely to his words. Provoked by their inattentiveness, he at once withdrew his grant of immortality and replied instead, that they should henceforth be subject to death. Then the Red People came down into the plain and dwelt around Nanih Wayah."

Prophet Chief smoothed one side of the seasoned wood with red and yellow sandstone. Presently, he began another story:

"Chahta and Chickasha were two brothers. One day they set forth with all their people from a land in the west—hvshi aiokatulla (the place where the sun falls into the water).[2] They traveled toward the rising sun, in search of a new country in which to live.

"They came to a muddy, slimy river and camped there. The next stop was on the banks of a bloody red stream. They remained by this river and lived on fish for two years. But the springs were low in that region so they followed down the course of the river.

"They heard a noise like thunder. They searched to find whence the noise came. At first they saw a red smoke, then a mountain which thundered. They heard music coming from the mountain. On top of the mountain, they found a whirling pole from which came the music. How could they stop the pole?

"Finally, Chahta took a motherless child and swung it against the pole. The whirling stopped. The child perished. The great Chahta called the pole 'fabussa' and gave it to Isht Ahullo, the wise leader and prophet.

"The Isht Ahullo tied his medicine bag to one end of the pole and

2. The Chahta (Choctaws) still refer to the west as hvshi aiokatulla, "the place where the sun falls into the water" [Wright's note].

planted the other end in the ground, telling the people the 'fabussa' was magic and the standard around which they should pitch their camps at evening. Morning after morning, the pole leaned toward the east, so Isht Ahullo called his followers to arise and march forward again and again.

"The journey continued many years over high mountains, great deserts and wide plains and through deep forests. Enemy tribes they encountered along the way but were overcome by strategy in warfare. Chahta with his men acting as advance guards made a charge. Then the people followed making attacks on the right and on the left, so the enemy was soon in retreat.

"During this time, some of the Isht Ahullos, other than their leader, admonished the people to be strict in observing their ancient customs, especially the sacred duty of caring for the dead. It was thought a sacrilege to leave the remains of those who died along the way to be desecrated by wild beasts in the wilderness. Surely, on account of such treatment at the hands of their children, the grieving spirits of the departed would hover around and bring sorrow to the whole tribe. For that reason, whenever a person died, his bones were carefully preserved, certain ones among the Isht Ahullos having been selected by the wise leader to be Na Foni Aiowah—bone gatherers. Those who were to fill this office were chosen because they were intelligent, trustworthy and had open countenances. Many of them were fine looking and had graceful hands and feet. The wise Isht Ahullo said their descendants through the years to come would also be like them in observing the sacred duties and remembering the lore to the honor of the nation."

Prophet Chief sat for a time, making smooth the other side of the wood for his bow. Then he continued his story.

"When they had traveled many years, however, the people who now called themselves Chahta after the great Chahta himself, began to murmur because the Isht Ahullos continued to advise such rigid respect for the dead. So many Chahta had died that their bones had become a burden.

"Just as they were approaching the banks of a wide river, the Mississippi, they encountered a tribe whose warriors were large and fierce. The Chahta shot over white arrows, the sign of peace. The enemy painted the arrows red and shot them back, a challenge of war. In the battle that followed, the Chahta were held at bay by the side of the mighty stream.

"In a council of war that night, the wise Isht Ahullo called for suggestions in defeating the enemy. The Na Foni Aiowah consulted together.

Then their spokesman suggested before the council that stones be cast into the water to bridge the river; that mice be caught and, at the right moment, turned loose among the enemy warriors to gnaw their bowstrings and render them helpless in battle. This suggestion was carried out. The following day, the Chahta marched forward victorious and crossed the mighty river.

"One morning, after crossing to the east side of the Mississippi, the wise Isht Ahullo, who had been the leader during the migration, pointed to the sacred pole standing straight in the midst of the encampment. Surely, this was a sign the Chahta should end their wandering. Having arrived in a fertile country where there were running streams, great forests and little prairies, all teeming with game, the people were delighted to make their homes there.

"Soon after the Chahta had arrived in the new country, the Mi^{n}ko, or Great Chief, ordered the bones of all those who had died during the long journey to be placed together in one spot and covered with moss and bark. To make the pile more secure, men and women worked for many days carrying earth in baskets to cover it until at last a huge mound had been erected.

"Then a great ceremony was held on top of the mound. The sacred emblem of the sun which had been carried from the Far West by the wise Isht Ahullo was set up and the Mi^{n}ko proclaimed the laws to the people, all of whom had gathered for the occasion. During the celebration, the mound was named Nanih Wayah,[3] calling to mind the mountain where the Red People were said first to have seen the light of day. Finally a feast was held at which the Chahta sang these words:

" 'Behold the wonderful work of our hands and let us be glad. Look upon the great mound; its top is above the trees and its black shadow lies on the ground a bowshot. It is surmounted by the golden emblem of the sun; its glitter dazzles the eyes of the multitude. It inhumes the bones of fathers and relatives; they died on our sojourn in the wilderness. They died in a far off wild country; they rest at Nanih Wayah. Our journey lasted many winters; it ends at Nanih Wayah.'

"Thus, the mound became hallowed ground, a place where the cherished bones of our ancestors had been cared for and the people had renewed the life of their nation.

---

3. The remains of Nanih Wayah, the sacred mound of the Chahta, may still be found in Winston County, Mississippi. The name Nanih Wayah means "Mountain that brings forth fruit" or "Fruitful Mountain," also, "Productive Mountain" [Wright's note].

"So, is it strange, oh Chahta youth, that the devoted warriors of our people through the ages have spoken of Nanih Wayah as 'Inholitopa Ishki' (Beloved Mother)? That, in token of their devotion, they often ascend the mound to place on its summit votive offerings—prizes taken in hunting and war?"

Prophet Chief selected a strong length of sinew and fastened it at one end of the seasoned wood which he had polished all day. He made a loop in the other end of the sinew for a bowstring.

"Omeh! Give ear! Oh, Chahta youth," the old man looked straight at the Dreamer. "I behold the fine light in your eyes. I see your graceful hands and feet. I wonder at your intelligence and your ability to attain knowledge. Yet all these attributes are natural, they are yours by inheritance. No one can take them away. The Na Foni Aiowah, our ancestors, held sacred their duties in memory of the dead, preserved the history and the lore of the nation. Remember well, oh youth! You also keep this trust!"

Prophet Chief's work was finished. How gracefully the seasoned wood had sprung in the bow! What power lay within the bowstring!

The Dreamer had arisen. A new strength seemed to have braced his slender figure. A look of joy was on his face.

"Chahta sia hoke! I am a Chahta!" he said proudly.

The next morning when the sun rose on the summit of Nanih Wayah, there lay the beautiful coat of the panther.

Undated

A Chieftain's "Farewell Letter" to the American People

With the signing of the Treaty at Dancing Rabbit Creek, September 27, 1830, the Choctaws gave up the last acre of their land in the state of Mississippi. Ten years previously, they had been induced to trade a part of their Mississippi lands for the country lying between the Canadian and Red rivers, west of Arkansas.

By the new treaty, they were to move to this region, the sixteenth article of the treaty providing that the United States government, at its own expense, should remove the some 20,000 members of the nation "in wagons; and with steamboats as may be found necessary." Within two days after the signing of the treaty, special government agents were being appointed in preparation to carry out these provisions.

Two weeks later, Colonel Greenwood LeFlore, a chief of the Choctaws, appointed certain leaders of his people to go without delay on an exploring expedition to the western country to reconnoiter and to select sites for settlement.

One of the members of this party was Colonel LeFlore's nephew, George W. Harkins, an educated young Choctaw, who upon his return from the expedition found that he had been appointed chief, as successor to his uncle, Colonel LeFlore. From this time the young man was prominent among his people, and was later elected district chief, in the Choctaw Nation, west. . . .

Colonel Greenwood LeFlore never came west to live, but remained in Mississippi where he was an influential citizen, being successfully elected to the House of Representatives and the Senate from that state.

When the news that the treaty for removal had been actually signed and approved consternation reigned among the Choctaws, the great mass of whom were against removal. "The very mainspring of their exertions" seemed to be cut off, and their hearts were filled with sullen despair. They felt they owned their beloved country, and could not believe they would be forced to leave their old homes. Here their ancestors had been buried in the centuries past; here was Nunih Waiya, the sacred mound, from whence the Choctaws had first come to see the light of day, according to the ancient tribal legend.

Though it was hoped that every member of the nation would go to the western country, provisions had also been made in the Treaty at Dancing Rabbit Creek, to grant any individual Choctaw, who wished to sever relations with the tribe could remain in Mississippi, and his allotment of land subject to the laws of the state.

Some of the members remained to take advantage of this offer in Mississippi, but with the passing of years most of them came to Oklahoma. Today, only a few hundred fullbloods remain in out-of-the-way sections of Mississippi, where, during the almost one hundred years since the treaty of 1830, they have erected, as it were, an impregnable wall against the progress of modern times. They still dance to the measured beats of the tom-tom and chant in plaintive wails, "Hinaushi pisali, Bok Chito onali, yayali," (I saw a trail to the big river and then I cried) in remembrance of the time when they bid their kinsmen farewell.

The Choctaw exploring party returned to Mississippi during the first week of December, 1830 and reported that already as many as 1,000 members of the tribe had passed them on their way westward "driving their cattle and hogs, and packing their horses with children, provisions, etc."

In the meantime, the government agents were gathering parties of Choctaws, numbering all the way from 100 to 1,000, and were concentrating them, principally, at Vicksburg, where steamboats were specially chartered to take the emigrants to Arkansas Post, situated fifty miles above the mouth and on the north bank of the Arkansas river.

Some of the parties gathered at Memphis, Helena, in Mississippi, and Point Chicot, from whence they, also, went by boat to Arkansas Post, though a few crossed the river at these points and proceeded overland to the west. From Arkansas Post, the emigrants traveled overland in wagons through Arkansas, or continued by boat to Little Rock or Fort Smith, then by wagon to their new home.

It was no small task for the government agents to move the Indians to the new country, through the sparsely settled region of Arkansas, at the time, since most of the parties were taken west during the winter months. Roads had to be cleared, bridges built, and horses and oxen and wagons hired for transportation. Thousands of pounds of salt pork and flour were purchased at Little Rock and Fort Smith and were given out as rations to the Indians as they passed on their journey.

Captain J. Brown, U. S. A., superintendent of removal and subsistence of the Indians, reported to the War Department, at Washington, in December, 1831, giving a glimpse of the responsibilities of his work. He wrote that the greater portion of the emigrants "have been sent to the Post of the Arkansas, and that, too, without any previous knowledge, or even intimation, that such would be the case. The consequence is an overland journey of three hundred and fifty miles, and in mid-winter without preparing for such a large number, and in a country where land transport is exceedingly scarce, having to send, in some instances, two hundred miles for teams, and then not obtaining more than about half the number required to move one thousand emigrants in October, will not now transport more than five hundred."

On account of the lack of transportation many of the emigrants had to walk, resulting in much suffering among the poorer Choctaws who lacked moccasins and sufficient clothing to protect them from the unprecedented rain and snow during the winters of '31 and '32. Many died from exposure and were buried along the way; hundreds of others were stricken with cholera that was raging in the United States at that time.

The leaders of the Choctaws had chosen the terms of the Treaty of Dancing Rabbit Creek as a matter of expediency, thinking it best to encourage the people to remove to the new country where the nation could have its own laws and government. Though these leaders made every effort to push matters toward this end, yet their hearts were filled with sadness at the scenes of departure from the homeland. They were aware of the hardships that lay before their people in the journey to the west and in the settlement of a wild country that was open to many enemies including the thousands of hostile Indians of the plains, of whom little was known even by the United States army officers of that time.

It was George W. Harkins who expressed the feelings of his people, when he left Mississippi in the early winter of 1832. His address was hurriedly written on board the steamship, *Huron*, and appeared in the press of the country without any revision.

"To the American People."

"It is with considerable diffidence that I attempt to address the American people, knowing and feeling sensibly my incompetency; and believing that your highly and well improved minds could not be well entertained by the address of a Choctaw. But having determined to emigrate west of the Mississippi river this fall, I have thought proper in bidding you farewell, to make a few remarks of my views and the feelings that actuate me on the subject of our removal.

"Believing that our all is at stake and knowing that you readily sympathize with the distressed of every country, I confidently throw myself on your indulgence and ask you to listen patiently. I do not arrogate to myself the prerogative of deciding upon the expediency of the late treaty, yet I feel bound as a Choctaw, to give a distinct expression of my feelings on that interesting, (and to the Choctaws) all important subject.

"We were hedged in by two evils, and we chose that which we thought least. Yet we could not recognize the right that the state of Mississippi had assumed to legislate for us. Although the legislature of the state were qualified to make laws for their own citizens, that did not qualify them to become law makers to a people who were so dissimilar in manners and customs as the Choctaws are to the Mississippians. Admitting that they understood the people, could they remove that mountain of prejudice that has ever obstructed the streams of justice, and prevented their salutary influence from reaching my devoted countrymen? We as Choctaws rather chose to suffer and be free, than live under the degrading influence of laws, where our voice could not be heard in their formation.

"Much as the state of Mississippi has wronged us, I cannot find in my heart any other sentiment than an ardent wish for her prosperity and happiness.

"I could cheerfully hope that those of another age and generation may not feel the effects of those oppressive measures that have been so illiberally dealt out to us; and that peace and happiness may be their reward. Amid the gloom and honors of the present separation, we are cheered with a hope that ere long we shall reach our destined home, and that nothing short of the basest acts of treachery will ever be able to wrest it from us, and that we may live free. Although your ancestors won freedom on the fields of danger and glory, our ancestors owned it as their birthright, and we have had to purchase it from you as the vilest slaves buy their freedom.

"Yet it is said that our present movements are our own voluntary acts—such is not the case. We found ourselves like a benighted stranger, following false guides, until he was surrounded on every side, with fire or water. The fire was certain destruction, and feeble hope was left him of escaping by water. A distant view of the opposite shore encourages the hope; to remain would be utter annihilation. Who would hesitate, or would say that his plunging into the water was his own voluntary act? Painful in the extreme is the mandate of our expulsion. We regret that it should proceed from the mouth of our professed friend, and for whom our blood was commingled with that of his bravest warriors, on the field of danger and death.

"But such is the instability of professions. The man who said that he would plant a stake and draw a line around us, that never should be passed, was the first to say he could not guard the lines, and drew up the stake and wiped out all traces of the line. I will not conceal from you my fears, that the present grounds may be removed—I have my foreboding—who of us can tell after witnessing what has already been done, what the next force may be.

"I ask you in the name of justice, for repose for myself and my injured people. Let us alone—we will not harm you, we want rest. We hope, in the name of justice, that another outrage may never be committed against us, and that we may for the future be cared for as children, and not driven about as beasts, which are benefitted by a change of posture.

"Taking an example from the American government, and knowing the happiness which its citizens enjoy, under the influence of mild republican institutions, it is the intention of our countrymen to form a government assimilated to that of our white brethren in the United States, as nearly as their condition will permit.

"We know that in order to protect the rights and secure the liberties of the people, no government approximates so nearly to perfection as the one to which we have alluded. As east of the Mississippi we have been friends, so west we will cherish the same feelings with additional fervor; and although we may be removed to the desert, still we shall look with fine regard, upon those who have promised us their protection. Let that feeling be reciprocated.

"Friends, my attachment to my native land is strong—that cord is now broken; and we must go forth as wanderers in a strange land! I must go—let me entreat you to regard us with feelings of kindness, and when the hand of oppression is stretched against us, let me hope that every part of the United States, filling the mountains and valleys, will echo and say stop, you have no power, we are the sovereign people, and our friends shall no more be disturbed. We ask you for nothing that is incompatible with your other duties.

"We go forth sorrowful, knowing that wrong has been done. Will you extend to us your sympathizing regards until all traces of disagreeable oppositions are obliterated, and we again shall have confidence in the professions of our white brethren.

"Here is the land of our progenitors, and here are their bones; they left them as a sacred deposit, and we have been compelled to venerate its trust; it is dear to us yet we cannot stay, my people are dear to me, with them I must go. Could I stay and forget them and leave them to struggle alone, unaided, unfriended, and forgotten by our great father? I should then be unworthy of the name of a Choctaw, and be a disgrace to my blood. I must go with them; my destiny is cast among the Choctaw people. If they suffer, so will I; if they prosper, then I will rejoice. Let me again ask you to regard us with feelings of kindness."

"Yours with respect,
"GEORGE W. HARKINS."

1926

Joseph Bruner

MUSCOGEE

(1872–?)

Joseph Bruner was a member of Lochapoka tribal town in the
Creek Nation, son of John and Lucy Bruner. Born at Tulsa, September 20, 1872, he attended area schools, including the Indian
Mission School at Wealaka. Later, Bruner attended Baptist Indian University, later Bacone College, at Muskogee, Creek Nation. He was elected to the Creek House of Warriors, the lower
house of the nation's council and represented his people in
Washington, D.C. He received his allotment in 1899, a hundred-
and-sixty-acre plot northwest of Sapulpa near what would later
become rich oil fields. After finishing college in 1903, he entered
the oil and gas business. In 1924, he was a Creek representative
in the Federal Court of Claims. In this period he became politically active. During the 1920s he was active in the Society of
Oklahoma Indians. In 1933, he was elected Principal Chief of
the National Indian Confederacy to garner support for his out-
spoken criticism of Commissioner of Indian Affairs John Collier
and his Indian policy and worked diligently to defeat the
Wheeler-Howard Act. This opposition finally galvanized in 1934
into a national organization, the American Indian Federation, of
which Bruner was president. Convinced that the communists
were behind Collier's policy and the New Deal, the federation
developed close ties to the German American Bund. The organization died out in the mid-1940s. Bruner was knowledgeable in
both the recent and traditional history of his people, some of the
latter of which is reprinted here.

Discovery of Tobacco

As I have mentioned, thousands of years ago the Spo-ko-kees lived as a nation in South America. Their form of government was like a monarchy. That is, they had a principal chief and many subordinate chieftains to reign over the people.

Me-chisk Emorther was the name of the great chieftain. He was powerful in a diplomatic way and was very generous and good to his people. He had a beautiful daughter, Nuchaga, which the name implies in the Indian language. Her hand was sought by every warrior of the tribe, but her father always turned a deaf ear when it came to such an invoking.

She had just reached womanhood, which constituted some 240 moons. And it was the wish of the old warriors of the tribe to see Nuchaga married to one of their promising warriors.

E-nah-Hinaha was a dashing young warrior who had always been a fearless fighter. He belonged to the Tiger clan. It was rumored by his relatives that it was time that he had a wife to help look after his aged mother and to take care of things around the tepee.

Three aged warriors went to Me-chisk Emorther and suggested E-nah-Hinaha as the best warrior for the hand of his daughter. The old chief said that it would take two days to ponder over the request. On the third day he said that E-nah-Hinaha was the logical suitor and that he had always supplied his mother with food and shelter. But to become a qualified warrior for the hand of his daughter it was necessary for him to go in quest of large game, he must go alone toward the setting sun, kill and dry meat with his own hands and be gone for four moons.

It was during springtime. E-nah-Hinaha's mother prepared him some Ehulwa (provisions) and two horses were required for the long journey. The agreement was kept a secret among all of the parties concerned, which is a custom among the Indians. The day came for E-nah to depart and the sun served as his guide reckoning.

E-nah traveled west for half a moon. He saw plenty of game. A camp was made under a sheltering rock which would protect him in all kinds of weather and from any vicious animals. He labored for two days getting his camp in shape before he was to venture forth in the search of game.

He scouted around the country and was very observing in making certain locations so as not to get lost when it came time to go forth and kill his expected game. He discovered a hive of bees and removed the honey to his camp to be taken back to Nuchaga.

The warrior next day killed a young buck deer. He skillfully slip-skinned it, removing the meat and bones out of the hide. He turned the skin wrong side out, washed it clean and tied the legs up with the sinews of the deer. Out of the deer's hide he made a bag into which he placed the honey so a bear could not steal it when he was away from camp.

Time passed. He ate wild meat and honey and sofkey. He was becoming very lonesome for his mother and his bride-to-be. During the third quarter of the fourth moon of time, he had killed a large buck and it was an arduous task to drag him to camp. After it had been dressed and he had feasted like a king, E-nah took a nap on the root of a tree.

He dreamed or saw a vision—that Nuchaga had come to his camp on the date of the full-of-the-moon and talked to him thusly: "E-nah, you and I will never be wedded. I have come all the way to tell you this and to reveal to you a great secret, that in the forest you have been hunting is the home of a great medicine. It is not only a great medicine but will afford a pleasure to our people. On your awakening you will see a bird flying around in the trees nearby. Don't lose sight of him and watch on which weed he lands, as it will be the great medicine bush promised to our people. Now I bid you goodbye forever." She gently patted him on the cheeks and vanished.

He awoke from his day dream and to his surprise saw the little bird in the tree just as Nuchaga had told him. He watched the bird fly off and followed him on and on until he lit on a great weed. All at once he disappeared in the sunlight. E-nah walked up to the weed and to his surprise it was a different kind from any that he had ever seen in his rambles. He took a few leaves back to camp with him. He watched the weed grow old and become a gold or orange color.

Next morning as he sat by his campfire he wondered what it could be good for. A few pieces of the leaves that had become dry were blown by a gust of wind into the fire. A strange smell came to his nose—an odor of burning crumbs. He wished that he might enjoy the flavor and resorted to the plan of fashioning a clay pipe. He took a joint of cane and fastened it to the pipe and put in a few dry crumbs. He lit his pipe and took a whiff or two, which had a strange effect on him—and was the first smoking of tobacco ever taken by man.

By the elapse of the fourth moon of his hunt he had gathered a great quantity of the leaves and seed from two kinds of the weed. One leaf was large and heavy, while the other was a dwarf kind which produced a great quality of flavor. The dwarf kind later proved to be the great medicine of the Creek race.

His horses were heavily laden as he started home. When he reached home it was dark and he drove directly to his mother's abode. She was very happy and notified the people of her son's arrival and of his good luck on the hunt. The next day was a rejoicing one in the camp for everyone except E-nah.

Nuchaga had died on the full of the fourth moon, just at the time she appeared to E-nah in his dream. A great council was called and the old chief related with tears in his eyes the sad incident to him, while E-nah stood with bowed head holding his hand. He was asked to tell of his great adventure, which he did not finish until late in the night. He later distributed the seed of the great medicine to the warriors and departed for his mother's camp.

He was very much grieved because of the loss of Nuchaga. He took a farewell look at his sleeping mother's face and departed. He mounted his favorite horse and rode away—thus closing the life of E-nah on earth and the discoverer of tobacco.

1927

Indian Fish Fable

An Indian learned long before anyone that a fish would bite at a worm, Cara-fa-maka, as he called the red earthworm. So he fashioned a hook out of a fish bone. How he got his first fish to get a bone is unknown to us, but he made his line thus:

He pulled several hairs out of the tail of his pony and out of the hairs he made a line, then went and by main strength with a burned stick, sharpened while burning, he dug up the worms, then he went to a cool shade of a creek and threw in his bone hook well baited. The fish raised at once, and in fact they hit so fast that he only had time to bait his hook and jerk them out and throw them over his head. His hook having no beard on it, the fish readily came loose from his hook while in the air above his head.

He sat and jerked out fish as fast as he could; in fact he mis-counted the number he had thrown over his head. When he thought he must have a couple of strings about four feet long, he stopped fishing to count and string them before proceeding to his tepee. He went upon the bank and looked all around for his fish, but found only one.

The Redman could not understand such luck; he knew he had caught a great lot of them, and to go home with only one fish did not look good to him. Having lots of bait, he decided to try another string. He stood and studied the situation. He had in his life seen flying fish, and thought maybe he had been catching flying fish all the time and maybe as they came unhooked they had flown off to some other part of the creek. So he thought he would be more careful and see where they were going. He was not long getting a bite; he gave a jerk and up came Mr. Fish. While between the earth and heaven and loose from the hook, a fish hawk swooped down and caught the fish on the fly and swallowed him right before the Redman's eyes.

He saw at once what had become of his big catch. Then it was Mr. Injun who planned to fool the fish hawk, so the next time he went fishing he made a long throw line and he caught and saved up all his catch. Since that time the Redman always uses a throw line. Moral—Don't jerk your fish too high up in the elements for fear of fish hawks.

1927

Another Indian Fable

The Redman did not at first like hog meat; he thought that the hogs were very dirty and unclean and were not good to eat. Although the Redman raised lots of hogs, but seldom ever killed one to eat. He liked his deer and other game that lived among the native woods.

A certain medicine man who had cultivated a taste for hog meat was very fond of it. The neighbors had lost several hogs, and on the quiet the medicine man was accused of getting the missing hogs. But no one wanted to come right out and publicly accuse the medicine man, as he was prominent in the community. But finally one of the neighbors had been missing too many hogs, which made him very angry and he made up his mind to watch as well as pray.

So one morning he was out watching his bunch of swine and at a distance he saw the medicine man coming in the direction of the herd. The owner of the herd hid himself and waited in patience. The medicine man arrived near the swine herd and proved to be a very kind and liberal medicine man, for he reached into the comprise of his buckskin shirt and unearthed some ears of corn and began to shell and distribute very freely among the herd, and all the time speaking kind words to the hogs, and all at once he plunged a knife into the heart of one of the fat ones.

Now as to where he got the knife is very easily solved. Christopher Columbus gave him this knife and instructed him how to use and it was good to kill a hog with as well as a man. The medicine man shouldered the hog and proceeded towards his house. The herd owner cast his eyes up and saw him advancing in the direction of his home and followed him. He saw the medicine man land his load or burden and he also saw the good wife heating water to clean the hog.

The medicine man cast a faraway look from whence he came with the hog and saw the swine owner coming, and the first thought that struck his mind was to hide his catch. He told the good wife to hasten hither with a buffalo hide at once, and the wife obediently came to the rescue with the article wanted. The medicine man spread the hide over the hog and after a time the herd owner came up and the medicine man very cordially invited him to have a seat. The herd owner seated himself on a log and waited for further developments.

The medicine man was very talkative, and among other things he said that the patient under the cover had been very sick and he was now trying to sweat his fever off. While saying this he went around on the opposite side from where the swine owner sat, raised the buffalo hide a little and inquired of the would-be patient if he was perspiring; then he came back to where the swine owner sat and in a low voice told him that he was afraid that he would lose his patient if he could not get up a sweat on him. The swine owner got up to go and the medicine man cautioned him not to disturb the patient, as that might prove fatal.

1927

Ben D. Locke

CHOCTAW

(1882–1928)

Ben D. Locke, the son of Victor M. and Susan McKinney Locke, attended school in the Choctaw nation. He began his professional career at age nineteen as a deputy United States marshal and later joined the United States Army, which he made his career. He commanded an all-Indian unit during the army's actions on the Mexican border in 1916 and in 1918 was transferred to the field artillery to command, at the rank of captain, an all-Indian battalion during the World War. After the war, Locke was stricken by a long-term illness and spent his last four years in the Veterans Hospital at Muskogee, Oklahoma. There he edited *Trench 90*, the hospital's newsletter, and began to submit works for publication, some of them under the names Illapotubbe and Kiamiti. He wrote a number of popular poems, including "The Doughboy," but he was also known for his storytelling and humorous anecdotes. One of the latter reprinted here appeared under the name Illapotubbe and was probably based on his personal experience.

Meeting with Reptiles

Eli Baldwin was a reckless, factional Choctaw. His enemies were afraid of him, so they voted to kill him by surprise and superior odds. Eli died on his front porch with his six shooter half cocked and twenty lead bullets in his body.

His people buried him, as was their custom, in the back yard of his home, and to stamp out the memory of his tragical death the family moved away and for many years the house stood vacant.

With one hundred and fifty cattle on the nearby range I decided to appropriate the old Eli Baldwin home for my own use. It was a hewn log structure of six rooms, a large front porch with an old fashioned bannister enclosure and suited generally to my convenience and needs.

I had a wagon load of household effects hauled to the place on a late afternoon and my horse and I landed later on, for my first night in the abandoned house. My housekeeping outfit had been carelessly dumped on the front porch and I began at once to sort my belongings in an effort to find my first essential to housekeeping—a lamp. But I just didn't have one. There was nothing to do but make the most of a dark situation.

About midnight I was awakened by the rapid flight, from wall to wall, of bats. Then a big wood rat galloped across the floor, but I persuaded myself that these pests were harmless, and I again slept. Suddenly the piercing shriek of a big rat in the middle of the floor just to right of my bed told me instinctively that hell was to pay.

The rat's screams were accompanied by the loud whirr of a tremendous rattlesnake. I reached for my rifle that was supposedly by the side of the bed. Ye gods, it was over in a corner of the room. The dying shrieks of that rat, as the rattler slowly choked him, disturbed the bats, a possible dozen of them, and they again took up a mad flight from wall to wall in their effort to gain freedom.

Simultaneously and just over me in the loft of cobwebs and wasps' nests another rattlesnake became aroused and his rattles signaled a vicious "no quarter." In the name of all that is good and bad was there ever a more defenseless position? The constant singing of the two rattlers told me positively the house was full of them.

I imagined I could see the eyes of twenty big snakes in that dark room and I was frightened beyond action; my presence of mind was fast fading and my general state of being becoming helpless. I could almost feel the strike of the poisonous fangs.

I would reach out in the dark with my hand thinking to hold off, for only one minute longer, the dozen reptiles that were slowly closing in. God in Heaven, I was choking to death with fright. Great beads of perspiration were popping out, and my hair seemed to be standing straight up and falling out in bunches.

Already chunks of poisonous flesh seemed ready to drop off my body.

With one last dying effort to control myself, I made the sign of the cross and with a Hail Mary Mother of God I looked upward and around and my sweeping vision caught the smiling face of Old Buck, my dog, reared up from outside endeavoring to look through the one small four-pane window.

Then he growled and barked, and with a spontaneous mental reaction, I realized there was still one chance for me. By standing up in bed and taking one leap to the floor I could, with one more long leap, go through that window.

"Actions speak louder than words." I landed in a bloody heap out in the front yard and with Old Buck joyously licking my hands I collected my faculties and dragged myself to my saddle and blankets and there, with my good dog's protection, spent the remainder of the night.

At sunup the following morning I hailed a man who was en route to an adjoining cattle range and together we entered the abandoned house of horrors. There was not a sign of the previous night's disturbance, but upon going in the back yard we found the wide trails made by the enormous snakes which led just sixty feet away, and disappeared under the little house that covered the Indian's grave.

And down in the bottom of that grave was the nest and home of the diamond rattlesnakes who bedded up with the bones of the Choctaw fighter, Eli Baldwin.

> The rattlesnake sleeps by the side of the trail,
> Look out, "Big Boy," don't step on his tail.

1928

Rachel Caroline Eaton

CHEROKEE

(1869–1938)

Rachel Caroline Eaton was born in the Cherokee Nation, the daughter of George W. and Nancy Willliams Eaton. Her father was white, and her mother was Cherokee, the namesake of Nancy Ward, well-known among the Cherokees for having received the title of "Beloved Woman," which gave her the privilege to speak and vote in Cherokee councils in the period before the Revolutionary War. Rachel Eaton was educated in Cherokee Nation schools. She graduated from the Cherokee Female Seminary in 1887, received a B.A. from Drury College (1895), and earned her M.A. (1911) and Ph.D. (1919) from Chicago University. Eaton was a teacher who spent a major portion of her life researching and writing the history of her people. She began her teaching career in Cherokee Nation schools, including the Female Seminary. She also taught at Lake Erie College, Ohio, and Trinity University, Texas. Upon returning to Oklahoma, Eaton became superintendent of schools for Rogers County. After her retirement, she turned to writing, building on her published doctoral dissertation, *John Ross and the Cherokee Indians*. "The Legend of the Battle of Claremore Mound," reprinted here, is Eaton's account of the well-known fight in 1818 between the Osages and Cherokees, who had removed from Georgia to western Arkansas, land traditionally claimed by the Osages. The author draws not only upon written accounts of the incident, but also on the oral tradition.

The Legend of the Battle of Claremore Mound

I

This story is a composite of many sources. The warp is authentic history based on the written records and on the hill which stands as the immutable background of this tragic encounter; the woof is fashioned of legends, traditions and fireside tales passed by word of mouth from generation to generation of each of the tribes that took part in the engagement; but the fabric woven of these elements is shot through with the memory [and] was embroidered with the imagery of one whose childhood was spent under the shadow of the historic hill, the grassy slopes and rock-rimmed summit of which furnished a marvelous playground where romantic youth seeking adventure could salvage, with eager interest, such relics of a vanished culture as arrow heads, battered tomahawks, and bits of colored beads; could gather gorgeous wild flowers to lay with childish reverence on the grave of the great chief who gave his name to the Mound where he is said to have fallen fighting; or garner great handfuls of fragrant blood-red berries that ripened in such profusion on the site of the village of Pasuga in the time of the Strawberry Moon.

II

The battle of Claremore Mound was fought between the Osages and the Cherokees in the spring of 1818 during the season of wild strawberries called by the Indians "Strawberry Moon." This bloody engagement was the culmination of a long-standing feud between the two tribes of different stock and cultural background, which, to some extent, may account for its savage fierceness.

The Osages were among the most impressive and picturesque of the wild tribes living west of the Father of Waters.

On November 10, 1808, by a treaty with the United States concluded at Fort Clark, Kansas, near Kansas City, Missouri, the Osages ceded to the United States all their lands east of a line running due south from Fort Clark to Arkansas river, and also all of their lands west of Missouri river, the whole comprising the larger part of what is now the state of Missouri and the northern part of Arkansas. The territory remaining to them, all of the present state of Oklahoma north of the Canadian and Arkansas rivers, was still further reduced by the provisions of treaties at Saint Louis, June 2, 1825; Fort Gibson, Indian Territory, January 11,

1839; and Canville, Kansas, September 29, 1865; and the limits of their reservation were established by Acts of Congress of July 15, 1870. This consisted (1906) of 1,470,058 acres.

The tribe numbered something like five thousand when, about 1800, the main body migrated to the valleys of the Grand and Verdigris in what is now eastern Oklahoma. Their two main villages in this region were Pasona or Black Dog's Town, near the present site of Claremore, and Pasuga at the foot of Claremore Mound where lived the hereditary war chief of the tribe called by the French and Osages Claremont and pronounced by the English Claremore.

The Osages were hunters, living in the barbarous stage of development. While their village-sites were more or less permanent, their houses, built of a framework of poles covered with bark and rushes, were frail structures requiring repairs and restoration after each return from the buffalo hunt to which, at stated seasons of the year, big, little, old and young betook themselves, leaving their lodges deserted for weeks at a time.

They were people of fine physique, tall, straight, and of commanding appearance. According to the artist Catlin, who visited their villages in the early thirties of the nineteenth century and painted portraits of some of their chiefs, they ranged from six to seven feet in stature, and were well proportioned in body. Their dress was simple, consisting of leggings and moccasins; the body from the waist up was unclothed except for the buffalo-robe thrown over the shoulders to protect them from the most rigorous weather of winter.

The scalp clean shaven, and the bare body were painted with some degree of artistic taste. Long strands of beads and elk's teeth hung around the neck, bracelets decorated the arms, and a peculiar style of head-dress completed their costume.

With these giants of the prairie the French had been on the most friendly terms for many years; had established trading posts in their country to which the Indians brought furs to exchange for supplies of beads, silver ornaments of various kind, kettles, knives and firearms. As early as 1798 Pierre Choteau of St. Louis had set up a trading post on the Grand River, which long remained a center of barter with the western Indians. A survival of this French influence is still to be found in such names as Choteau, Salina, Sallisaw, Poteau and Verdigris.

Unlike the French, the Cherokees were not held in high regard by the Osages but were considered intruders, aliens, if not apostates whose strange ways and mediocre stature furnished targets for the pungent wit and dry sarcasm for which the "Big People" were noted.

A fragment of the most powerful and progressive mountain tribe of the Appalachian Highland was known as the Cherokee Nation; these western Cherokees had left home for various reasons and for more than a quarter of a century had drifted in by families or by groups of kin and located in settlements along the streams of the Arkansas and White rivers until in 1817 they numbered between two and three thousand souls. In the east the Cherokees were a sedentary, agricultural people, hunting being only secondary. These families had brought with them from the east, some of the essential elements of civilization and their gardens, orchards and grain fields, together with their horses, hogs and cattle furnished them an abundant and assured subsistence.

Nor were they illiterate. Had not their great Sequoyah given them an alphabet, himself teaching them its use in order that they might communicate with one another and with friends and kin in Georgia and Tennessee?

The naturalist, Thomas Nuttall, who visited this band in 1819, found them living in houses of logs or lumber, comfortable and furnished with a degree of good taste beyond that of most pioneer white settlers of the time. This he tells us in his "Journals of Travel in the Arkansas Territory."

These Cherokees for years were settlers without title to their homes, however, a status which had begun to disturb them greatly as time went on.

Not only did the Osages despise these Cherokees, but they looked upon them as intruders. Nor was the heavy hand of the "Big People" long in descending upon the hapless heads of the "alien people," as the Cherokees were considered by the wild plainsmen who made forays into the Cherokee settlement, stealing horses, carrying off captives and murdering in cold blood. The Cherokees retaliated in kind, even invading Osage territory. This border warfare continued for several years, making life hideous for all concerned.

Such was the state of affairs when in 1817 word reached the Osages that a treaty was pending between the United States Government and the Western Cherokees. The great Indian fighter, Andrew Jackson, representing the Federal Government, had charge of the negotiations and was pressing the Cherokees for a cession of land in Georgia in exchange for a tract between the Arkansas and White Rivers in the Arkansas Territory, land which the Osages had ceded to the United States, but which they still claimed because, they said, the treaty had never been ratified in Washington. Regardless of all opposition the treaty was concluded July 8, 1817, which changed the status of the Arkansas band of Cherokee from settlers without title to their homes to that of the Cherokee Nation West.

The Osages, furious over the culmination of affairs, began a series of depredations calculated to show to all concerned what they thought of it.

A pathetic letter sent to the Governor of the Missouri Territory in 1817 by the old chief Tah-lun-tees-ky is the source of this information. It was written in Cherokee and translated by an interpreter. "We wish you to pity us, for the Osages are deaf to all we can say or do. They have stolen two of our best horses and killed two of our young men," he wrote, adding that the Cherokees had stood about all of this sort of thing they could endure. Something must be done about it. The rivers were running red with blood of the Cherokees. They, the Cherokees were going to Osage country and get their horses, and while there would "do mischief" to those Indians. Would the governor, when he heard of it, be pleased to remember "the piling up" of their provocations and not be too hard on the Cherokees?

But week after week passed and still the Cherokees failed to make good their threat. On the other hand Osage raids into Cherokee country continued on a small scale through the fall and winter. The big coup, however, was being reserved for spring, when grass was plentiful and the corn-fed horses of the Cherokee would be turned out to graze at night. Moreover, a foray depriving the Cherokees of their horses at a critical period of their crops would desolate the country, prostrate the tribe, and drive them back to Georgia, leaving the Osages to recover their lost territory.

So the great drive was made. A hundred warriors are reported to have participated in it. Viewed by the Osages it was a huge success, a raid of unprecedented magnitude. While the Cherokees, weary from their farm work, slept the sleep of the just, the Osages collected and drove off all their best horses. It was done so deftly, with such silent precision, that not even the dogs were disturbed to give warning. The horses vanished between suns as if by magic, forty from one small neighborhood alone, leaving only a few of the poorer sort to be used in pursuit.

And so without let or hindrance the wily marauders drove their booty in triumph across the Six Bulls or Grand River and thence to safe pasturage in the vicinity of their own towns.

But, this once, the bold prairie warriors had overshot their mark, had reckoned without their host in relying upon the supine helplessness of their enemies. The Cherokees had their backs to the wall.

On awakening to the realization of their loss, the Cherokees determined on a prompt course of action. Too-an-tuh, their war chief, called a council of war and plans were laid for the long promised punitive expedition into the country of the marauders to recover their horses and chastise the enemy.

Preparations began without delay; guns and ammunition were made ready, hunting knives were sharpened, and a sufficient number of horses borrowed as mounts for the warriors from white renters who had not been molested and a strong coalition was formed with several other tribes unfriendly to the Osages.

To the women of the tribe fell the task of provisioning the little army. It was a simple task to prepare a sufficient quantity of kewees-tah, ancient war ration of the tribe and a diet admirably suited to such an undertaking. This was made by first parching grains of maize or corn in the ashes until they were brown and crisp, and then pounding them into a meal in a mortar. Eaten dry by the handful or mixed with a little water it was a palatable, nutritious, and wholesome food.

The war-party of six hundred fighting men and scouts that finally started on the march up the Arkansas to the Osage country was composed not only of Cherokees but of Choctaws, Shawnees, and warriors of other tribes which had suffered at the hands of the marauders. With them were eleven white men who also cherished grievances against the Osages. The trail of the Osages was easy to follow. "There was such a large herd of the stolen horses that a road was made as they went along," so well beaten out that there was small danger of losing it or of being misled by any strategy of the marauders. Approaching the villages of the Osages, the Cherokees had need of the utmost caution. Halting in the hollow of a little creek, they rested and waited for darkness to conceal their movements. Scouts returning reported that "all was clear." Resuming the advance they arrived by midnight at Black Dogs creek on the western bank of which stood the village of Pasona. Here all was silent and deserted. The Indians had gone on a buffalo-hunt.

Again taking up the trail of the horses which led north-westward and following it under cover of darkness the silent but determined Cherokees

and their allies advanced toward Pasuga where the great warchief, Claremont, with his four wives and thirty-seven children, together with the
rest of the village, slept on, all unconscious of the approaching disaster.
A halt was called in the shelter of a grove of trees while scouts went
forward to reconnoiter. Returning almost immediately, they reported
that the horses were grazing just beyond the grove, herded by a few
sleepy Osages. A sudden impetuous attack on the part of the Cherokees
took these herdsmen utterly unaware, who, leaving their horses, took to
their heels, running in mad haste toward the village to warn the sleeping
inhabitants that the "foul fiends" were upon them. One, braver than the
rest, stayed to try conclusions with the foe. Mounting his pony, at a single
bound he dashed full-speed into the thick of the enemy, killing one man
as he went. The next instant he fell mortally wounded, shouting the tribal
war-cry with his last breath. So die brave warriors of every clime and
creed and race.

Thus began the bloody massacre. Revenge was sweet to the suffering
Cherokees whose blood was up at last. The sun, glancing over the eastern
rim of the prairie, beheld a strange sight. The peaceful village of yesterday
had become a shambles. The motley group of silent, serene, civilized red
men who so calmly followed the trail the day before had been transformed into a mad melee of furies.

Through the panic-stricken herd of horses the avenging host charged,
stampeding them in every direction to increase the disorder. On toward
the village they swept where now reigned confusion worse confounded.
The surprise was so complete as to demoralize the Osages from the start,
causing them to give way at the approach of the Cherokees. Men, women
and children fled in the greatest disorder, the latter hiding behind boulders, trees or underbrush while the warriors retreated up the hill where
the rock-rimmed summit formed a natural rampart and the steep slopes
gave every advantage for defensive fighting.

Armed with bows and arrows and with guns, and occupying a strategic
position, with the Cherokees exposed to their open fire, the Osages
should have won the encounter by every token of Indian warfare. But
this they failed to do. For the Cherokees, long accustomed to the use
of firearms, were skilled marksmen, aiming their muskets with deadly
precision, picking off any unwary Osage who exposed himself to their
fire. Moreover, exasperated by continued loss of property, smarting from
taunts of their inferiority, remembering friends and kinsmen murdered in

cold blood, at last they found themselves worked up to a pitch of passion little short of madness.

Gone berserk with revenge and excitement, they charged madly up the slope, driving the Osages from every cover, until they had gained a foothold on the very summit and could thus come to a death-grip with the enemy. The Osages, stricken helpless with fear, threw away their empty guns, rushed headlong down the further slope, and plunged blindly into the seething current of the river, swollen from the spring rains and filled with floating driftwood. The weak and wounded perished. Those who reached the farther bank continued their flight to hide in the rocky ravines or in the scanty underbrush of the neighboring streams.

For a part of two days the Cherokees pursued the fugitives and, rejecting all overtures of peace, slew without mercy, or captured all who were overtaken. Scores of men, women, and children thus perished from the relentless fury of the foe, victims of one of the bloodiest Indian massacres of modern history.

Satisfied at last that their work was well done, the victorious Cherokees rounded up their horses and, driving them before them and leading their captives beside them, turned their faces homeward. Moving in triumphal procession, the battle-stained cavalcade followed the well-trodden trail of the stolen horses back to the Six Bulls and beyond to the settlement on the Arkansas and White Rivers, where a joyous welcome awaited them from anxious wives and children.

After the Cherokees were well on their way homeward, the remnant of the beaten Osages returned to repair their homes, reorganize the band and take up life again on the scene of the great disaster. One of their first acts was to bury their great and beloved war-chief who in the early part of the conflict fell mortally wounded near the southern rim of the hill. Here a shallow grave was made after the custom of the tribe and the body of the warrior laid reverently to rest near the place where he fell, after the ritual and according to the ceremonies of his people.

A cairn of white limestone, heaped above his body, rose as a fitting monument to the war leader of the great Osages, one of the most distinguished and picturesque of America's aboriginal peoples.

1930

Sources for Headnotes

FOLSOM: Angie Debo, *The Rise and Fall of the Choctaw Republic* (University of Oklahoma Press, 1961), 2–4; Choctaw—Folsom Family File, Grant Foreman Collection, Archives and Manuscripts Division, Oklahoma Historical Society, Oklahoma City; Christine Bates (interview) *Indian-Pioneer History* (Archives and Manuscripts Division, Oklahoma Historical Society), 14: 11–17.   BROWN: *Indian Journal*, February 6, 1879; *Cherokee Advocate*, February 12 and 26, 1879; *Twin Territories* 2 (June 1900): 113.   GUY: H. F. O'Beirne, *Leaders and Leading Men of the Indian Territory with Interesting Biographical Sketches* (Chicago: American Publishers' Association, 1891): 213; *Daily Ardmoreite*, August 18, 1907; Joe T. Roff, "Reminiscences of Early Days in the Chickasaw Nation," *Chronicles of Oklahoma* 13 (June 1935): 169–90.   ADAIR: H. F. O'Beirne and E. S. O'Beirne, *The Indian Territory: Its Chiefs, Legislators, and Leading Men* (St. Louis: C. B. Woodward Co., 1892), 463–66.   CANUP: O'Beirne and O'Beirne, *The Indian Territory*, 430; Foreman, *Oklahoma Imprints, 1835–1907* (Norman: University of Oklahoma Press, 1936), 67, 87, 89–92.   EUBANKS, W.: R. Roger Eubanks (interview), *Indian-Pioneer History*, 74: 98; *Muskogee Phoenix*, September 14, 1893; *Cherokee Telephone*, May 14, 1891; Nathan E. Bender, "Cherokee Shorthand: As Derived from Pitman Shorthand and in Relation to the Dot-Notation Variant of the Sac and Fox Syllabary," *American Indian Culture and Research Journal* 15:3 (1991): 63–76.   DUNCAN: Kathleen Garrett, "Dartmouth Alumni in the Indian Territory," *Chronicles of Oklahoma* 32 (Summer 1954): 130–32; Carolyn Thomas Foreman, "Notes on DeWitt Clinton Duncan and a Recently Discovered History of the Cherokees," *Chronicles of Oklahoma* 47 (Autumn 1959): 305–11; Mary Hays Marable and Elaine Boylan, *Handbook of Oklahoma Writers* (Norman: University of Oklahoma Press, 1939), 55–56.   ANDERSON: *Pryor Jeffersonian*, September 22, 1949; Gretchen M. Bataille, ed., *Native American Women: A Biographical Dictionary* (New York: Garland Publishing, 1993), 9–10.   OSKISON: Daniel F. Littlefield, Jr., and James W. Parins, "Short Fiction Writers of the Indian Territory," *American Studies* 23 (Spring 1982): 23–38; Gretchen Ronnow, "John Milton Oskison, Cherokee Journalist: Singer of the Semiotics of Power," *Native Press Research Journal* No. 4 (Spring 1987): 1–14.   GREGORY: D. C. Gideon, *The Indian Territory* (New York: Lewis Publishing Co., 1901), 543–44; James Roane Gregory Manuscripts, Archives and Manuscripts Division, Oklahoma Historical Society.   POSEY: Littlefield, *Alex Posey: Creek Poet, Journalist, and Humorist* (Lincoln: University of Nebraska Press, 1992); Littlefield and Carol A. Petty Hunter, eds., *The Fus Fixico Letters* (Lincoln: University of Nebraska Press, 1994).   PORTER: John Bartlett Meserve, "Chief Pleasant Porter," *Chronicles of Oklahoma* 9 (September 1931): 318–34.   GIBSON: O'Beirne and O'Beirne, *The Indian Territory*, 296–98; Gideon, *Indian Territory*, 891–92.   McCOMBS: "Reverend William McCombs," *Chronicles of Oklahoma* 8 (March 1930): 137–40.   COLBERT: *Daily Oklahoman*, December 18, 1921; Colbert Vertical File, Oklahoma Historical Society Library, Oklahoma City, Oklahoma; Rex T. Harlow, *Makers of Government in Oklahoma* (Oklahoma City: Harlow Publishing Co., 1930), 484.   McCURTAIN: John P. Dilday and Mark H. Scott, eds., *Oklahoma History South of the Canadian* (Chicago: S. J. Clarke Publishing Co., 1925), 3: 1199–1200; Meserve, "The McCurtains," *Chronicles of Oklahoma* 13 (September 1935): 297–312; Marion E. Gridley, *Indians of Today* (Chicago: Indian Council Fire Publications, 1947), 58.   REED: Daryl Morrison, "Twin Territories: The Indian Magazine and Its Editor, Ora Eddleman Reed," *Chronicles of Oklahoma* 60 (Summer 1982): 136–66.   EUBANKS, R.: Eubanks (interview), *Indian-Pioneer History*, 74: 98; Cherokee National Records, Archives and Manuscripts Division, Oklahoma Historical Society.   LANDRUM: Gideon, *The Indian Territory*, 271–72; Joseph B. Thoburn, *A Standard History of Oklahoma* (Chicago: The American Historical Society, 1916), 1434–35. McDERMOTT: *Muskogee Times-Democrat*, March 22, 1910; Brown Family Papers, Manuscripts and Archives Division, Oklahoma Historical Society.   PARKER: Oscar H. Lipps, "Gabe E. Parker: An Appreciation," *Red Man* 7 (December 1914), 115–16; Gideon, *Indian Territory*, 694–95.   CARTER: *Who Was Who in America* (Chicago: The A. N. Marquis Co., 1942), 4:199.   ROGERS: Dixon Wecter, "Will Rogers" in Harris E. Starr, ed., *Dictionary of American Biography* (New York: Charles Scribner's Sons, 1944), 21: 635–37.   RIGGS: Phyllis Cole Braunlich, *Haunted by Home: The Life and Letters of Lynn Riggs* (Norman: University of Oklahoma Press, 1988); Thomas A. Erhard, "(Rolla) Lynn Riggs" in Andrew Wiget, ed., *Dictionary of Native American Literature* (New York: Garland Publishing, Inc., 1994), 289–93.   WRIGHT: Ruth Arrington, "Muriel Hazel Wright," in *Notable American Women, The Mod-*

ern Period: A Biographical Dictionary, ed. Barbara Secheman and Carol Hurd Green (Cambridge: The Belknap Press of Harvard University, 1980), 751–52; LeRoy H. Fischer, "Muriel H. Wright, Historian of Oklahoma," *Chronicles of Oklahoma* 52 (Spring 1974): 3–29 (contains a bibliography); Bataille, ed., *Native American Women*, 286–87.   BRUNER: *Muskogee Daily Phoenix*, May 20, 1934; Luther B. Hill, *A History of the State of Oklahoma* (Chicago: The Lewis Publishing Co., 1909), 2: 212–13; Richard M. Caldwell, "Joe Bruner, American Indian," *Holland's Magazine* (October 1936): 7, 35.   LOCKE: "Capt. Ben Locke, Noted Indian Soldier-Writer, Passes Away," *American Indian* 2 (January 1928): 6; Carolyn Thomas Foreman, "St. Agnes Academy for Choctaws," *Chronicles of Oklahoma* 48 (Autumn 1970): 323–30.   EATON: Wright, "Rachel Caroline Eaton," *Chronicles of Oklahoma* 16 (December, 1938): 509–510; Bataille, ed., *Native American Women*, 85.

Sources for Selections

FOLSOM: "Lo! the Poor Indian's Hope," *Vindicator* (Atoka, Choctaw Nation), May 1, 1875; "Choctaw Traditions: Introductory Remarks," *Vindicator*, November 3, 1875; "Choctaw Traditions: Name and Migration from the West," *Vindicator*, November 10, 1875.   BROWN: *Cherokee Advocate*, February 26, 1879.   GUY: "The White Man Wants the Indians' Land," *Council Fire* 1 (July 1878): 113; "Lament of Tishomingo," *Council Fire* 2 (January 1879): 15; "Fort Arbuckle" in H. F. O'Beirne, *Leaders and Leading Men of the Indian Territory with Interesting Biographical Sketches* (Chicago: American Publishers' Association, 1891), 213.   ADAIR: H. F. O'Beirne and E. S. O'Beirne, *The Indian Territory: Its Chiefs, Legislators and Leading Men* (St. Louis: C. B. Woodward Co., 1892), 466–68.   CANUP: *Telephone* (Tahlequah, Cherokee Nation), November 5, 1891.   EUBANKS, W.: "For Lands in Severalty, and Statehood," *Cherokee Advocate* (Tahlequah, Cherokee Nation), April 18, 1894; "Measure for Measure," *Cherokee Advocate*, July 11, 1894.   DUNCAN: "A Momentous Occasion," *Indian Chieftain* (Vinita, Cherokee Nation), June 24, 1897; "The Indian's Hard Lot," *Indian Chieftain*, June 2, 1898; "Passage of Curtis Bill," *Indian Chieftain*, June 21, 1900; "The Dead Nation," *Indian Chieftain*, April 27, 1899; "Sequoyah," *Vinita Weekly Chieftain*, June 2, 1904.   ANDERSON: "An Osage Niobe," *Tahlequah Arrow*, May 17, 1900; "General Stand Watie," *Chronicles of Oklahoma* 10 (December 1932): 540–48.   OSKISON: "Tookh Steh's Mistake," *Indian Chieftain*, July 22, 1897; " 'Only the Master Shall Praise,' " *Century Magazine* 59 (January 1900): 327–35; "When the Grass Grew Long," *Century Magazine* 62 (June 1901): 247–50; "The Problem of Old Harjo," *Southern Workman* 36 (April 1907): 235–41.   GREGORY: "The Green Corn Dance" and "Nineteenth Century Finality," *Wagoner Record* (Wagoner, Creek Nation), August 9, 1900; "Some Early History of the Creek Nation," *Wagoner Record*, January 24, 1901; "Traditions of the Creeks," *Indian Journal* (Eufaula, Creek Nation), February 22, 1901.   POSEY: "Fancy" and "Coyote,"

Posey Manuscripts, Thomas Gilcrease Institute of American History and Art, Tulsa, Oklahoma; "Tulledega," Posey Scrapbook, Thomas Gilcrease Institute of American History and Art; "Ode to Sequoyah," *Twin Territories* 1 (April 1899): 102; "Hotgun on the Death of Yadeka Harjo" and "The Passing of Hotgun," *Indian Journal*, January 24, 1908; "Fus Fixico's Letter," *Muskogee Daily Phoenix*, April 17, 1904, and April 16, 1905, and *Cherokee Advocate*, May 28, 1904.   PORTER: *Muskogee Phoenix*, September 18, 1902.   GIBSON: "The Passing of the Indian," *Indian Journal*, January 3, 1902; "The Indian—His Past," *Indian Journal*, May 16, 1902; "The Indian—His Present," *Indian Journal*, May 23, 1902; "The Indian—His Future," *Indian Journal*, June 6, 1902; "The Way of the Spokogee," *Indian Journal*, July 4, 1902; "Wild Cat's Long Swim," *Indian Journal*, October 17, 1902; "Why the Lion Eats His Meat Raw," *Twin Territories*, 5 (February 1903): 61–62.   McCOMBS: *Tahlequah Arrow*, May 16, 1903. COLBERT: *New-State Tribune* (Muskogee, Creek Nation), July 26, 1906.   McCURTAIN: *New-State Tribune*, August 9, 1906.   REED: "Father of 90,000 Indians," *Sturm's Oklahoma Magazine* 2 (July, 1906): 81–83; "Indian Tales Between Pipes," *Sturm's Oklahoma Magazine* 3 (November 1906): 86–88; "Billy Bearclaws, Aid to Cupid," *Sturm's Oklahoma Magazine* 9 (September 1909): 47–53.   EUBANKS, R.: "The Middle Man," *Sturm's Oklahoma Magazine* 8 (July 1909): 38–42; "Nights with Uncle Ti-ault-ly: How the Terrapin Beat the Rabbit," *Osage Magazine* 1 (May 1910): 72–74; "Nights with Uncle Ti-ault-ly: The Ball Game of the Birds and Animals," *Osage Magazine* 2 (September 1910): 45–47.   LANDRUM: *Tahlequah Arrow*, May 26, 1910.   McDERMOTT: "Legends of the Creeks," *Muskogee Times-Democrat*, March 15, 1910; "Oklahoma Justice as Seen by a Fullblood," *Daily Oklahoman* (Oklahoma City), November 23, 1913.   PARKER: *Quarterly Journal of the Society of American Indians* 2 (January–March 1914): 60–63. CARTER: *American Indian* 1 (October 1926): 14–15.   ROGERS: "Slipping the Lariat Over," *New York Times*, July 29 and September 9, 1923; "Wild Movie Titles," *Tulsa Daily World*, May 17, 1931; "Educational Frills," *Tulsa Daily World*, July 31, 1931.   RIGGS: "Spring Morning—Santa Fe," "Santo Domingo Corn Dance," and "The Deer," *The Iron Dish* (Garden City, NY: Doubleday, Doran and Company, Inc., 1930), 6, 8–10, 16; "Knives from Syria" in *One-Act Plays for Stage and Study* 3rd Series (New York: Samuel French, Inc., 1927), 193–207.   WRIGHT: "Legend of Nanih Wayah," undated broadside in Lee Harkins Papers, Archives and Manuscripts Division, Oklahoma Historical Society, Oklahoma City; "A Chieftain's 'Farewell Letter' to the American People," *American Indian* 1 (December 1926): 7, 12.   BRUNER: "Indian Fish Fable" and "Another Indian Fable," *American Indian* 1 (August 1927): 10–11; "Discovery of Tobacco," *American Indian* 1 (September 1927): 6.   LOCKE: *American Indian* 2 (February 1928): 14.   EATON: *Chronicles of Oklahoma* 8 (December 1930): 369–77.